WHOREMASTER

A Biography

wendy cole

Abacus & Quill™
Books

INTRODUCTION

Whatever anyone else thought of him, Walter Plankinton considered himself an honorable, decent man. That he had business savvy and was virtually fearless is unquestionable.

When he was very young, he recognized and assimilated the difference between the absolute truth of his childhood and that which is commonly practiced within American business and among politicians, i.e., stretched, creatively distorted, convenient truths. However, he sincerely believed that he rejected lies of any measure when it came to the American right to function within the letter of the law.

This was a man who took his well-honed business and marketing skills into a usually hidden enterprise, however legal, and succeeded—to the dismay of his competitors and the politicians who demanded control over him and the brothel industry he entered.

For those who might scoff at the corruption levels discussed in this book, two earlier books and a made-for-TV movie were produced, specifically on the subject of the unethical shenanigans of those in political/judicial control of Nye County, both related and unrelated to the "legal" brothel network.

As for "brothel shenanigans," Walter Plankinton was a humorless man, in the generally accepted sense, which makes some episodes in this book even better for the reader with any level of imagination and a funny bone.

Wendy Cole

ONE

The second child born to Chester (Chet) and Faye Ola (nee Merritt) Plankinton on October 22, 1928, Walter's entry into the world was made in the same house—maybe the same room—as his father, and his father's father. Walter's great-grandfather built the house over 100 years earlier, after he arrived in Pohattan, Kansas. from Pennsylvania with John Brown and the Abolitionists.

The six-room house, made of beautiful old oak trees that his great-grandfather cut down from the forest he found there, sat on 100 acres of lush farmland. On hot summer nights Walter's family slept in the yard; pure adventure to his sister, Donna Pearl, fourteen months older, and him.

The year 1928 was called the *Good Times*, although in rural America money was scarce, as usual. To a farmer, good times meant just a little more cash, nothing resembling affluence.

The Plankintons were typical Midwest farmers: able to do fair at best, capable of survival at least. Walter was taught, as well as shown by example by his parents, that all was well as long as they had the land, their home, hard work to keep them busy, each other to make them happy, and God to teach them right from wrong. They were a healthy and—by regional standards—prosperous family.

Stocks were at an all-time high, twenty-three million cars crowded American roads, and almost everyone had a newfangled home radio. Eddie Cantor was *Making Whoopee*, Mae West was starring in *Pleasure Man*, and a fascinating Joan Crawford was up on the astounding new giant movie screens. It was a real boom period. Experts predicted there would "never again be a 'bust' as in the 1840s and 1893."

The Plankintons were not churchgoers but taught Donna Pearl and Walter to believe in God, never tell a lie, and follow *the Golden Rule*. Chet and Faye were hard-working, law-abiding, honorable people. Walter was born when a man's word was his bond. His first year was in a good world, a prosperous country. He was a safe, happy baby.

Then on October 23, 1929, *Black Wednesday,* the day after his first birthday, stocks tumbled. The next day, the bottom dropped out of the market, called *Black Thursday,* and the following week was added *Black Tuesday,* when over sixteen million shares were traded. Three billion dollars in market value was destroyed. Men jumped from buildings, shot themselves, or fell into quasi- or total silence for life.

Although the words *depression* and *panic* were first used in the United States referring to earlier panics, none were like this one. In those others, victims were men of wealth. They were more financial panics, not a general depression.

In 1929, bread lines had to be organized to keep whole city populations from starving. What was first stated a panic was finally admitted to and called *The Great Depression*.

Still, life on the Plankinton farm was simple and sweet. There were dances and Sunday dinners, when adults indulged in their favorite pastime, conversation, and children played games with sticks or ropes. But weekdays (including Saturday) were busy. Even small children had chores—which grew as they did. It was a long walk to the school. Then home to feeding pigs or chickens, milking cows, fetching water (Walter's job as soon as he could carry a full bucket), pitching hay, and many more tasks to ensure efficiency on the farm. After chores came homework.

Rainy days made working the land impossible. Walter chuckled whenever he recalled his father's favorite rainy-day pastime. He would stand at the crank-up wall phone listening in on the eight-party line, particularly to old Mrs. Hall. One day, Chet decided he could hook up the old crystal (radio) set to the phone. Then instead of standing long periods eavesdropping on the gossip, he could sit and listen over the old crystal set. He hooked up the jury-rigged contraption, then waited for the first rainy day. He grumbled until the phone finally rang, then turned on his cleverly devised system. Electricity flowed through just as he intended. What followed, however, was not part of the plan. The radio caught fire and almost burned to a crisp before Chet could douse it with water. No radio was allowed in the Plankinton household for ten long years.

By 1932, people blamed President Herbert Hoover for *the Depression*. Songs reflected the tone of the nation: *Brother, Can You Spare A Dime, Shanty In Old Shantytown, Time On My Hands*. Some were written to cheer people such as *Wrap Your Troubles In Dreams* and *Life Is Just A Bowl Of Cherries*. Ironically, a song written in 1929 for the movie *Chasing Rainbows* became the theme of *the Great Depression: Happy Days Are Here Again*. But *Shanty In Old Shantytown* was the favorite of the Plankinton clan.

As *the Great Depression* knocked the nation to its knees, something else, started about 1914, would cause a cataclysm in the Midwest. In their primitive state, Midwest plains were held in place by grasslands used for grazing stock.

4

But as homesteading increased, cattle diminished. Rains flowing from the Rocky Mountains were no longer held by wild grass. Some ninety-six million acres (comprising parts of Kansas, Oklahoma, Texas, New Mexico, and Colorado) became parched, due not only to the extreme changes in use of the land, but also to a drought period, the simple and natural changing character of the soil, and a series of crop failures.

Another cause for the disaster points directly to the frantic need to grow wheat for soldiers fighting in Europe during *World War I* (1914-1918). More grasslands had been cleared to farm than would have been in a natural evolution. Soil began to blow away, seen in massive clouds that journeyed as far as the Atlantic Coast. Walter recalled the quarter-inch layer of dirt that each dust storm left on tables inside the farmhouse. Some days the wind blew so hard, the Plankintons couldn't go outside without wet cloths over their noses to keep from breathing the powder into their lungs. Huge red dust clouds from Oklahoma blocked the sunlight, making it look more like night. People said they were as high as fifty thousand feet. Walter said, "Our farm got so dry you couldn't raise hell on it with a gallon of whiskey."

When banks held auctions to sell the stock on neighbors' lost farms, friends refused to bid over a dollar or two. The banks had to accept the bids since they were preannounced auctions. Those with a few dollars would buy a cow or horse or hog for a dollar, then give it back to its original owner. It fed a few a little longer, but it didn't stop the bankruptcies or the destitution that followed.

By the early 1930s, there was little money for seed. Even those with seed couldn't grow anything in the dead, loose dust. Walter remembered seeing corn go to six inches, then just wilt to the ground for lack of rain. In the midst of this came the grasshoppers. In one disastrous sweep, anything green was consumed by millions of the dreaded insects. Then man struck with even more cruelty. One example was etched in Walter's youthful memory.

There was a surplus of hogs. President Franklin Delano Roosevelt decided that if he could eliminate that surplus, prices could be raised. Chet sold his hogs to the government for surplus. Later, friends and neighbors told him the government was killing the animals just to get them off the market. The whole Plankinton family went to see for themselves. What they saw in St. Joseph was a sight that Walter never forgot.

Men knocked the hogs in their heads, then threw train- and truckloads of animals into the river, while hundreds of near-starving people stood on the river's edge frantically trying to fish out the still bleeding carcasses. The National Guard, with rifles poised, threatened to shoot those people, driving them off so they would stop pulling out the hogs. This was 1934, when not

5

only rural America was starving, but tens of thousands in the cities; people had no money to buy anything. Walter never understood how depriving already starving, penniless people by inflating costs could be the only way to turn an economy around.

The Plankinton nest egg dwindled. It wasn't easy to get *Relief*, the 1930s name for welfare; and Chet, a proud man, couldn't ask. Faye, while no less proud, was more practical. Walter clearly remembered the day that he, Faye, and Donna went to the county seat in Hiawatha. Everyone had to appear before an appointed board to explain their plights. The board then determined what each should be given—in funds and/or food. The process was demeaning and painful for hard-working people who had been self-reliant all of their lives.

When the three Plankintons arrived at nine in the morning, the secretary behind a huge desk told Faye to sit down and wait. Donna and Walter went through different intervals of restless, whiny, and sleepy, but were consistently bored. By midafternoon another element was added: hunger.

All through the day, people who came in and out talked to the secretary, or exchanged papers. The phone rang continuously and, throughout, she spoke loud and clear so that everyone heard her. She told people—in person and on the phone—things such as: "I'll get to it as soon as I can get rid of all the white trash in my office." The words *white trash* were used repeatedly. Faye near choked trying to control her humiliation, pain, and anger. Finally, after hours of sitting in that strange, uncomfortable place with two small, tired, hungry children who could hear the constant assaults on theirs, as well as her dignity, rage overtook reason.

Without a glimmer of warning, this two hundred twenty-five pound mostly muscle farm laborer leaped to her feet and said very precisely to the woman (who barely acknowledged Faye's rising): "You refer to me one more time as 'white trash,' and I'll knock your head off." Foolishly, the small woman behind the desk said something condescending. Like a bullet, Faye, until then several feet away, was in front of that desk with a long arm extended over it gripping the woman's throat with one hand, fairly lifting her out of her seat, while she slapped her back and forth across the face with the other hand.

Everything came to a dead stop until the door of the meeting room flew open. The commissioners ran out to see what the commotion was about. Walter knew there were noises, but he could never remember what they were, recalling only a sort of din. He assumed that his mother was shouting and the woman screaming. He clearly recalled his mother becoming a wild woman. One of the commissioners, John (who would later become Walter's good friend), made the mistake of grabbing Faye to stop the assault on the secretary.

She let go of the woman as soon as she felt him trying to overpower her, turned toward him, and hit him so hard in the jaw with her fist that he flew back against the wall, half unconscious as he slid slowly to the floor. Two other commissioners dove at her to suppress any further violence, but were no match for this strong woman who, in her frenzy, became a powerhouse. As she hurled them off of her in a single thrust, Donna and Walter screamed in terror, certain that the animals were hurting their mama.

By then sheriff's deputies had run up the flight of stairs from their office just below. It took several to finally subdue Faye. They led her down to the jail where they booked her on assault charges. Once she was calm again, they listened to the whole story of what first appeared to them an unprovoked assault. People for miles around heard the story. She became revered. Walter's first examples of otherwise impotent, bureaucratic employees who used the power of their jobs to bully defenseless people, were viewed through the very small boy's eyes.

The morning after the fracas, a county truck drove up to the Plankinton house. They all watched through a window as the driver went around to the rear and lifted a sack off the truck. He approached the door just as Faye opened it. It was rice from the county relief office. Apparently the commission recognized the secretary's abuse and understood Faye's reaction. It likely kept them from starving that winter. Afterward, however, the greatest living chef could probably have not camouflaged rice to get Walter to eat it.

Faye set high standards for herself and her children. Being the lady Walter always felt she was never kept her from standing up for herself, or her family. Chet was a gentle man, but strong. Nothing could have stopped him from defending his family or its honor. Although quieter and softer than Faye, Chet said things only once in his home. Walter's ears were boxed many times, but never when he hadn't made every possible effort to earn it. They taught their children, by example mostly, to defend themselves if they felt wronged, and help others who might not be as strong. At an early age, they were bequeathed a code of honor and dignity. Surely it's why it became almost impossible to intimidate Walter.

The wolf eventually found the Plankinton door. No prayers, hope, or hard work changed that. Chet sold what he could, loaded the old sedan with everything possible, and like so many before them, the Plankintons headed for California. They said goodbye to friends and relatives who were desperately hanging on. The family home and security were no longer theirs.

As they drove off that morning in the summer of 1934, Chet and Faye turned back to their little house and town with looks on their faces that their children had never seen; nor had they ever seen their mama cry before. Both parents were silent for a long time. Donna and Walter knew to keep quiet, too.

To a six-year-old boy, however, the move was quite another matter. Walter remembered sadness at leaving his friends and the farm, but was too young to share his parents' fears or sense of loss. This was adventure. He was going beyond what he had seen every day of his life from his own front yard, the horizon. At last, he knew that he would find out if the stories he heard were true. He was going to see the world!

TWO

In his late twenties, Chet had never been more than twenty miles from his hometown. The Plankintons were lost almost immediately. He finally got a map from a general store in one of the towns they passed through. He knew the National Guard was turning people back on old Hwy 66. The roads were giant waves of people heading west, hopefully to survival. At the borders of some western states, guardsmen were ordered to stop both migration and transmigration. Allowed to continue unchecked, the glut of people would strip other states of their own fast-depleting resources, plunging the West into the same chaos as the Midwest.

Chet decided that Denver and Utah would be safer and a less-congested route than Hwy 66 through Amarillo, the route most chosen—as depicted in the classic movie of that era, *The Grapes of Wrath*. The trip was fascinating. Walter never lost any of his vivid memories even though he wasn't quite six.

They traveled on a gravel road (Hwy 36), twenty to twenty-five miles an hour. No one traveled after dark, and there were few motels. Most towns had a small park or square where travelers with little or no money slept at night. Or, they pulled off the road on the outskirts of town. Just about everyone slept on pallets on the bare ground.

The little boy could sense that the spirit of adventure and determination slowly began to replace Faye and Chet's sadness and apprehension. Then, east of St. Francis, Kansas, the car broke down. Chet left his small brood to buy parts in the next town.

As they happily and simultaneously chattered—as children do when a parent will sit and listen—they saw something moving a short distance away. Right down the middle of the road came longhorn cattle. Donna and Walter giggled as they approached (grazing animals still owned the countryside and roads). But instead of passing, they stopped and started milling around, bumping and pushing the car. Fear replaced glee. The top of the car was only canvas and their horns were up to three feet long. What was worse, as they recognized the cattle very slowly coming toward them, Faye had told the children a short story about some people who found themselves in much the same situation. Those cattle overturned the vehicle, practically demolishing it.

They all huddled, Donna and Walter holding tight to their mama. They sat in almost breathless silence, knowing that any menacing move by one of those giant beasts would be followed by the rest. They bumped and gawked for over an hour. Surrounded, with no avenue of escape, the trio knew that out of the car they would be mauled or trampled. The fear was bone-chilling. They were at the mercy of those awesome, brainless creatures, like being spied upon by animals outside a cage, in complete control of the lives of people inside. Finally, the gigantic beasts started moving away as quietly as they came, their curiosity apparently satisfied. The children had a lot to tell their papa when he got back.

Although people had radios, there were few radio stations and even fewer weather reports, particularly in rural areas. Weather news was circulated by truck drivers and travelers at filling (gas) stations along highways. People driving any direction depended on the friendly, well-informed attendants to tell them what was ahead.

At daybreak of the third morning, the travelers anxiously continued until they finally reached a *modern* road (oiled asphalt). They saw more and more cattle, and the farms looked healthy.

Just west of Bennett, Colorado, Chet stopped the car. Silently, he got out and walked around to Faye's side, leaned over and pointed ahead. He said, "Look up there, more rain clouds, I think, and they're really black. It must be stormin' up ahead." But as Faye looked in the direction he pointed, she said, "You know, Chet, I believe that ain't no cloud, that's the mountains we heard about here in Colorado." With no more assurance than his wife's usually extraordinary instinct, he continued on without a word. Of course she was dead right.

As they approached Denver, silence fell over the group, awed by the sight before them. Although the plains were not then quite as *fruited* as in better times, the mountains still held their overwhelming *purple majesty* spoken of in *America the Beautiful* as the sun set behind them. Every time Walter saw them again, the memory of that first sight enhanced even more the full breadth of the beauty of the mountain range.

All four were stunned by the vastness and crowds of Denver (some 60,000 people in 1934), never having seen anything larger than Holton, Kansas (2,792 in 1933).

That night the little family stayed at Leaches Park, green and lush with sweet-smelling alfalfa, also housing something they had never before seen, an amusement park. Their eyes near popped out of their heads when they saw the roller coasters and ferris wheel. They had no money to go in, but just seeing the rides from their campsite thrilled them all sufficiently.

10

The moon was huge and the mountains stood out clearly against the star-filled, moon-bright sky. The small boy fell asleep with a mind filled with wagon trains, soldiers, and majestic red men on regal ponies standing up there, looking down on him from countless mountain ridges.

They left Denver at dawn and were soon in those mysterious mountains, a prism of colors reflecting the rising sun. The other three forever swore that Chet figured that once they got to the top of those mountains, they could coast all the way to California, because they certainly didn't have the money for gas to get them there. Not at fourteen cents a gallon.

The impression the mountains made on the flatlanders was extraordinary. They were terrified of the steep hills and winding roads, but dazzled by the beauty enfolding them. Occasionally, a young deer ran through the trees, or they saw a valley full of horses that must have been wild. There were birds everywhere with plumage they had never before seen, which sang songs just as strange and new to them. Streams alongside the road were clear as crystal. Sometimes Chet stopped alongside one just to inhale the beauty as well as the clean, mountain air. Strange fish darted about in their own wonderful sea. The liquid was like ice when they knelt next to the rushing streams to catch the remarkable-tasting water into their cupped hands. They ooh'd and ah'd at every turn, wanting to talk and share, but so enchanted by the sight that the next moment brought, they were mostly silent as they climbed.

It was not only hard to gain speed going up, Chet, equally entranced with their surroundings, drove even slower than necessary. It took a whole day to get as far as Idaho Springs, only thirty-six miles from Denver. They stopped just outside the town and set up their little makeshift camp, each of them flushed with the excitement of this magical place. Walter knew, with the absolute certainty of a little boy, that he would not be able to fall asleep, his mind was so filled with delight and marvel. Of course, by the time his small head touched the pallet, he was already in the dream world that only the very young may enter.

It took the better part of the next day to reach the foot of Loveland Pass, just sixty miles west of Denver. Once again they hit gravel roads. In mountains, there is no way of telling the altitude without road signs, and there were very few back then. Feeling a bit short-winded is almost the only indication. Not knowing was probably just as well because Loveland Pass is twelve thousand feet high. Walter later suspected that his father knew, but never told the rest of them.

The next morning, rested and refreshed, they started out even more lighthearted than before; but it would be awhile before Walter would get to climb that next hill. The car refused to pull. They unloaded everything and tried pushing it, but one man, a woman (however strong), and two small children could not generate the horsepower it took to move that vehicle upward. Eventually they had to give up.

Suddenly feeling very grown up, Walter listened intently to his parents. This was new since they did not usually discuss serious matters in front of their children. Chet mentioned a man they had met in Denver, who told him about a farming town not far away with a few jobs left for men willing to work. Faye spoke of how green it looked at the foot of the mountain, and how pleasant the people seemed. The decision was made: they would turn back and find that town. Chet turned the car around and headed eastward. Walter was disappointed, but the letdown was soon replaced by the excitement of seeing the beautiful place he knew they were heading toward. They found Longmont, Colorado—about fifteen miles from Boulder, the home of the University of Colorado. Just as Mr. Jenkins said, it was quiet, small, peaceful.

Chet then confided to his family that they had only two dollars and fifty cents left, which meant nothing to the boy who knew it would be easy for his papa to care for them now that they had found this place. Walter would learn later what his parents felt, almost penniless, with no family, no home, far from everything safe and familiar.

After searching for awhile, Chet found an old boxcar once used as a granary. Faye scrubbed it all up and found gunnysacks for the windows. They used nail kegs for chairs, and a camper-type kerosene stove which they filled with precious fuel. The pallets used in roadside camps became their beds. They had a home. They were safe again.

THREE

Walter's memory fast-forwarded forty-one years, to Loveland Pass, still climbing hills, anxious to see what he could from the top. He drove until he approached Las Vegas. As he reached the summit of the last hill, the sight ahead nearly took his breath away. He had been to Las Vegas before, but the lights were never as bright as they seemed that night.

Las Vegas is the perfect playground for pleasure-seekers, and Walter played for the next two weeks, often around the clock. He didn't gamble, but there was always something to see or do. It was his *Disneyland*. For Walter, Las Vegas never stopped being the most exciting, glamorous place in the world. He roamed around, sitting in on lounge shows, always amused by gamblers who thought they could win. A few did, and big. He needed little sleep in Las Vegas, and never tired of the beautiful showgirls. And of course, hookers were everywhere. The prostitutes fascinated him, and were always much more beautiful and desirable than any of the showgirls.

After a few days, he decided to take a drive. He had heard stories about a once-famous brothel called Ash Meadows near Las Vegas, so early one morning, he got into the car and headed there. The brothel was closed, but just seeing it filled him with an air of romance as he drove through the beautiful, open countryside.

Whenever people asked Walter why he patronized brothels, and what made them seem so romantic to him, especially "With so much around free for the taking?" his response was always the same: "While there for the taking, make no mistake, it's never free, not ever. There's always some kind of chain attached."

It was easy to get him to elaborate. He would tell the listeners that in most cases, the desire for a simple roll in the hay would be followed by the assumption that the words to follow would be a proposal. He insisted that to some girls, the act of getting laid is a declaration of fidelity, especially if it's repeated regularly. Picking up girls in a bar might also result in a sexual disease, a confrontation with her boyfriend, or some such situation. There may be problems with her kids. And of course, there are those perpetual matchmakers among family and friends. If you date one of those matches and find you do want to sleep with her, everyone is in on it, and you are

13

bulldogged if you get even close to a church.

No strings or chains are placed on a man in a brothel. He knows that a young, pretty girl will make him feel nine feet tall, or at least an object of lust. When he leaves, no one will follow him around trying to hog-tie him. He gets the best of both worlds: (a) a girl available whenever he wishes, for sex or to do the town; (b) freedom to determine for himself, without pressure, if he wants to court a girl or just continue his life of single bliss.

As for married men in brothels, a man can realize almost any sexual fantasy without fear of ridicule, or shock on the part of a wife who is Victorian, insensitive, or too cold to really care about what sex means to him. A man often needs no more than someone to talk to who really listens, or someone who will simply tell him he's wonderful. Some wives won't even try to deal with temporary impotence. A prostitute will.

After a leisurely drive, Walter found himself climbing a small hill. At the summit, he looked out on a green valley. He was as awestruck as he had been that day at Loveland Pass years before as his family turned around and went back down the gorgeous mountain toward Longmont. The little valley staring out at him looked much like the one he grew up in. Alfalfa was knee-deep, and he even saw cotton, there, in the middle of the desert. He pulled off the road, got out of the car, and just stood looking at the Pahrump Valley, an emerald in the middle of a vast, brown desert.

In the months that followed, Walter returned again and again, always standing in the same spot gazing down at the splendor below. Finally, he knew he had to have land there. He would have a house and land in the midst of this beauty, a place where he could grow vegetables, fruit, cotton, anything. A place to which he could return from the traveling he knew he would do. It was perfect. At long last he had found it: home!

In April 1976, Walter spotted a ten-acre parcel on the Hafen Ranch Road. The price was right so he bought it. When the deal was closed, he went into Las Vegas and purchased two mobile homes to combine into a house. Once the well was dug and electricity pulled onto his lot, he would connect the units.

In May, feeling a need for a break, he went to San Francisco. While sightseeing, he experienced chest pain. He went straight to Stanford Medical Center and checked in. After a series of tests, the doctors discussed a bypass, or possibly a transplant. Since they could not tell him if he would live one day longer with a bypass, coupled with a statistical mortality rate of five percent, he determined that if he fell into that five percent ratio, he would be one hundred percent dead.

While lying there feeling ill or weak only occasionally, time was endless, and depression plagued him. His mind kept drifting back to the early years, particularly those in Colorado during the 1930s.

Living in a boxcar wasn't much to return to at the end of long, laborious days. But it was home, after all. The hardships endured by the Plankinton family during their five years in Longmont made permanent impressions on all of them. He learned self-discipline, self-sacrifice, and became a hard, determined boy—and man.

His mother finally got a steady job in the *City Cafe*, always filled with obnoxious, dirty men, owned by a slob of a man. She was subjected to indignities that even Walter could understand. She frequently went home in a rage because the men would openly proposition her, using gutter talk she had never heard before. Other times, she was close to tears because a man grabbed or pinched her breast, or slapped her butt, or reached up under her skirt to try to touch her crotch. Her boss, worse than the customers, laughed along with them. She dreaded every minute in that place, swallowing insult and soul-shredding humiliation. But with times as they were, she had to make a living since Chet did not yet earn enough. Walter often remembered his father's face and clenched fists silently hitting his thighs.

The next summer, Chet, Faye, Donna, and Walter all hoed corn for one dollar an acre. Etched in Walter's memory was the picture of Faye hoeing a row, sitting down on the ground to cry a little, then getting angry and jumping to her feet, and together, they'd hoe up a storm. Walter could not understand why they were being mistreated—by life, as well as people. A deep bitterness was seeded watching his mother, sister, and father (not to mention himself) work as hard as mules simply to survive. He always considered this time as a disheartening, cruel period in the history of the country. But it made him what he eventually called conservative. No matter how much money he had, he'd worry about how much he had for tomorrow. He often deprived himself of simple pleasures—the kind most people take for granted—to save money.

Later in his life, Walter admitted to doing things to obtain money and property that cost him dearly in many ways. He finally realized that his insatiable need for wealth was the result of a gnawing fear that the poverty he once knew might return.

Things slowly improved, although Faye continued working in that terrible restaurant. Chet worked for a cement contractor, and all four of them hoed corn each summer. At last, through their joint efforts, Chet and Faye were able to buy a tiny plot of land. He never forgot the address: 1048 Ogden Street. As they saved more, Chet bought materials to build a small house. Eventually, the family moved into it with equal parts of relief and excitement.

One bright, Sunday morning, a car pulled up in front of the house. Chet's brother Rosie and his family were packed into their Model T Ford; even their old hound in the *turtleback (rumble) seat*. Uncle Rosie (named for Teddy Roosevelt) had kept his farm a little longer than Chet. When he lost it, he determined from the Plankinton's letters that things were better in Longmont. Uncle Rosie's family made Longmont their permanent home.

Donna, Cousin Glenn, and Walter attended a one-room school which had a crack between a wall and the chimney. Their teacher sent them outside for fifteen minutes each day regardless of temperature or their clothing. She then went back inside and locked the door. Since Walter was frozen within moments of hitting the often below-freezing temperatures, he did not "play," instead jamming himself into that crack between the chimney and the wall to get any warmth it might afford. It never occurred to him to resent not having a coat one year. Nor did it occur to him, then, just how heartless the teacher was.

The winter of his ninth year remained vivid in his mind. That Christmas he got a small framed picture of a little dog with a bandage on its tiny leg. He loved it. Donna got a rubber doll about six inches long. The children amused themselves making clothes for Donna's doll out of scraps of rags. Walter got pretty good at sewing. They spent hours pouring over the Wards catalogue, studying current fashions. Copying them kept them busy through many cold winter and rainy spring days.

Walter was always an ambitious kid. Any way he could make a few pennies, he did. He trapped muskrats and skunks which he sold for skins. When he was ten, he carried shingles up a ladder for a neighbor doing his roof. He was certain he had struck a gold mine. He always found jobs on his own, but every fall the Plankintons picked pumpkins; in spring, cherries; and each summer, watermelons.

As soon as Chet and Faye were convinced things were returning to normal in Kansas, they started planning the family's return. They sold their house, and with what they had saved made a total of five hundred and twenty dollars. That was a lot of money, enough to begin farming again, the only life they wanted. Five years after they moved into Longmont, Colorado, the Plankintons were on their way home, with a lot more than when they arrived.

They moved to Netawaka, Kansas, not far from their original home. Despite the hardships they had endured, Walter missed Longmont. Colorado was home to him, not Kansas. Still, being with his family made him feel content, at least for awhile. And some of his memories were cherished.

One day, Chet was cleaning his lot bordering the highway, shoveling manure and putting it into the spreader to haul into the fields. His wife was in the house. A man came to the door selling magazines—common in those days. Faye wasn't buying but the man wouldn't give up. After a time he began to irritate her. She finally said, "Oh hell, I wish you'd stop bothering me, I don't read." The salesman instantly countered with, "Well, maybe your husband would like to read them." She looked him square in the eye and said, "My husband's deaf and dumb; and he don't read, either." The man finally left. She was pleased with her ruse.

But instead of leaving, the salesman went to where Chet was shoveling manure and started trying to communicate with him. He waved his arms in the air, pointing and moving his hands about. Chet, assuming the man was a deaf mute, responded in kind. The two men flailed about in the middle of the open field of manure in total silence. After what seemed like at least ten minutes, a neighbor came across the field toward the two men engaged in their silly, noncommunicative dance. As he approached he called out, "Hey Chet, could you come and help me?" to which Chet answered, "Sure, just as soon as I get rid of this dumb son of a bitch." The whole town, and beyond, laughed at the story for years.

Walter soon realized that while farming might be his parents' way of life, it definitely was not his. To him it was little more than slave labor. He milked cows, fed hogs, chopped wood, toiled in the fields, and worked a garden for what felt like endless hours, days, weeks, and months. From the day the family returned to Kansas, anything resembling boyhood was ended for Walter.

He shucked corn for neighbors to make money for Christmas. Not instead of regular chores, in addition to them—which already took up most waking hours except for school. By thirteen, he was so good at shucking corn he claimed to have produced more than most grown men. Big and strong, he was expected to work long hours and just as hard as any man. Yet, he was an obedient *child*, seen but rarely ever heard. It was a natural role for a boy his age in that period in the U.S. Hard work was a family tradition so it never entered Walter's mind to resent anything in his life.

Walter started setting traps for muskrats and skunks just as he had done in Colorado, in his one and only pair of shoes. The smell made the kids call him *Skunk*, and the teacher never allowed him to sit anywhere close to the heater. Nevertheless, he was respected; he was the world traveler. He'd been to faraway Colorado. Although the name-calling hurt, he enjoyed the limelight.

In Colorado, Walter had not been much of a student, but in Kansas something happened. His teachers, Mr. and Mrs. Boone, who had also been to Colorado, began talking to their student about Colorado. His schoolwork improved. He finally wanted to learn, and began working hard to achieve the highest grades in elementary, and later in high school.

About eighth grade he discovered girls. He was wild about Alma. She was smart and achieved top grades, too, but Walter claimed that he always bested her. Although competitive in schoolwork, he also insisted that it never affected their "puppy love," a claim difficult to swallow for anyone knowing Walter.

That winter, Walter worked harder on his traps than ever before. He wanted to make Christmas special for his family. He had a good haul and often went to the barn just to look at the hides hung there to dry. He knew he would get a good price from the buyer, Mr. Holton. One cold morning just days before Mr. Holton was due in town, Walter stopped to take a quick look at his gold mine before starting for school. He walked into the barn thinking about all the things he would buy for Christmas.

They were gone. The skins were all gone. He ran to the kitchen where his mother was clearing the breakfast dishes, gasping that someone had stolen his precious hides. To his youthful hysteria, she said unceremoniously and without explanation, "Your dad took them. Go on now, you'll be late for school." The boy was devastated. For weeks, he agonized over the unfairness. He was the one who left a warm bed before dawn to go into that terrible morning cold. He withstood the jibes of friends and classmates who nicknamed him Skunk. He spent his few free hours, often late at night, skinning those horrendous carcasses with their sickening smell. He could not believe his own father could be so cruel, so dishonest. To make matters worse, Chet never once mentioned it. He never told his son that he was sorry. Nor did he explain how after teaching the boy to be honest he could just take his property. Walter was crushed and bewildered. Every attempt to question his parents was met with stony silence.

Christmas was sad that year, with no spectacular dinner and few sparse gifts. What saved the day for Walter was a friend from Longmont coming to visit. It caused many feelings to erupt. Walter had been happy with his family, seeing both parents content to be home among their old friends and relatives. But what happened with the skunk pelts made him sad, angry, and suddenly aware of how much he disliked Kansas and wished to be back in Colorado. He borrowed fifteen dollars for bus fare and three days after Christmas, he ran away—*home* to Longmont.

When he stepped off the bus he headed straight for his Uncle Rosie, who contacted Chet and Faye. Walter found a job with an old couple who paid him thirty dollars a month, plus room and board. They liked him and he liked them. They were older, with grown children long gone from their farm. Their new hand did everything there was to do, and thoroughly enjoyed being pampered by this lovely woman who probably missed having her own children and grandchildren around.

Something else was happening. Young men were disappearing. Every time he went into town, someone asked if he could work for them. It was March 1942 and World War II was raging. Walter helped wherever he could, but even a boy needs rest. He was getting tired, and not just from long hours of hard work. Farming was never his favorite job in the first place. He was feeling the first stages of wanderlust, a compulsion affecting the rest of his life.

FOUR

Once again it was goodbye to Longmont. With one dollar in his pocket, Walter started hitchhiking west. The first night he got to Raton, New Mexico, over two hundred miles. When it started raining he crawled under a railroad trestle, curled up and fell asleep.

He awoke with the bitter cold reaching clear through ill-protected flesh to clutch his bones. He jumped up and walked as fast as he could. About a mile down the road was an open filling station. He spent his last dollar on something to eat out of vending machines.

At dawn, back on the highway, his shivering thumb pointed west. By noon he reached Santa Fe. Although Walter had little interest in reading, he liked American history. He took full advantage of being in the historic city, roaming around soaking up as much as his youthful energy and enthusiasm allowed before he returned to the highway. On the main road outside Albuquerque by dusk, an old truck carrying about thirty Mexican sheepherders picked him up. They invited him to go on to Utah, assuring him that he could get a job. He said no. They parted at a truck stop in Gallup, New Mexico, where the truck turned north. Since he had not eaten since before dawn, he was hungry, and tired. Too proud to ask for a handout and not yet road-wise enough to know how to work for a meal, he sneaked into a truck stop, crawled into a back booth and fell sound asleep.

At sunup the waitress woke him up holding a cup of very hot coffee in her outstretched hand. He used most of the sugar and all of the cream on the table in that one small cup. The coffee warmed his stomach and rejuvenated his spirits. He was going to the place with lush green valleys, a body of water so vast he wouldn't see the end of it, glamorous movie stars, exciting and wonderful things he had only read about. Waiting for him to conquer it, all he had to do was get there. With spirits again soaring, he pointed his thumb toward the great unknown.

Within minutes on the road, a brand new Lincoln Zephyr passed him going ninety, continuing on for another half mile or so. Then it stopped and backed up at an incredible rate of speed until it stood in front of him. The driver asked, "Hey kid, can you drive?" Walter told him, "Well, I never drove no fancy car like yours, but I can drive. If you show me how, I'll take a whirl at it." The stranger pointed to the driver's side and the boy obeyed with youthful zeal. He had driven through from Chicago and was bone tired. The man said he'd give Walter a ride if he'd drive so he could sleep. They were soon moving down the road. The man told Walter not to worry about gas (which was rationed) because the trunk was filled with tanks, and they could go two thousand miles without refills. Before long the stranger was sound asleep.

He finally woke up and told the boy to pull into a hotel up ahead. It was the place where Clark Gable and Carol Lombard had recently spent their honeymoon: Oakman, Arizona, forty-five miles west of Kingman, Arizona. They stayed only long enough for the man to eat. Although Walter went into the cafe with him, he had no money. The man never asked why the boy didn't order anything. He simply ignored it. The boy was almost faint with hunger, but would never have admitted that. Instead, he concentrated on the surroundings, listening to an older couple talking about how much money was being made from the old gold mines around there. It helped him to ignore his growling stomach.

Back on the road, with the owner of the car again driving, he finally fell asleep wondering how this man could not hear the ferocious roars bellowing from the starving gut. Walter saw his roll of money; he was just incredibly cheap.

When the boy woke up it was dark. He had no idea where they were except that it was a mountain pass. Later, he'd recognize it as Cajon Pass, California. The man bragged about being in the movie business, then asked where Walter wanted to be dropped off. Knowing nothing about California, he just said downtown. They drove to the corner of East Sixth and Los Angeles Street and he dropped the boy off without even a thank you or good luck. Throughout his life, Walter said that every young hitchhiker brought back the memory of the selfish bastard who left a young kid in the center of skid row.

Walter watched the taillight as it disappeared down the street, leaving him alone in that sleazy place. He stood cemented to the small square of concrete sidewalk under his feet. His mind was blank. He had no idea what to do. He was so lost and scared his eyes began to fill with tears, but he knew he couldn't cry.

After what seemed forever he began walking, aimlessly. Ahead was a brawl in front of one of the many bars. As he approached, a group of derelicts and passersby (he never could figure out what normal-looking people were doing on that block) were gathering to watch the free show. Eventually the police came and dispersed the onlookers.

As the crowd thinned, the boy's attention reluctantly returned to his own predicament. He stood still, bewildered and terrified. After a couple of minutes, a man with a severe limp walked toward him. He said, "Hey, Kid, you lookin' for a job?" Walter said yes, quickly and in dead earnest. The man's name was Lenny, and he was the manager of a ranch on a river not too far away, near Ojai. He needed a "sort of all-round man who can milk cows and wrangle horses." The tall, gangly boy was flattered. It was the first time anyone had addressed him as a man. He had done both since he was raised on a farm. Lenny said, "I'll give you thirty dollars a month, plus room and board. What do you say?" In a split second, the boy could hear his own roar saying "Yes, Sir!"

They started down the sidewalk toward Lenny's car. As they passed a diner, the man said, "By the way, Kid, you hungry?" Even faster, and louder, the boy repeated, "Yes, Sir!" He steered Walter into the diner. Lenny said, "Order anything you want, Kid." Those were the most wonderful words ever spoken. He looked down at the remarkable list as he breathed in all the aromas engulfing him.

Walter near inhaled the ham, eggs, toast, and coffee. When he finished they walked back into the street. The moment the boy hit the air, he got so sick he almost doubled up. He rushed toward an alleyway, but before he could reach it, vomited on the sidewalk. When he finally stopped he was utterly humiliated and embarrassed. He tried to explain to his new boss who stood waiting, patiently, that he had not eaten for awhile, then too fast. In contrast to the thoughtless bastard who left a young kid to fend for himself in a dangerous place, this kind man turned Walter around and marched him back into that same diner saying, "Okay, let's try again." The second helping, eaten slowly, stayed down. As he ate, Lenny talked about how his ankle was broken in an accident years before and never healed properly.

They drove to Lenny's house on Highland Street in North Hollywood, where they stayed a couple of days. While Lenny took care of business, Walter wandered around sightseeing and eating (Lenny gave him money for bus fare and meals). When they left for the ranch, Walter was his healthy, robust self again.

The *dude ranch* housed twenty-five guests in cabins. The main structure was a large house with the biggest dining room Walter had ever seen, except in movies. One day while wrangling some donkeys, the boy bragged to Lenny that he wanted to ride the lead burro, a huge animal. Lenny advised against it because that particular critter would buck him off. Being a cocky kid, Walter assured him he could ride anything with four legs. Lenny laughed, which only spurred the boy on. He'd show him. A few minutes later, Lenny howled watching Walter pick himself up from the other side of the fence. Walter would say, "I swear that donkey hardly moved a muscle to make my large frame fly through the air with the greatest of ease, until it hit the ground with such a thud, I was certain that ass had broken this ass."

After a month, an older boy came to work on the ranch. He told Walter how in Lake Tahoe, Nevada, he could easily make two hundred dollars a month because the war made the hotels busier than usual. The more he talked the more excited Walter got about the glamorous resort town, and the big money.

Walter told Lenny he was leaving. Lenny tried to convince him to stay, telling him that he had a secure job on the ranch with a good future, and that he didn't know what he'd find in Lake Tahoe. He insisted the kid filling him with stories was a drunk (which Walter already saw), and was exaggerating. Although it was common in those days for a young teenager to be on his own, a thirteen-year-old was still only a boy. And the prospects along the open road definitely enchanted that boy. Security was a word, not a reality. Lenny insisted he would get into trouble out there with that other kid, and that Walter was ungrateful. Walter believed Lenny was just saying those things because he was angry. When he looked back years later, he recognized that Lenny was only trying to protect him. Lenny finally relented and offered to drive the two boys to the highway to catch a ride to Walter's Shangri-la.

The road seemed less forbidding than before. Of course this time the thirteen-year-old had a traveling companion who was older, maybe three or four years his senior, consequently wiser. Between them, absolutely nothing was impossible. They were two enterprising young men rushing into the world to seek their fortunes.

As they stood there, thumbs outstretched, Walter felt a rush of pride and fervor. Then, just as easily recalled, he watched his new-found sidekick pull out a fifth of whiskey and a bottle of coke. Upon his insistence, Walter sat down next to him along the roadside. He offered the boy some hooch. Walter had never tasted whiskey so it was all strange to him and, of course, adventurous. While the kid held the cup, Walter poured some of the nectar into it. He sat there drinking, the sun on his head, the heat penetrating his body as the liquid settled into an early morning stomach. Within minutes, Walter heaved up every drop of the "nectar," plus his entire breakfast. His companion howled.

The kid finished the rest of his bottle alone. They went to the side of the road. Soon, Walter's companion walked over to a tree, laid down on the ground using a roll of clothes he carried as a pillow, and passed out cold, seemingly proving how much more grown up he was. For the rest of the day, not one driver responded to Walter's tired thumb.

Well into the evening, an elderly couple stopped and asked if the boy wanted a ride. He roused his besotted confederate. They drove them to a town with a bus depot. Although Walter had some money, he decided hitchhiking was as good as riding. His new-found friend agreed so they headed northeast toward Sacramento. As they progressed, the companion proved he was much more interested in drinking than making time. Finally disgusted, Walter went on alone. After awhile, feeling tired of the road, he finally got on a bus.

It was natural in those days to talk with bus drivers, and his was exceptionally friendly. The boy explained to Mickey that he was going to Lake Tahoe to get a job in a hotel his friend told him about, adding that it would have to be fast since he was almost broke. Mickey let the boy finish his moneymaking tale, then lowered the boom. There were no jobs in Tahoe because the hotels were not open. He explained that it was cold there, and that tourists would not arrive for another month or so, depending on the weather. Walter was desolate and suddenly scared again. Apparently recognizing his fear and feeling sorry for the young boy out on the road alone, Mickey invited him to Truckee, where he could stay until the season started. The boy willingly postponed his dream of great riches and went home with the bus driver.

People who have never hitchhiked, traveling under the open ski, living—as it were—on the road, might not realize that such a lifestyle is not conducive to staying clean and sweet-smelling. Myra, Mickey's wife, was as kind as he was. When she saw how, shall we say, unkempt the boy was, without benefit of discussion, she heated some water (there was no running hot water in most homes in those days). When the first teakettle was hot, she poured it into a basin, told the boy to bend over, and scrubbed his head. When he saw the black water, he was embarrassed. Maybe the thirteen-year-old thought he was a man, but to Myra he was just another kid. To his dismay, she filled the tub and told him to strip, give her his clothes, and get into the tub. It was not a request. She bathed him. Maybe a better term would be scoured him. Walter wore Mickey's clothes while she washed, dried, and pressed his.

After about a week with the wonderful family, Mickey told Walter that he might have found a job for him in a Lake Tahoe gas station. The owner, who also owned a motel, had been stricken with an illness that left him a virtual invalid, and his wife could not operate the service station. When Mickey took him there, Walter was hired on the spot.

While supposedly working for the wife, she dumped all responsibility on the thirteen-year-old boy. They paid him very little, although part of an extremely wealthy family. He slept in their motel and ate in their restaurant, all family-owned.

They were condescending, treating the boy like a beast of burden. Walter had worked like a mule since childhood, but had never been treated like one before he met these people. The crippled husband was uncivilized. Taught compassion for anyone who was sick or disadvantaged in any way, Walter had never seen his kind of bestiality much less been subjected to it. Although honest to a fault, the owner questioned and challenged the boy's every move. He later learned that stealing in the area was the rule rather than exception, so paranoia in the man in the wheelchair was somewhat justified. The boy never stopped looking for another job.

In June, the hotels began to open, and he found a job in one which paid much more money. He washed pots and pans in the bakery for a sweet old lady, sharing a clean room with another boy, Tommy. He also ate very well. Tommy was only a bit older than Walter. He was from San Francisco. He explained that he was not on his own, but came from a family that believed in their sons learning to work for others from a very early age. Walter didn't quite understand the reasoning too well, but just accepted what the other boy said. They became good friends.

Tahoe was a different place in 1942. There were no jet planes to move people cross-country in hours. People took trains from the east coast, traveling several days. Vacationers stayed a month or six weeks. Only the very wealthy stayed in Tahoe, so its hotels were elegant. The war had not yet cut into their way of life as it did after another year, when the town closed up for the duration of the war.

After a month or so, Tommy left, but not before he invited Walter to visit him. At the end of the season Walter took a bus to San Francisco. He decided to spend some money on decent clothes, but overdid it just a little. It was worth it, particularly when he found Tommy's address. Walter described it as straight out of a movie, perched on a cliff overlooking the entrance to San Francisco Bay. The servants were as elegant as the house. He claimed that he was awestruck. This brief tale was undoubtedly a well-padded exaggeration, or perhaps an outright lie. While some very wealthy families believe in their sons learning to work for others, it is be unlikely that a rich thirteen or fourteen-year-old would have been sent away from home, unsupervised by any family member or close friend, into a resort town to room with strangers of possibly questionable backgrounds, during a raging world war. His exaggerated descriptions of the family's cultured demeanor further widens the doubts.

Tommy's mother was kind and gracious, almost regal. The next few days were like a fairy tale to a rough and tumble boy from a Kansas farm. He didn't recognize their prominence until he was much older, and kept in touch with them throughout the years, although Walter would never tell anyone the name of the family. Because everything Walter talked about had at least a small measure of basis in fact, there likely was a Tommy, and a pleasant, even affluent, family living in San Francisco. But reality probably stopped at "very wealthy."

After awhile, Walter determined that while he was enjoying his "fantasy," it was time to move on. He had to find work. His cash was almost gone. He said farewell to his generous hosts and caught a bus to Los Angeles with his last few dollars. Had his hosts actually been both wealthy and generous, it is unlikely they would have allowed a thirteen-year-old boy to leave for some unknown place with limited funds.

When Walter got off of the bus on that overcast, dismal day, he gasped. He was almost exactly where he had been just a few short months before when the man in the Zephyr drove off. He sat down on a bench in the depot almost dazed by his predicament. He had not moved one step forward. He made good money by working extremely hard for a whole summer, yet, there he was again: no cash, no job, no place to live, and no idea what to do next.

All at once, he knew that he was still only a boy, not a man; at least not yet. He also acknowledged to himself that he was homesick. He needed his parents' assurance that they still loved and wanted him. He needed the sister who believed in him no matter what. After sitting there thinking for a very long time, he got up and walked over to a public phone and stood looking at it, choking on the pride that was arguing with the panic inside him. In his pocket were his last three coins. He asked the operator to reverse the charges.

It had been eight months since he left Uncle Rosie's in Colorado; no one knew where he was. Relief and joy were in his mother's voice. He told her that he was broke and wanted to come home. They were *hard up* but she told him not to worry, that she would get the money somewhere. She told him to stay in the depot and she would wire the cash there. Walter went into the Western Union office again and again to see if it had arrived. It finally came the next morning. She had managed, somehow, to send three extra dollars. He could eat.

The last few miles were the longest. He fought back tears and a huge lump in his throat. The Plankinton farm was one mile north of Netawaka, Kansas, right on the highway. The driver dropped the boy off directly in front of their property. As the bus slowly pulled away, he stood there staring at the house up on the hill. Nothing before ever looked quite so beautiful.

It was about seven in the morning. As he began to walk, impulse and thrill made him begin to run. He stopped suddenly as he caught the first sight of his mother coming out of the storm cellar, a milk pail in each hand. It was what he had seen countless times before, but it never looked quite like this. Nothing could hold back the tears. He couldn't move; his feet were planted solid into the earth, that sight erasing everything else from his mind.

As if sensing something, Faye turned slowly toward him. The pails clattered to the ground. She started running toward Walter as she called out to Chet. The boy dropped his pack and started to run, too. When they met, they threw their arms around each other, laughing and crying at the same time. Never before that moment did he realize how deeply he loved his mother.

Seconds later, Chet reached them, also running. He put his arm around his young son and said, "Sure glad to have you home, Boy." Walter was stunned. It was the most demonstrative, dramatic indication of feelings his father ever made to him. Later in his life, he admitted that he had never even thought about his father loving him before that day. Public displays of love were unheard of in those days, and certainly never discussed within families. Midwestern farmers simply didn't show affection. The one great exception may have been when boys came home from WWII. Usual demeanor seemed to be thrown to the wind, at least for awhile, before it settled back into what was then considered normal, emotionally detached behavior.

Times were still hard so Walter shucked corn that fall. Faye felt it absolutely necessary that he return to school, so she went to the principal and somehow convinced him to give the boy some tests so he could rejoin his own class, even though he missed his entire ninth grade. Almost immediately, school bored him. The just-turned fourteen-year-old knew he had to seek a life outside this sleepy little Kansas town. The lifestyle was (and still is) a small piece of heaven for many, including his parents, but he was certain it would never be for him.

After Christmas he took a job with some neighbors, moving in with them for convenience (commonplace then). On school days he milked cows and on weekends hauled hay and shoveled manure. They were good to the boy and he worked as hard as he could for them. By April 1943, however, school stretched beyond boring into nerve-racking, pursued closely by a recurrence of wanderlust.

Walter finally told his parents that he wanted to return to Colorado. They weren't too pleased with the idea but knew that he would leave one way or another. They also recognized that the boy was reasonably capable of taking care of himself. Certainly there were potential dangers, but not nearly as many, nor the same kind, as exist today. If a fourteen-year-old who looked eighteen was aggressive and strong, and Walter Plankinton definitely was, it was not likely anyone would bother him. There were sex deviates around, no doubt, but they were not as unrestricted nor as enterprising as they seem to be now, at least not in terms of males. Drugs were available, too, but were all but invisible in the company Walter kept and the environment in which he existed. Parents feared for their children, but nowhere near as much as they must today.

Donna didn't want her brother to leave either. But, she was his rock and staunch supporter, no matter what. She wrote to him wherever he went. Walter hated leaving them and the security of his home, but he had to go. He was too ambitious to be a low-paid farm hand, content to spend his life in fear every time it rained too hard, or not at all. And, although unafraid of hard work, he had already seen places he liked more, where hard work paid much better.

On the bus heading for Longmont, he looked out the window with mixed emotions: While yearning to go just as he had that first time when he was only six, he was sad to leave a family he loved, knowing he would never again live with them. This would be his last time to "leave home." This time, he would make his fortune, and home would be in another—however then unknown—place.

Walter went straight to Uncle Rosie's, but didn't stay. There was a war on and male help was near impossible to find. First, he went to work for a local farmer but soon started working in a small dairy.

FIVE

Walter claimed to have wondered from the time he was a small child why farmers stacked hay manually since every year there seemed to be more new machines to do everything else in farming. Certainly someone had ideas to improve the stacking process. Discussions about this and things like it came close to arguments with his father. He claimed to have spent a great deal of his spare time reading farming catalogues and books on agriculture, trying to show his father what was available. But Chet would not accept modern machines or new agricultural ideas over tried and true ways. And coming from a boy, he likely considered his authority, and perhaps manhood, being challenged. There was a loud ring of exaggeration here, particularly when Walter was questioned as to how old he was when he was giving all this sage advice. His answers, or nonanswers, spoke much louder than his "memory" of what happened.

He said he remembered watching men at the dairy in Longmont (during the very brief period there with his uncle) tediously collecting hay using a *sweep rig* pulled by two horses, then piling it with an overhead stacker. After awhile, he knew what to do. In those years, a fourteen-year-old could buy a car without a parent's consent or a license. So Walter bought an old car, borrowed a welder, and rigged a power rake to push the hay into a stack. To turn in tight corners, he drove backwards, which also kept hay away from the radiator. It took a while, but when it was finally perfected he began his first entrepreneurial venture.

His *buck rake* was an instant success, easily outdoing the slow-moving horses pulling the sweep rig. He swore he earned sixty dollars a day when men made forty a week, which had to be another exaggeration. Even the amount he claimed that men made, forty dollars a week, is highly suspect. Men in rural America made even less than in cities, and minimum wage in cities did not reach $1 an hour until 1956. It took even longer for that rate to reach the rural areas. Only the shortage of manpower due to the war made the need for his services genuinely pressing. Whatever amount he really earned, Walter was dizzy with power and wealth.

At the same time of this first foray into commerce, Walter said, "the sap started to run." He pushed hay ten hours a day and chased Margaret the rest of the time. Soon he knew he had to make a choice. At fourteen, there was no contest. He sold the buck rake to devote all of his time to Margaret.

Here, Walter's story became even more questionable. Even at this age, he claimed to have had a passion for money, above almost anything else. Granted, a young boy can easily become smitten, but for him to just arbitrarily give up what he remembered was an above average adult, full-time income, is also very suspicious. When challenged for his rationalization regarding this contradiction in his personality, as well as the dollar numbers he claimed, he first displayed anger, apparently to intimidate, but when that didn't work, he simply refused to discuss the issue further.

While it is believed that there were fragments of truth in Walter's stories of his early life, mostly because Walter had little *creative* imagination, there is no doubt that there were many embellishments. It didn't take long before it was relatively easy to spot exaggeration and grandstanding. Often his body language revealed truth-stretching, but for want of a better expression, cross-examination quickly raised anger if he had no reasonable answer.

Within two weeks and without a backward glance, Margaret brushed him off. Walter was desolate. Scorned by the woman he had sacrificed so much for. He couldn't understand how she could stop loving him, and for no apparent reason, at least none that he could see. The hours crept by. He spent most of his time brooding, alone, and when he got tired of that, he soulfully roamed around town hoping to catch a glimpse of her.

For weeks, the real world hardly existed for him. Walter was not used to giving up what he wanted, nor what he believed belonged to him. Then he noticed something he didn't understand. It seemed like all of the girls in town would near swoon whenever a serviceman came home on leave. He began to watch, and tried to figure out what the fascination was. He firmly believed that he was more handsome than most men, and certainly much smarter; so other boys, even those years older than he was, should not have been capable of offering him any competition. Besides, the same men and boys who had lived there all their lives were the ones the girls seemed to notice for the first time. He soon realized that it wasn't the boys the girls were falling all over. It was the uniform. That was the answer, and it certainly made more sense. It had nothing to do with him, his good looks, great intelligence, or enormous charm. He needed a uniform. Certainly then he would win the fair Margaret back. But how was a boy of fourteen going to pull this off?

After changing the date on his birth certificate, he took a bus into Denver. All the way, he visualized himself sailing around the world. He headed straight for the Navy Recruiting Office. With one glance, the officer behind the desk spotted the clumsy erasures on the birth certificate. With a sly grin he simply dismissed Walter. The boy was shocked. He stepped back from the officer's desk and just stood there, embarrassed as never before. And the disappointment burned into his mind. Any hope to recapture Margaret's love was swept away with the wave of this stranger's hand. He stepped back, out of the way of the next person waiting, but just stood there, almost paralyzed.

He realized someone was speaking. It was a young man telling the recruiting officer that he was from Arkansas and had no birth certificate. He explained that he was born on a farm without a doctor in attendance, and his parents never had one recorded. It worked. The officer filled out the papers and told the boy that he was on his way into the Navy, providing everything checked out and he passed the physical. It appeared almost magical. Walter's hopes were rekindled. He knew he'd never get by the same officer a second time. The Marines! They sailed around the world, too, and their uniform was even more impressive.

Walter ran to the Marine Recruiting Office and repeated the story he heard in the Navy office, but gave his name as "Donald Allen" Plankinton. He was never able to determine where that name came from. When the Marine Corps ran its check through the Kansas Office of Vital Statistics, there would be no Donald Allen Plankinton on file. The officer handed the boy the enlistment papers, which included affidavits for his parents to sign, verifying his date of birth as October 22, 1925—instead of 1928.

Back in Longmont, Walter forged his father's name; a girl he knew signed Faye's name. He remembered that a friend of his parents', a real estate man in Longmont, was also a Notary Public. He had to be in his eighties and didn't see too well anymore. Walter's young friend called him pretending to be Faye. She told him that Walter was joining the Marines—with her blessing of course—and that she would count it a favor if he'd notarize the signatures. He told her to send the boy right over. He ran all the way. Since everyone in Longmont always called Walter "Sonny," he was almost certain that old Mr. Dobson probably never knew his real name. If he did, he counted on his ability to fast-talk almost anyone to get around the old man. In July 1943, he was on a train for San Diego. He was three months shy of being fifteen.

Boot Camp was a revelation. They had six short weeks to turn gawky kids and unskilled men into combat soldiers with only two purposes: to kill and to survive. Walter had the typical sergeant who, had he gone overseas with his men, would likely never have been seen alive again. He worked the *Boots* twenty hours a day. He had every tree and every bump on the ground memorized. He forced the *Boots* to be silent when there was no reason, and screamed in their faces even when they did what he asked. Eventually, like all servicemen, Walter and the others realized the sergeant probably saved many of their lives.

Walter's platoon joined an invasion force heading for one of the large Pacific islands held by the Japanese. The island was quickly secured. As the troops sat around drinking beer (they depended on the Navy for beer), they watched the wounded being prepared to go home. Walter saw a boy who seemed familiar. As he approached the injured young man, he realized that he was from Netawaka. They talked. Knowing Walter's real age, the young man was surprised to see him. Walter explained everything, and asked him to see his folks and tell them he was safe since, once again, they had no idea where their son was. Afraid they might try to get him out of the service, Walter hadn't written to anyone.

True to his word, as soon as the young man hit Netawaka he went to the farm to let the Plankintons know about their boy. Faye went straight through the roof knowing her young son was in combat. She was in the Kansas City Marine Corps office like a shot. By then Walter was in a place called Ulithia. That invasion was quite different from the first. It claimed many in the first assault wave. By the time Walter's whereabouts were pinpointed he was on Saipan. There were no computers in the 1940s.

For three days and nights, Walter's platoon was pinned down in the middle of a sugar cane field by a sniper holed up in a smoke stack of the sugar factory which bordered the field. For seventy-two interminable hours, he lay in one spot watching men being killed all around him. The sniper picked out one man at a time and just kept shooting until he hit his mark. If it took too long, it seemed he must have gotten bored because he'd move on to another target; like playing a game. If a man raised his head, the sniper swung that wand and killed him.

Walter had been afraid, but in that flat sugar cane field, he learned about terror, as well as his own sense of survival. Those two things, terror and survival, blocked everything else from his mind. Food and sleep didn't matter. Living, only living mattered.

Their only cover was young, not very high sugar cane stalks. Fortunately, the soil was soft. With as little movement as possible, Walter kept digging the dirt out from under his body, piling it up into a small mound directly in front of him. This had to be done very slowly because a sudden move could draw the sniper's attention.

Learning about the unbelievable self-control it takes to overcome the impulse to jump up when a friend is hit, not knowing if he's alive and in pain, maybe in desperate need of help, or if he's already dead, was very quickly, and prematurely, turning a boy into a man. Periodically, panic made him tremble convulsively, which in turn led him almost into hysteria, which had to be choked down. He thought about his family, and wondered if he would ever see them again. He was never aware of sleeping, although he suspected he must have. He kept asking himself over and over what he was doing in this God-forsaken place clear across the world.

He didn't dare move. The sense of survival he learned lying there in that shooting gallery was both fragile and powerful. He came to believe that such a situation literally takes over mind and body; even the soul. He would later say that, "We think we are always in control, but I found out at fifteen that no one is ever in total control. The desire to live helps us face indescribable fear not with courage, really, more with abandon. Yet something keeps us from doing anything mindlessly stupid, or suicidal."

He went from despair to hope and to despair again. After what seemed an eternity, he heard a plane. As the sound got closer and louder, he knew that no music, no voice would ever again compare with the awesome beauty of those U.S. Navy dive bomber engines. His invisible rescuer dropped a bomb into the center of that smoke stack. The son of a bitch was off his ass, and the other 500 men pinned down in that strange, terrible place.

When his platoon returned to base, the colonel called Walter in and told him he knew his real age, his real name, and how he had pulled off his little charade. He also told him that his mother was raising all kinds of hell about her fifteen-year-old son being in combat. Walter's thoughts while the colonel spoke went from panic, to rage with his mother for trying (at least in his mind) to keep him a baby, to regret that his little scheme was over. Then to his complete surprise, the colonel added, "Son, you've proven yourself a man, and we've decided to leave the decision up to you. Do you want to go home or continue on as a Marine?" By then Walter was a *gung ho Marine*. Of course he said, "Sir, I'm a Marine, and I'll stay till the job is finished." Within days he was on his way back to the States. He went straight to Longmont because by then, to him, that was his real home. There he met Maxine, and miraculously, Margaret fell to oblivion. Walter was *really* in love. Again. The portion of the thirty days he spent there went by like a streak of lightning.

Soon after reporting back to Port Hueneme, California, he was on another ship heading toward the Pacific. Two weeks of nothing but lying in the sun, eating, sleeping, watching movies, and playing *Red Dog*, a card game.

This time, however, they never even slowed down as they passed Diamond Head. Soon, they were waiting offshore of another unknown island while the Navy pounded away at the beach with their big guns. As they approached the beach the enemy fired at them with everything they had. Their defenses were so enormous that each foot the Marines gained seemed to take forever.

For four days, they were pinned at the base of a mountain. Once more Walter watched helplessly as one man after another dropped around him. He expected a *seasoned* soldier to adapt to the realities of war. He never stopped wondering how many ever do. After about a week his platoon was relieved. As they passed some of the reinforcement troops coming up, a young, fresh-faced boy told them where they were: Iwo Jima.

In the spring of 1945, just off Guam, they joined the largest convoy Walter had yet seen. It turned north. The sight was breathtaking: ships of every description in every direction as far as the eye could see. No one had to tell any of the men that this was going to be one big dogfight.

As they neared the island, they heard gunfire so loud, and what seemed so far-reaching, they couldn't help but wonder if the Navy planned to blow the island right out of the ocean. The assault wave was well ahead of Walter's ship so that their landing was relatively uneventful. They moved inland. Litter-bearers passed them trying first to remove the wounded, then the dead, from what seemed to Walter an ocean of bodies. He already knew the name of this place, Okinawa.

The Navy had leveled the island so as even the early wave of troops moved in resistance was minimal. They came upon what must have been a commercial area. A bank was blown away except for a huge safe that stood in the rubble, completely intact. As luck would have it, there was a fellow in Walter's outfit called "Skeeter." Skeeter was forty-nine, with a wife and seven kids back home. He was in prison when the war broke out. Certain convicts were offered deals by the government: If Skeeter entered the Marines he would get a full pardon. He needed no more prodding than that to *volunteer*. Skeeter was a safecracker. His name naturally came up when the boys spotted the safe. It took little to find him. Skeeter took command. His fellow Marines followed his orders to the letter.

Some dynamite was *acquired* to cook up nitroglycerine. Using a bird feather, he painted the cracks and locks of the safe with the nitro extract, then drew a sort of line around to the side of it. He was ready. The troops all moved as far as Skeeter ordered them to, while he stayed just in front of his target. Carefully, he raised his rifle, and with the butt end hit it lightly. The door sailed off about 300 feet.

The men were into the open steel box like a swarm of bees. They stuffed their pockets with precious Japanese yen. Merchant Marines on ships fresh out of the States would happily trade cigarettes, milk, steaks, vegetables, almost anything. The Marines also gathered up old parachutes (which they cut the size of flags and painted red circles on) and the Japanese rifles found all over the combat zones. They took them to the piers and traded them for cases of whiskey—always in good supply on ships.

They moved toward the southern tip of the island near a raging battle. The troops were trying to take Conoco Hill, where the Japanese had a gun emplacement commanding the sea for miles around. The enemy had already wiped out eighteen platoons, but with marines lying out there, the powerful adversary had been softened up.

Walter tried to think up ways to keep from following so many dead men up that hill. He considered hiding, or "getting lost" in another part of the island, anything to stay out of that deathtrap. He was sixteen and terrified. He didn't know how to hide from probable death.

His platoon was ordered up the hill to take the gun. He was a corporal leading a twelve-man squad. Near the top, they drew intense gunfire. Men began dropping all around the young corporal. Suddenly, for some reason he never quite understood, he felt invincible. Bullets whizzed by so close he could feel their breeze. Just in front of him a three-man team carrying a Browning Automatic Rifle fell. Walter picked it up along with all the ammunition he could carry. As he moved, he started firing. The piece he carried was as hot as fire. But he was almost hypnotized by the force of the shooting machine pressed against his body. Round after round, he never stopped moving toward that gun.

Suddenly he realized he was the only one shooting. He stopped firing. It was silent. Japanese soldiers lay dead and dying all around him. He was alone, the big gun directly in front of him. Calmly, he dropped two magnesium grenades down the throat of the awesome killer, disabling the gun forever. As he turned around and started down the hill, he saw men dead, dying, and wounded. He could find only seven still alive. By helping each other they got down the hill safely. There was no explanation for Walter's survival.

A few days later he was called into the colonel's tent. He was recommending the boy for a medal. Walter received a battlefield commission to first lieutenant. He was proud, but had witnessed hundreds of acts of heroism. He knew that only a few men (or boys) could represent that collective courage. Walter was one of those chosen.

Three days after V-J Day, Walter left Okinawa on an old liberty ship named the *Henry J. Sanford,* heading home. He went straight to Longmont to see Maxine. She had written every day he was overseas. He stayed with her family at their ranch.

At the end of his leave Walter was ordered to Washington, D.C., where on October 1, 1945, he was presented to President Harry Truman in the White House twenty-one days before his seventeenth birthday. That memory remained fresh in his mind forever. President Truman told him that he would be a first-class citizen of the United States as long as he lived, and that the whole nation was grateful for the things he did in defense of freedom. As he pinned a medal on Walter's chest, the sixteen-year-old almost burst with pride. He swore he would always fight for the freedom he saw so many men die for. From there, along with four other servicemen bestowed with the same honor, he went on a tour of the country, promoting the sale of War Bonds.

Walter tried hard to imply that he received the *Congressional Medal of Honor* which, of course, it was not. He apparently was honored with a medal, but could never be pinpointed as to which medal. Had it been the *Congressional Medal of Honor*, he would have carried it everywhere he went and shown it to everyone, forever. What was genuine, however, was his powerful sense of patriotism. Whatever else he was or became, Walter Plankinton considered himself a true American.

Each furlough he headed back to Maxine. She was pretty and sweet, and Walter was the most important person to her, the center of her world. He could no longer imagine the rest of his life without her.

Slowly, Walter sensed something was wrong but couldn't decide what it was. At the beginning, Maxine's mother seemed to like him. But her attitude gradually changed until it was obvious that she wanted to break the young couple up. Walter was deeply disappointed, but it made no difference in his relationship with Maxine. He loved her, and no one would interfere with that.

During 1946, Walter continued traveling, but now he was selling Bonds. As a result, he couldn't get back to Maxine as often as he wished. In August, he met his parents and did a bit of traveling with them. Although in Colorado during that trip, he made no attempt to see Maxine. He was aware that while he didn't give a hoot about her mother's attitude, the girl was strongly influenced by it. Walter didn't think he should press the issue even though he was deeply hurt and missed Maxine desperately. At the end of the trip with his parents, he returned to San Diego.

One day his commanding officer informed Walter that his records had finally been straightened out, and that he was officially reinducted into the Marines under his own name and age. It was October 18, 1946.

The first of December, Maxine called him. She told Walter that he had a three-month-old son. He was shocked, but thrilled beyond words. He loved Maxine. Nothing could have made him happier. Walter told her he would be there as soon as he could get a leave, and they would get married.

On December 10, 1946, Walter saw Douglas Eugene for the first time. He was a beautiful, healthy, and happy boy. The young father was as proud as a peacock. Maxine's father took them to Laramie, Wyoming, where they were married in a little church across from the courthouse.

They had only two days before Walter had to return to San Diego. He assumed she would go back with him so that they could start their lives as a family. Walter was surprised, and deeply hurt, when she said she wanted to stay in Colorado. Maxine was just seventeen.

After receiving an Honorable Discharge on February 21, 1947, Walter went straight to his new family. They lived with Maxine's parents while he looked for a job (a rather common arrangement following the war, when housing was a problem for the thousands of new veterans coming home and marrying). Walter was offered a coveted job with the Denver Mint. He even found an apartment. To his dismay, Maxine said she had no desire to leave her parents' home. Her mother took complete care of Doug and all household duties. Maxine preferred the easy life. Without hesitation, Walter turned down the job at the Mint and found a construction job in Estes Park, about twenty miles from Lyons. Over unpaved mountain roads, commuting soon became tedious, so he stayed at the jobsite, going home only on weekends.

The following summer he farmed on a sharecrop basis. Maxine still refused to move into a place of their own, so Walter stayed with her uncle, a bachelor. In the fall he rode a tractor day and night to get the plowing and planting done. In the winter, he worked in Estes Park on the water tunnels being constructed for the Bureau of Reclamation. He saved every dime to convince Maxine that they could do just fine on their own, but she still wouldn't leave her mother.

The next spring Walter returned to sharecropping. This time he decided not to live with Maxine's parents. He rented an apartment, and told her that they were in good financial shape, so she didn't have to be afraid. Also, the apartment was not far from her mother's house so she would not be deprived of their relationship. Maxine refused. Walter told her that if she and the baby were not in their new home by ten o'clock the next morning, he would have to be free. Walter tried to explain that they were not living a normal life, that it was time for her to grow up, time for her to be his wife and Doug's full-time mother. Maxine and Doug never showed up. Walter went to an attorney.

After harvesting his crop, he found he netted one hundred and sixty-six dollars for the hardest year's work he ever imagined. He was depressed. His marriage and business were failures. He still loved Maxine, but he finally accepted that he would never pry her loose from her mother's nest, whatever the reason. After some serious thinking, he knew that it was time to move on.

SIX

September 1948, single, and again heading west; this time with a friend. They hitchhiked to Oregon and got jobs on a ranch. Soon, the young friend became ill and left. As it grew colder, Walter knew being there was a mistake. He got into the old Ford he had just bought and drove south.

Just across the California state line, a wheel fell off the car. The garage owner in Alturas told Walter he'd order the part and said to come back in ten days. Walter decided to go to Reno by bus and pick the car up later. He was different from that boy who had bummed around the country. Distance was no longer forbidding.

In Reno he wandered into some gambling joints. For the first time he watched the gamblers exchanging enormous amounts of money with dealers. He was all eyes. Walter knew that he was as smart as any of them, and his luck would equal theirs and turn his money into big bucks. Very quickly, he discovered the truth in "A fool and his money is soon parted" (James Howell, 1629). That 17th Century quotation became very clear on a 20th Century cold, hard park bench that night.

His thoughts as he lay there burned into his memory. He never again wanted to be a loser. From that night, whenever he saw casinos, he was reminded of the lesson he learned in Reno the winter of 1948: Those magnificent buildings which house *games of chance* were not built on winners, but from the pockets of losers.

When a person is hungry, it takes no time to find work, at least that was the way it was then. He drove a dump truck in a placer mine in the desert until the freeze set in. The November day he returned to Reno was the eve of the presidential election. Truman, his idol, beat Dewey. Walter was thrilled. Since he had a little money he wasn't desperate. This time, he could be choosy about a job. He went to work in an animal hospital which paid one hundred fifty dollars a month, plus a nice apartment above the combination office and hospital.

As soon as he went to work for the vet, he called the garage in Alturas. The owner told Walter the car had been stolen from their lot right after they fixed it, and he had put in a police report. Since Walter had no insurance (normal at that time), the garage owner suggested he consider it a loss. Walter was still too young and inexperienced to ask about their insurance, which certainly they had to carry, or if not, they would have been held liable in any courtroom. Walter just accepted it as a loss and forgot about it.

Two weeks later, two FBI agents came into the vet's office asking about the car. Walter explained what the garage owner told him. They said thieves used it in a crime spree, finally wrapping the car around a telephone pole in El Paso, Texas. The police shot one to death; the second was killed in the crash ending a high-speed chase.

He only stayed at the animal hospital about six months, complaining that it was below zero every night and snowed every day. At least that's how he remembered the winter of 1948-1949.

Walter began noticing girls again, and he believed forever after that it was then and there, in Reno, that he formed his permanent ideas about women. It was fun to be with straight girls, but he used prostitutes, too, and clearly recognized the difference between them. A *straight* girl demanded concentration on her. If he took one to dinner or a show, all he might get was a handshake or good-night kiss at the door. Walter never considered his expense worth it. He always felt that spending money on a girl was an investment, and that she "owed" him a roll in the hay after an evening out. Instead, he believed that each and every one of them was desperate to marry him. While some may have wanted to get married, that every women he ever met considered him a great catch and a gorgeous hunk was a self-designed illusion he held the rest of his life.

For five dollars a prostitute not only satisfied his sexual needs, she "genuinely appreciated" his manliness and always let him know it. What made it even better was that he never had to bother trying to flatter her, or seduce her. "Whores seduced me," he would say with a huge grin. And she was no more interested in a permanent relationship than he was. It didn't take long before Walter realized that he much preferred hookers on a day-to-day basis.

Although he had no desire to get involved, he met one girl he liked somewhat. She was not a prostitute, but Olga was lustful and a great lay. Just what he needed: someone who enjoyed going out and drinking, then home to bed, to play. American girls were raised for marriage, and there were lots of virgins around. In gambling cities it was very different. Showgirls, waitresses, and change girls were everywhere. And those who were single, which was most of them, had little else to do for entertainment during free time. While they may have arrived in Reno virgins, following the excitement and glamour (or in some cases to get quickie divorces), most of the women who lived and worked there were as free with sex as any man.

Walter also met George, who became a friend. They talked about how they should go to California and dig for gold. Neither of them knew a thing about mining, of course, but they were both twenty and bursting with get-rich-quick dreams.

Walter bought a 1938 Willys and both young men quit their jobs. On their journey to becoming wealthy mining prospectors, George and Walter stopped in French Gulch. In the local cafe, they met some old-timers who enjoyed talking about their mining experiences. They made the stories of the *Gold Rush* days sound like a romantic adventure novel. None mentioned anything about the work. Within a very few days, George and Walter were settled into an old cabin, ready to "strike it rich."

Olga—whom Walter had written to—showed up one day, much to their surprise. Walter was so involved in their great adventure in the wild that he had all but forgotten her. She stayed and kept house for them most of the summer. Walter worked a garden and trapped a couple of bears. The young men hunted and fished, sat and talked, and lived off the land. Walter also had the pleasure of Olga. He remembered the nights as idyllic and sex-filled. Of course, little mining got done.

Mining, it turned out, hardly resembled what the youths had been led to imagine. It was backbreaking, only slightly productive, boring work. One day when the two miners returned to the cabin after a day of hunting in the wild, Olga was gone, as easily as she appeared three months earlier. Walter never saw her again.

In February (1950), they decided to get back to reality. They plowed through four miles of snow four feet deep to get to a main road. George went to Cleveland to visit his family, and Walter went to Kansas to see his. Before they parted, they made plans to go back to the cabin in the spring to try again.

Walter was with his folks about a week when he received a call from George's cousin. He had arrived home safely and was telling his mother about their adventures. He complained of pain in his stomach and said he must have an ulcer. Moments later, he clutched his stomach, turned white and slumped to the floor, dead. An ulcer ripped into a vein causing him to bleed to death. Walter never went back to the mine, nor that cabin.

Walter stayed at the family farm in Kansas for awhile, then found a job as a truck driver for a meat-packing company in Topeka. He knew nothing about driving a semi, but learned fast. He hauled meat scraps through Nebraska, Iowa, and Kansas, returning to Topeka with loads of horses for slaughter. By spring, he was on a *sleeper*, hauling meat to the dog tracks in Florida carrying juice on return trips.

Bob, his partner, was about the same age and they got along well. They enjoyed the Florida trips. Their egos made a few trips, too. They laid a lot o girls in every town, but never let their *Don Juan* statuses interfere with their schedules.

In Topeka, Walter met Darlene. She drank heavily and was promiscuous. By the standards of those days, she was considered wild. Walter liked her more each time he saw her. After a couple of months, they decided to get married. Darlene had a good office job, and Walter was doing well. They moved into a little apartment.

Later that summer, Walter bought a tractor through the G.I. Bill, and pulled trailers. But by November, he realized he was falling into a hole so he sold the tractor. The company he hauled for offered him a job working on their docks in Denver. He snatched it up since he hated Topeka. They decided that a pregnant Darlene should stay near her family until their baby was born. The marriage wasn't too good, so making that decision was easy. Walter applied to a large freight line as a cross-country driver. On December 27, 1950, they called him to work driving Denver to Chicago.

On March 2, 1951, Pamela was born, and Darlene and Pam arrived in Denver. Things got better. Walter liked his job, Pam was a beautiful, healthy baby, and Darlene seemed happy in her role as wife and mother. He was away for two days then home two days. He looked with pleasure to the future.

One beautiful day in June, Walter arrived home from a Chicago run. As he entered their apartment, he enthusiastically called out "I'm home." He called Darlene and Pam's names as he walked into the bedroom. Pam was sound asleep in her crib. He leaned over to kiss her. She was warm, dry, and obviously in a peaceful, well-fed sleep. A little surprised to find the baby alone in the apartment, he concluded that Darlene had gone to a neighbor's. Walter went into the kitchen, got something to eat, and sat down to read the newspaper. He assumed Darlene heard him come in so she wasn't concerned about the baby being alone. After an hour and no Darlene, Walter began to get angry, then worried.

He went to the neighbor he was sure she was with; she wasn't. She wasn't on their floor. One after another said no, adding that they hadn't seen her all that day. Slowly, fear turned to panic as he began to imagine the possibilities. After speaking to every tenant in the building, he decided to ask the landlady who lived at the back end. He doubted she could have seen anything because of the placement of her apartment, but he had nothing to lose and it was the last possibility before calling the police. Walter stopped back into their apartment for the tenth time to check on Pam, but she slept the sleep of all contented babies.

Unceremoniously, the old woman told Walter that just as she heard him coming through the outside front door, Darlene left out the back end with a man she had never seen before. Walter's blood ran cold. He ran back to the apartment. Holding his breath, he went to the closet and stood rigid in front of it. Finally, he opened the door. Darlene's clothes were gone. Tears filling his eyes, he went to the dresser. Empty. Looking in those places had not occurred to him earlier.

At first he was shocked. She walked out on that adorable baby, her own tiny baby. He was crushed for both of them. He wondered if he could possibly be so terrible that a woman not only abandoned him, but their child. He knew that he didn't love her as he should have, and being on the road they never had a real relationship. He knew he married her for sexual convenience and little more. But, he never cheated on her. He felt very strongly that if he had a need to sleep around, he should not be married. Maybe the stronger reason, which also occurred to him, was that he could never have handled the intrigue. He was a loud, blustery kind of person who demanded respect while giving it to few others.

His morale plunged as he tried to recall every incident that might justify a young woman walking away from a small, innocent child. It never occurred to him that he had chosen an irresponsible tramp, even when her actions proved she felt no responsibility to anyone, not even her own child. Walter suddenly felt that the only love he could depend on was the little darling in the next room. He was absolutely certain of Pam's love. He went to the crib and carefully lifted her so as not to wake her. He carried her to a chair, sat down and looked into her tiny face. He finally let all the tears flow for both of them.

This time he wanted, and got, an annulment. He had unrestricted custody of the infant, not that her mother ever showed up again much less to oppose such custody. Walter quickly found the handicapped daughter of a judge who used the top floor of her father's house as a nursery to care for children. When Walter dropped off his truck, he picked Pam up and took her home. He swore that he spent every free hour with Pam, and enjoyed every moment. The routine worked well, and he watched as she grew month-by-month.

When Pam was about a year old, nine months with the sitter, Walter saw that the baby had begun to form a deep attachment for her sitter. He determined that the baby needed a mother. He began a "systematic search" everywhere he went. In a town about fifty miles outside of Denver, he met a sweet farm girl who worked in a truck stop cafe. He stopped in each time he came back home, talking to her, asking lots of questions. He could see that she was seriously smitten, which was very important, although he really didn't think about his own feelings toward her since that was not the issue. He soon knew she was the right one. After only two dates, they got married.

Nola was eighteen, worshipped the ground Walter walked on, genuinely

42

loved Pam and took good care of her. The baby adored her, too. Nola was an excellent wife. Walter couldn't ask for more. After about four years, they had Michael. Nola was a decent, religious girl, a Jehovah's Witness, so Walter never once drank or smoked in her house. He was twenty-six with a perfect family, a good job, and a bright future. He took responsibility much more serious than most and began saving, consciously dedicating himself to the goal of "getting rich."

He bought a small dairy farm in North Denver and hired Nola's father and brother to run it for him. Eventually, they moved to a larger dairy farm (100 head of Holstein cows) north of Boulder. Things not only looked promising to Walter, but to the banker who had arranged loans to cover the operation. Then a group of large dairy farmers, recognizing the sudden dip in the economy could hurt them, went to Walter's customers and told them that if they wanted their supply at all, they must buy from them. Independents were out of business in the wink of an eye. Walter auctioned off everything. The bank got their money and he had five hundred dollars. Fortunately, he had never given up his job driving a truck for the freight line so they were secure, if disappointed. While sorry to see the dairy go, Walter was not discouraged.

Mining again grabbed Walter's interest because uranium was causing a stir. With the five hundred dollars from the dairy he bought three old mining claims in Blackhawk, Colorado. It was 1954. Somehow, without working capital, he managed to interest a few people and they started digging. He called it *Treasure Key Tunnel*. He was always convinced the name sold more stock than his salesmanship. He owned one hundred thousand shares. Nola kept the books, and every day the mailman dumped a bag or two of checks for stock. Soon, there was well over three hundred thousand dollars deposited in the bank in the corporate account.

One day Walter needed some cash. In coveralls and boots he headed into town, and the bank. The teller refused to cash his check despite his identification. She referred to one person after another asking them what to do since he persisted, ending at the bank president's desk. In his usual blustery, intimidating voice, Walter told the terrified man that he had three hundred and eighty-six thousand dollars in his bank, but he had been shuffled from one clerk or officer to another like any poor fool. Walter roared, filling the whole bank with his voice, that he suspected he was among his largest depositors and that the president should at least have an idea of who he was. He added, "I'll tell you what. You have three hundred and eighty-six thousand dollars of mine in this bank, all in a noninterest-bearing checking account, brought here in secured checks and cash, and I want it, now, in cash."

Almost hysterically the man said, "Mr. Plankinton, I would have to call the Federal Reserve Bank for money; we don't keep that kind of cash here. If we had to close while I arrange this, the depositors will surely panic. It could be catastrophic. You cannot allow this to happen." He choked and sputtered. When the man was humiliated and groveling to his satisfaction, Walter told him that he would withdraw the request for all of his money, but that in the future, whenever he walked through the front door, he expected the president to be on his way to greet him by the time he was half-way through the bank. Walter took pleasure in the story, and only returned to that bank two or three more times, but swore that each time, that was exactly what happened. Shortly thereafter, he sold all of his stock and left with three hundred thousand dollars in profit.

Again, Walter had kept his driving job, and during that entire time other drivers on the freight line razzed him. The day he went to quit his job and laugh in their faces, he drove up in a fancy new convertible when he knew most of them would be there. Their eyes almost popped and Walter felt like a conqueror. When asked where he got the car, he happily told them from his gold mine. He said good-bye, and told them he hoped they continued to do well as truck drivers.

Soon thereafter, a man came to Walter with a sure-bet vibrating mattress deal and a chance to make real money. It was an opportunity the retired truck driver/miner couldn't pass up; this man had the patent. As it turned out, someone else had an earlier one. There were patent and infringement suits, and inevitable legal fees. Within six months, Walter was broke.

His pride would not permit driving in Denver. He went to California, leaving Nola and the kids behind until he was established. For some reason, none of them adjusted to California. After a few months, they decided to return to Colorado. They drove the northern route, stopping in Salt Lake City. Both Walter and Nola were impressed with the clean, quiet city, and decided to stay. It was 1956. Walter found a driving job, but was laid off on Thanksgiving Day. He found odd jobs to keep the family going reasonably well until he was called back in February. The following Thanksgiving, the layoff was repeated. He found another driving job.

It was on the next job that he became aware of a situation he found fascinating. There were permit problems when hauling anything onto Indian Reservations. The loads had to be zig-zagged between truck lines causing so many delays that some of the food spoiled. It was inefficient and costly. Walter took an interest in the complexities and found logical solutions. He studied every ICC regulation governing trucking, which strengthened his belief that his ideas were feasible. When he was certain he was right, he went to the owner of the truck line.

The man recognized the value and agreed to give Walter "one-third interest in anything realized within the next three years" culminating from his ideas and labor. Walter started working what seemed like twenty-four-hour, seven-day weeks. He built an express line between Salt Lake City, Grand Junction, Colorado, and Phoenix, drawing a regular salary.

Under his management, the business multiplied ten times, and money rolled in like a tidal wave. After awhile, the owner and Walter *jointly* decided to sell the line to a larger carrier since it could mean a substantial profit overall. After the sale, he went to his *limited* partner for his one-third share. Laughing, the man refused to pay Walter anything. His naivete had allowed him to believe the owner when the man told Walter that it was his policy to use *gentlemen's agreements,* and that the truck driver could certainly trust him since he was a "good Mormon Bishop." After filing suit, Walter quickly discovered in the courts that all of the judges were also good Mormons. Walter called his position *hometowned,* with no recourse anywhere in the State of Utah. They also knew the truck driver with a family didn't have the money to fight on a federal level.

From his upbringing Walter felt religion stood for honor and integrity. He was raised in a town that practiced business ethics; any other behavior would have been disgraceful, and condemned by the whole community. This successful, pious businessman first exposed the naive husband and father to what he would eventually learn a lot about, *Tartuffe,* "a hypocritical pretender to religion." This incident convinced him that he should never again trust a Mormon. Nola, the children, and Walter returned to Colorado.

He had no problem finding a job with a man who advertised as a "devout Seventh-day Adventist," meaning he could be trusted. He, too, had the conscience of a barracuda. Employers had, and still have, the advantage of a man in need of a job. By then, Walter had been given an extraordinary education in double standards, that as long as a man pretended to be pious he was free to do absolutely anything he wished in the name of money.

The next company that hired him was in trouble so Walter easily convinced the owner of his abilities. That owner gave the ambitious, hardworking young man complete autonomy. By then, Walter understood the territory so was able to put the company back up on its feet. This man was honorable, and compensated Walter well.

During his tenure with the carrier, he met Chuck and his sister-in-law, Maxine, partners in a small moving and storage company, agents for several national moving companies. As he observed how the two firms interlocked, he began to recognize that there were better ways of utilizing their operating permits, some of which were not even being used. After it was all clear in his mind, Walter went to Maxine and Chuck with a plan which proved a moneymaking venture for both their company and the carrier, his employer.

In the summer of 1963, Walter saw the relationship with his boss deteriorating. He believed that in most one-man operations, a too-ambitious employee, or one like him with better ideas than *the big man*, especially if they proved successful, caused embarrassment. Before it could escalate, he quit and went to work for a meat hauler.

Hired as a driver/supervisor, he did quite well for the company. He bought a permit to drive from Colorado to California and Nebraska. As soon as his boss found out, he demanded the permit. When Walter refused to turn it over, he was fired. Before too long, Walter realized that it was the best thing that ever happened to him, forcing him to finally consider trucking on his own.

Roaming around seeing people he knew, looking into various things for sale or lease, Walter ran into Chuck again, who told him about an operating authority available which required a cash purchase. They worked a deal where Walter would end up with fifty percent of Chuck's company; he would keep forty-five percent, and his sister-in-law, Maxine, retained her five percent. It was a fine match, each with different skills—Maxine took care of the books and money; Chuck was a good salesman; Walter ran the hub of the operation and did all of the developing. The day he legally joined with the company and new partners, October 22, 1964, was Walter's thirty-sixth birthday.

All of the efforts in previous jobs began to pay off. Walter had always *romanced* shipping clerks and managers. He had taken lower-management people to lunch and worked hard to make them feel more important than they were. He had always spent time with drivers under him, asking them how they felt about things going on within the business, and the industry in general. He rarely followed any of their suggestions, believing no one could possibly know anything better than he did, but his tactics were effective.

Now, in his own business, he had a small army of willing allies. They gave him inside information and ideas. His efforts started paying off in contracts with plum accounts. In a short time, they were into extensive warehousing and a lot of governmental contract work (his wartime achievements provided at least an introduction to purchasing directors; and the joint skills of Walter, Chuck, and Maxine maintained those contracts). Soon, his goal was being met: He was making real money.

There was just one fly in the ointment. From the day Walter went into this business, Nola complained constantly. She wanted him to get a job like her brother had, working for Western Electric. He worked regular hours, and at the end of fifteen years, he'd get a three-week, paid vacation. The more Walter was away from home, the more Nola complained. There was no longer a threat of loss—as in the mattress deal. They were secure no matter what happened from that point. Nothing he said mattered. That he was working toward total financial independence not only for himself, but for her and the kids, all fell on deaf ears. He was passionate about what he was doing and never once considered giving it up. He was completely bewildered by Nola's feelings. The more she complained, the more he stayed away, working longer hours than he had to. He couldn't tolerate the nagging. There was only one thing really important to him, to be rich, really rich.

Nola never had an interest in wealth, nor did she understand Walter's ambition. People without ambition cannot possibly understand the zeal that drives a person like Walter, any more than people with such a drive understand how others are content standing still or moving ahead at a snail's pace. Walter claimed that he never criticized Nola, saying that they were just different, mismatched, and that in every other way, she was the perfect wife for him. It's difficult to believe that he didn't criticize her because she was, after all, just a woman, and admittedly, he controlled every single relationship he had, if not at first, soon thereafter. He had trouble accepting Nola's attitude since it was his career that was central to his future, and therefore, should have been central to her life. He moved into the office.

On September 8, 1965, a truck pulled into the warehouse to pick up some soap products. No one was in the warehouse. Rather than delay the driver, Walter carried out a one hundred ten-pound bag of soap and put it on the truck. It was nothing unusual, he did it all the time. He went back into the office and was talking on the phone. Suddenly, he felt terrible pain in his chest and down both arms. He couldn't catch his breath and lost consciousness. Maxine called a doctor who instantly diagnosed a heart attack. He told her to drive Walter to the hospital as fast as she could. She and their mechanic dragged his two hundred pounds of dead weight to a car since they could not carry him.

On the way to the hospital, Walter regained consciousness and sat up. They were going close to one hundred miles an hour, reeling in and out of heavy freeway traffic. He told his very frightened mechanic that he really didn't plan on dying unless the mechanic killed him in a high-speed chase.

The doctor stabilized Walter then called Nola, telling her to call anyone who wanted to see him alive. Chet, Faye, and Donna came immediately. Walter survived, although barely. He hovered between life and death for two weeks. Then, without warning or explanation considered medically sound, he began to recover. When he finally left the hospital, he was told to expect to live his life as a semi-invalid since he would never return to a normal life. He laughed, and in his superior way told them all they were crazy.

47

During the following weeks recuperating at home with his wife and kids, Nola was a loving, efficient nurse, and seemed to thrive on the role as protector of this invalid man/child. At first, it was what Walter needed. But instead of encouraging him to do things for himself, Nola tried to keep him from assuming any normal functions. She kept telling him that between a good job with a big corporation, and perhaps her getting a job, they could live quite nicely. Finally, Walter insisted on going to the office. Reluctantly, and silently, she chauffeured him. He stayed short periods at first, but gradually, the time increased. Soon he drove myself. By February 1966 he was working full-time. The couple knew they could not live together. Walter moved into a motel near the office.

The business seemed invincible. They purchased more operating authorities, expanding constantly. Walter made it his priority to learn rates and how to file for government tonnage. It paid off. For the next few years, it all seemed like dumb luck. The rest was due to the fact that the trio diligently learned their business down to the last, minute detail. At least Maxine and Walter worked long and hard. They were a perfect team. They also became good friends, and on occasion lovers.

SEVEN

One day in 1968 at a party, Walter saw a beautiful woman completely surrounded by men. He told the host he wanted to meet her because after being out of circulation so long, he didn't trust his own ability to approach her, particularly in view of the admiring audience she commanded. Walter claimed that, instantly, she was as taken with him as he was with her. They made a date. Soon inseparable, marriage was inevitable. Nola, too, had started seeing someone and wanted to marry him. Their divorce was amicable.

There was no question about where Pam would stay. Although never legally, Nola had become her mother, and Walter wouldn't consider taking Pam away from Nola or her brother. Of course, Walter freely admitted with no sense of responsibility or guilt that Nola's willingness to keep the little girl totally relieved him of any day-to-day care of Pam. He was free again, genuinely unincumbered even though he had three children. Although Walter recognized that he should support these two children, he had reached a stage in his career and character where any interference in his time, direction, and life were just plain intolerable.

The path was open to marry Oneta, but he held one reservation. While he was deeply in love with her, there was Maxine. He and Maxine had developed a powerful relationship. While he had deep love for her, it didn't have the passion or irrational *in love* everyone wants. More than once, he considered marrying Maxine, although he never asked her how she felt about it. They had so much in common. The business they built with joint energies and devotion was like their child. They talked about it endlessly, with great pleasure, and he thoroughly enjoyed her company during those times. He was torn between two very different loves, although he admitted he never loved Maxine the way he wanted to. She would have been a great convenience as a mate. As a result, he had a few misgivings about marrying Oneta right up to the ceremony in the Spring of 1968. After the wedding, he threw doubt to the wind and followed only his heart.

They entered an enjoyable social whirl. Men continued vying for her attention. She was personable, thoroughly enjoyed the attention of men, and was invited to every party. Walter enjoyed nonstop pleasure with her. His ego soared to an all-time high, inflated by her obvious popularity with so many men. Walter felt that their marriage was a total success. They bought a beautiful house and hosted dinners and parties there. Oneta was a gracious hostess, and to Walter, their marriage was pure joy.

Business was also fulfilling Walter's dreams. He became involved with, and was subsequently appointed a director on, the Transport Clearing Board. All of the large trucking companies belonged to the co-op generating one hundred eighteen million dollars in gross yearly earnings. Walter was active in the decisions made in methods of spreading the revenue.

In 1969, he got wind of opportunities in Belize, Central America, so he set up a corporation there. They represented a line of farm equipment and trucks, and eventually became involved in an oil mill that produced cooking oil from copra and cohune nuts.

Then in 1970, friends and business acquaintances encouraged him to run for Governor of Colorado, which he did, on the American Independent ticket. Walter would spout an almost rehearsed speech about it not being so much the idea of being elected that made him enter the race, that he really did it to put himself into a position where he might be able to influence decisions made in his state. He would go on saying that when he lost, he accomplished his ultimate goal—access to power; that doors never before accessible were thrown open. In the end, he would insist that he achieved some good for the people of Colorado. Upon some intense and fast questioning, the facade was penetrated, and the answers evolved, exposing a deep disappointment in people too stupid to recognize him for what he was, and a deep-seated, growling rage that they had humiliated him. He admitted that he had hidden a tremendous hope to win. It's unlikely that anyone would have had the nerve to tell him that he was a typical bull in a china shop, and likely would have embarrassed the State of Colorado had he been elected.

He expanded their holdings in Belize, acquiring a pipe plant, the largest hog farm in Central America, and a ranch. They had one hundred twenty-one locations across America and were handling overseas shipments to military bases. Walter and Maxine, then alone in their partnership (Chuck had withdrawn), were grossing twelve million dollars a year.

Thanksgiving in 1971, Walter reluctantly faced the fact that Oneta was seeing other men. At first, he pretended it was impossible, a mistake, a phase she was going through. By Christmas, it was impossible to continue to lie to each other, or themselves. She admitted that she had found someone else and wanted to end the marriage.

Walter was devastated, and furious. She was privy to outrageous dreams, his doubts and fears, strengths and weaknesses. He had trusted her, certain their love would go on forever. His world crashed around him, he would tell anyone who would listen. On Christmas Day, he drove to Colorado Springs and checked into the Broadmoor Hotel. He sat the entire day looking out at the mountains, and cried until there was nothing left inside. At the end of that day it was over. His simple explanation was that the love didn't end, nor the grief, but good sense took over. He would not allow a woman stop him at the peak of his abilities. He had given Oneta his all and assumed she trusted him with all that she was. He was wrong, or she lied, because it couldn't have anything to do with him. How could any woman not be content with what he offered. He was no longer sad, just revolted by her stupidity.

On New Year's Eve, he went to several parties, determined to forget everything except a good time, and he did. He knew he would never trust another woman.

By February 1972, the house was sold but Oneta's two grown sons moved into the apartment Walter leased—with him. It never for one moment occurred to Walter that his money might have at least something to do with that. In his mind, they very wisely loved him more than their mother. On the fifth of May, Oneta got her divorce. On May 10, the doorbell rang and Walter answered it. There stood Oneta. Her new lover had dumped her, had thrown her out of his apartment with only the clothes on her back. Walter let her move right back in, but without a marriage license.

Later that year she went to Belize with him and fell in love with the country. She gave wonderful parties and soon knew everyone in the government, the country's intellectuals and wealthiest citizens—likely another gross exaggeration. The attorney general became Walter's "good friend." A black man educated in England, Walter claimed he was probably the kindest person he had ever known.

In spring, another friend in the government told him that their services were about to be suspended. Before it could happen Walter began pulling out. It meant bankruptcy for that phase of the business, which was independent of their base operation. Transworld—the company formed for the Belize business—was broke, and Maxine had to fend off all of the angry creditors while Walter remained in Belize.

The next year, Maxine and Walter discussed splitting the partnership. There was no problem, they just knew it was time. She took most American properties and cash; Walter took the cash in Mexico, and Belize International. Maxine's son then joined her in the business, and they continued to have great success. Walter knew that if he ever had thoughts of a partner again, it would have had to be another Maxine.

Walter returned to Belize and living with Oneta. Now that much of the business was gone, he could rest and leisurely run the operation. One day in

September, Oneta said she wanted to go home to Colorado. Leaving Oneta's son Sam in charge of the Belize operation, the couple returned to Denver. Walter rented a luxurious apartment and furnished it befitting the elegance of their new surroundings. Walter's business interests were profitable, and he and Oneta were happy.

After one month, Walter arrived home on a typically beautiful Colorado October afternoon to find Oneta waiting impatiently for him. The apartment was stripped. There wasn't a piece of furniture in it. Walter was shocked, his first thought being burglars, and he was absolutely right. There had been a theft, all right, but not by strangers. Oneta very calmly explained that she decided to leave, and she certainly needed cash to start her new life. She had called a used furniture dealer who gave her ten cents on the tens of thousands of dollars Walter had just spent. He didn't believe Oneta could shock him a second time, but this overwhelmed him. He finally had to accept that she was an actress, not the fine lady he saw her as. Not even considering prosecuting her for theft, he boarded the first plane back to Belize.

It took weeks for him to calm down. Everything there reminded him of Oneta. He sold all of it. When the sale was complete, he called Sam—who still ran the company for him—and told him to give the new owner the keys, get into his car, and meet him in El Paso on November 16 (1973). They partied their way through Mexico, Arizona, and Las Vegas. When Walter was bored, they returned to Colorado for the holidays.

Two days after Christmas, Pam called to tell Walter that Mike had married the day before. He called Nola and, as he so quaintly put it, " spoke to her more sharply than I ever had." It's quite likely that she could have heard him without the phone regardless of how far away she was. She tried to explain but he went into a rage at being ignored so totally by his son, daughter, and ex-wife. A few days later, Sam told Walter that he was returning to Belize to get married. He knew he would miss his young friend, but he left with Walter's best wishes. On his way out of town, Walter gave Oneta some cash to buy Sam wedding gifts, then drove straight through to Carson City, Nevada. After a few days, he went on to California.

He wasn't there two days when his heart acted up again. He drove himself to the hospital, quite ill. On the fourth day, he opened his eyes to see Sam and his new bride at his bedside. No one knew he was going into the hospital. He had given Pam his new apartment address. When Sam tried to reach Walter and couldn't, he called the police who traced him to the hospital. Sam used all of the money Walter had meant for wedding gifts to get there. Walter was touched. The newlyweds stayed until Walter was out of the hospital and feeling his old self again, then left to start their new lives in Colorado.

Walter remained in California until spring, then returned to Denver. Nothing quelled his restlessness. He knew he had to work. He went up to Clear Creek at Blackhawk, Colorado, and set up a sand and gravel operation. About the time it began to make a little profit, the Bureau of Land Management notified him that he could not remove any more sand or gravel. It seemed that he owned only the mineral rights, which didn't include the other elements. He shut down the operation.

He returned to Belize and visited friends who encouraged him to start another business. He decided to raise cucumbers on land that the government would gladly lease. He found a young man to return with him to Colorado to help drive back the equipment he had to purchase for the new farm. They loaded the farming equipment onto a large flatbed truck. He also bought an air-conditioned pickup. They left for Belize.

It was slow going once they entered Mexico because of customs and bonds he had to post. About the tenth day, they stopped for gas and food. When they came out, Walter noticed that one of the tractors was about to slide off the flatbed. They rounded up six Mexican men and started straightening out the load. They lifted and pushed, including Walter with all of his enormous strength.

Suddenly his heart revolted, beating at an incredible rate—which he later learned was ventricular fibrillation. He became violently nauseated, but was able to get into the cab of the pickup and turned on the air conditioning. The cool air helped. After an hour, he felt a little better, and decided to go on to Vera Cruz to find a doctor. After two hours, he again became ill and pulled off to the side of the road. He told Emmanuel that if I should die, to call Maxine and she would know what to do about everything. Then he just lay back in the truck and waited for what he believed was inevitable. At daybreak he felt better, so they continued toward Vera Cruz. By the time they arrived, he felt so much better that he decided to go on.

On Friday, they arrived at the Rio Hondo at Chetamel in the Yucatan Peninsula, just across the border from Belize. The customs officer informed Walter that he would not clear them to cross until Monday because it was too late. It did mean a stack of paperwork, and it was evident that he didn't feel like working anymore that day. Walter told him that either he cleared an exit or he would drive over the bridge into Belize without clearance. The scene that followed might have been funny had it not been a life and death situation for the man who realized how ill he really was.

The guard ceremoniously told Walter that if he attempted to cross over, he would be shot. Threats and arguments followed until Walter was finally able to make the Mexican guard understand that there was a very good chance

53

that he was about to die anyway, particularly if he could not get medical help, so their threats to kill him were falling on deaf ears. Walter told him to go ahead and shoot, but that he was crossing over that bridge. There is little doubt that watching Walter turn colors, the guard began to believe that if he did not let him cross, and he died on the Mexican side of the border, he would have an even greater problem to deal with. He signed the necessary papers.

Walter went straight to a doctor who advised him to return to the United States as quickly as possible. Neither he nor the Belize hospitals were equipped to deal with such a heart condition. Walter was finally able to get reservations for the next Tuesday. At the Houston airport, he ordered the cab driver straight to Methodist Hospital.

He recognized that he was in grave jeopardy as he watched them sticking tubes and needles into him from every conceivable direction, almost frantically. Walter's heart stopped as they transferred him from a gurney into a bed in intensive care. He told the nurse the monitor stopped. Suddenly, people converged on him like locusts as they zapped him again and again. Walter watched and listened with interest to everything going on. He was later told that was impossible; that he could not have watched them since he was dead for three minutes. Unlike stories he read and heard about regarding out-of-body experiences, he never saw himself above looking down on himself. But he always insisted that he was on the table watching them. Finally he just drifted off to sleep.

Walter awoke the next afternoon with Pam and Maxine at his bedside. Seeing them thrilled him. The hospital called Pam and she called Maxine. They were told that Walter had little chance of surviving. By then, having had a total of fifteen cardiac incidents, his heart was "simply worn out."

They did an angiogram and verified that the damage was too widespread for surgery. They gave Walter huge quantities of medication, and prescriptions for a lot more. They told him to forget Belize because the strain would tax his body beyond its capacity. But he had equipment to dispose of and loose ends to tie so, ignoring the doctors' advice, he flew to Belize, sold everything, got in his car and headed for Denver.

The trip took seventeen days. He went slow and easy, playing tourist all the way. He arrived in Denver in early December and stayed with Maxine. A few days later, he had another heart attack. Back into a hospital and again out in a few days, he firmly believed that this would be his last Christmas, if he could last that couple more days, of course. He went shopping as never before for everyone he loved. He bought Pam's five-year-old son a huge bicycle. Sadly, he thought about the absurdity of giving a small boy a bike he would not ride for years. After he placed it carefully into the trunk, he just sat in his car and cried until there were no more tears.

After Christmas, he drove to Texas just to see the country. He was quite taken with the Rio Grande Valley. Denver was still cold when he returned. He spent time with Maxine who was patient with him, but was also running a busy trucking line. Somewhat reluctantly, he sold his latest mining venture and left for Brownsville, Texas. One day in the harbor at Port Isabel, Walter spotted a for sale sign on a shrimp boat. He went to the library and read, and started asking questions, determined to learn everything he could about shrimping. When he was satisfied he bought the boat. He called Mike and asked him how he felt about becoming a shrimper. He said he would give it a try. He came with his friend (leaving his wife and baby behind). Walter hired a seasoned captain to show the trio the ropes.

Third morning out, Walter's heart started fibrillating. The Coast Guard had to be called out to transport him to the hospital, where a doctor tried all day to convert his symptoms with medication. When Mike arrived, Walter told him to find a good cardiologist before they killed him. The physician arrived and on first sight, started barking orders. He hit Walter with four hundred volts without benefit of pain killers. Mike said he heard his father's scream four floors below. Up in a couple of days, the doctor told him the fastest way for him to die would be to go back on that boat. This time Walter listened. He stayed on shore and tried to keep busy with all of the business aspects of shrimping.

His folks visited him in Brownsville. For three weeks, Chet followed Walter everywhere. Father and son got to know each other all over again, better than ever before. One day as they sat alone talking, Walter asked his father why he took the skunk pelts out of the barn. Chet spoke in a voice Walter hardly recognized, and the sad look that replaced the one he'd seen for the last few days made him regret he ever brought it up. They were about to lose their farm. They'd had a bad crop that fall and Chet couldn't pay the mortgage. He'd already convinced the bank to accept an interest payment, which he didn't have either. The interest was fifty dollars. Then he remembered Walter's pelts. He knew the buyer was already in town. He sold them all for fifty dollars. His pride just wouldn't allow him to tell his young son. He was better able to put Walter into the role subject to his command, or whims. It was painfully difficult for Chet to tell his son. Walter was able to let go of most of his resentment, at long last. Many things were clearer, finally. He saw much of his father in himself. It was a good feeling to know that he was just a little like the man he so respected.

One Sunday afternoon Chet and Walter went across the border to their first bullfight. They watched the bulls being chased around, then mutilated with spears. The happy pair believed it an inequitable match with the wounded bull chasing all those different, armed men around in total confusion, not to mention what must have been excruciating pain. They decided the bulls needed some encouragement, too. Every time the critter seemed to score a point, Chet and Walter jumped up and cheered at the top of their lungs. They quickly learned that *they* were the ones who might be in mortal danger. They left the stands barely escaping an angry crowd. Once safely away from the arena filled with fanatic, blood-thirsty, two-legged animals, they both laughed until the tears ran.

Soon after Chet and Faye left, Walter and his son both knew that Mike and the sea would never get along. Mike and his family left for Denver. Alone again, Walter soon tired of Brownsville. He turned the boat over to the captain on a share deal and headed home. On the way, he thought about moving back to Denver. There were so many painful memories of life with Oneta that he knew he wouldn't stay. Besides, the climate was not good for his heart.

After a few days, he decided to go west, maybe to Nevada. The year was 1976, and it was Spring.

EIGHT

In Pahrump, Walter began putting his house in order. He needed cement work so he contacted a local company. Pete, a mining engineer-turned-contractor, was a pleasant, interesting man. They had much in common and talked endlessly. One day they turned to Nye County politics, politics in general being a mutual interest. Walter was adopting the new community as his own; he had been there awhile. His local political orientation would be through his new-found friend.

He needed gravel for his long driveway, and Pete's truck was inoperable so he suggested Walter hire another contractor. He used the one his new friend recommended. After years in the trucking business—and out of plain old habit when his money was involved—he easily judged the time the truck took from the community gravel pit (ten miles) and back, including loading and dumping. When it turned out much less than his calculations, he asked the truck driver how he did the run so quickly. His answer shocked Walter.

He got the gravel at the county pit where it was dug, graded, and loaded for him by the county road crew. He just slipped the man a few dollars. He said it had "been going on for years; not too hard when my boss and a county commissioner are brothers-in-law." He kept talking about conspicuous graft. Even with a history in trucking, Walter was taken aback by the blatant theft of enormous quantities of county property. He was resentful because of what it meant to him as a new county taxpayer.

He told the driver the gravel he brought was stolen and that he would not allow it on his property. He demanded that the driver remove it since he would not "accept stolen goods." Visibly shaken, the man got into his truck and left.

When Walter related incidents such as this, you could hear the echo in the hollowness of the stories. These situations did happen, but probably not precisely the way he explained them. He enjoyed painting himself as kind, virtuous, and always above anything corrupt or illegal. The closer he lived to the edge of illegality, the more saintly he presented himself. Again, when pressed, he was a virtual expert on the corruption within the trucking industry. He didn't just know the surface practices that most business people do, or even truck drivers who kept themselves somewhat naive to live with themselves. He knew down and dirty facts about the backside of the industry.

When pulled into machine-gun-type questions and answers, he would choose his words carefully, but would sneer, or laugh slightly in a deep, low way that said as clearly as he was using words, *Whatever I do is all right because I'm smarter than everyone else, therefore, above everyone else. Why do you question me? See, you're not smart enough to recognize my superior cleverness and intelligence.*

In a short time the owner of the gravel company was at Walter's door. He repeated what he told the driver. The owner said they would not remove the gravel, and that Walter would pay for it. In later years, Walter would count that as the very first mistake he made in Nye County. He regretted not having kept his mouth shut and going along with their graft. Undoubtedly, the all-powerful *Good Old Boys*—who controlled the valley he fell in love with and was adopting as his home—knew of Walter Plankinton's existence by that day's end.

He refused to pay for the stolen gravel. When he told his new friend, Pete explained that he had learned about it upon his arrival in Pahrump, and that it had made his survival near impossible since, "I have to dig, grade, load, and pay for all of the gravel I legally remove from the community pit, while it's all free to them at taxpayers' expense."

Walter continued working on his house. As his curiosity about how this group got away with such enormous theft grew in his mind, he decided to try to find out. Whenever he needed a break, he drove to the county pit, or found roadside jobs, and just sat and watched. He followed trucks and watched where they dumped their loads. He soon understood the formula; it centered around two companies.

Walter computed estimates, then translated them into the years Pete knew of the practice, although they suspected it had gone on longer. His calculations showed that over two hundred fifty thousand tons of county gravel had been hauled away. That meant that approximately seven hundred fifty thousand dollars of taxpayers' money had already been stolen. Adding insult to injury, there was no attempt to hide it. Even worse, everyone in the legal system was aware of it.

But before he knew that for a fact, he decided to talk to the sheriff in Tonopah. He walked into his office like a naive child. There stood a man about forty, wearing a ten-gallon hat larger than Walter had seen anywhere in his entire life. The size of the hat was surpassed only by the dimensions of his gut which drooped repulsively over a belt practically hidden by the mass of undulating suet. On the belt was a holster, and in it a gun so big, it literally hung all the way down to his knee. It took every shred of training to be well-mannered regardless of the situation, plus years of using tact in business and

58

political arenas, to keep from collapsing into a heap of hysteria. The self-caricature's first words further threatened Walter's already shaky self-control.

As he continued his inward battle to get through this predicament, Walter began to recognize that this rolling hulk perceived himself as a latter day *Marshall Dillon*. Walter would learn soon enough, however, that there was no resemblance between him and the legendary marshall. As he stood there trying to prepare himself to speak without breaking apart, he used the sheriff's gigantic badge as his focus to regain his composure. He introduced himself to this *lawman* from another era.

Walter told him what he had seen, and skimmed through the estimates of what he translated into grand theft. The sheriff stared at the man across from him as if unbelieving, and the thought that maybe he didn't know about the thefts crossed Walter's mind. After all, his office was a long way off, in Tonopah. He was in Pahrump only occasionally.

When Walter finished, he sat back. The silence was deafening. After what seemed like three full minutes, the undulating hulk said, in a tone unbefitting a sheriff, "Plankinton, all you want to do is stir up a stink. Why don't you get out of here before I throw you in jail."

The look was disbelief all right, but not for the reason Walter had speculated. This mound of sweaty flab was dead serious about putting him in jail. Never easily pushed around, Walter was not a fool, either. He left. It was clear now how these people were getting away with wholesale stealing.

When Walter told Pete about it, they knew something had to be done and obviously no one else would ever do it. For weeks, they collected pictures of trucks loading county gravel into privately owned vehicles. They continued until they were certain they had unimpeachable evidence. Walter went to the Bureau of Land Management (BLM) and spoke with an agent. He asked about their role in the county gravel pit since it was on federal land. The agent explained that when the county hauled away sand and gravel, it paid the BLM a fee. Walter gave him his estimates, based on fair market prices, of what was being stolen. The agent told him that if the county kept no records, the BLM would not recognize pilferage; and that he needed proof. When Walter produced the pictures, the agent's face dropped. He pulled out a large file folder. What the BLM had been paid didn't even approach the estimates. The agent advised Walter to go to the U.S. Attorney's office. He did, and repeated his story there, showing that agent the pictures, and explained the difference between BLM records and his estimates. The agent thanked Walter and said an investigation would be implemented.

Soon after, Walter and Pete saw two men taking pictures and watching. Once they had matching data, they opened an investigation. They took depositions, including Walter and Pete's. The truck drivers were not willing to commit (federal) perjury to protect their bosses. By the time the federal agents got to the owners, they admitted everything.

To Walter and Pete's dismay, a federal officer went to the district attorney in Pahrump and told him to have the practice stopped. It seemed that the feds had no jurisdiction in the matter. The two men had to surmise that unpaid federal fees was of no consequence to the U.S. Attorney's office. Once placed into the district attorney's hands, the subject was closed. No charges, no fines, no repayment of taxpayers' money, neither on a federal nor local level. Nothing showed up in any newspaper about the findings of the U.S. Attorney's office.

Walter never reconciled himself to the fact that these thieves who openly stole taxpayers' property remained above laws everyone else had to abide by. He learned, soon enough, that the perpetrators were the primary supporters of the men in those public offices. This was only his first exposure to the depth of the *Good Old Boys'* power.

The two men decided one of them should run for county commissioner in the upcoming election, and of course with his past experience running for office, and certainly superior intellect—at least in Walter's own mind—he was the obvious choice. He knew that this valley would be his permanent home, and felt strongly that he would probably die there. The idea that a couple of power-hungry men could twist and turn laws to their own benefit made him angry. And when the truth was told, he felt much worse because they could control *his* life. In June 1976, Walter drove into Tonopah, the county seat, to file for a seat being vacated by one of the *in-group*.

He had driven there before, but maybe because of the reason for this trip, he was particularly irritated by the county seat being one hundred eighty-five miles away, while Las Vegas was only fifty-five miles from Pahrump. Pahrump was under remote control from Tonopah, like a robot.

About then, Walter met Arthur, near his own age, who lived a mile from his place. Arthur's son, Art, was in his early thirties and single. One thing led to another, and Art and Walter began visiting brothels in Lincoln County; two in particular. They had great times and their friendship grew.

In July, Walter went to Colorado to see his former partner, Chuck. He had put up twenty-five thousand dollars for him to go into the firewood business. Walter wanted to see how things were going. It was obvious that his cash had been dropped into a bottomless pit. He went back to Pahrump and threw himself into the campaign for the upcoming primary.

One morning as Walter walked into a coffee shop, the editor of the Pahrump newspaper stopped him. She blurted out a story circulating that he planned to open a brothel in Pahrump. Walter laughed out loud and told her, with some show of pride, that he visited one every week but hadn't given any thought to being a part of one. He added (putting in a plug for his campaign—he thought) that he was much too busy being a politician to consider running a brothel. But as he traveled around the county, the same question kept coming up. He couldn't escape what he called "a ridiculous rumor," and it soon became tiresome denying it.

Since he was unknown, he believed it necessary to speak with every voter in the county. It was easier for him than for someone who worked. He soon had a first-hand view of the third largest county in the Continental United States; eighteen thousand square miles of nothing. He learned that Nye County, approximately three hundred miles wide and one hundred fifty miles long, had less than thirty-five hundred voters. It cost him time and gas to see them all, but he felt it was only fair that they meet each of their candidates; and it was damned good politics. He worked diligently despite the negative reaction to the unfounded brothel gossip which he was unable to escape.

In mid August, he checked into a motel in Tonopah so he could call on voters there. His first stop was the courthouse. After he had spoken to everyone on the main floor, he went to the second level of the antique building right out of the Old West. The first door he saw showed "District Attorney." He walked in. A surprisingly young man sat behind a huge desk. With hand extended and a broad smile, he said, "I'm Walt Plankinton from Pahrump, and I'm running for county commission from that district." When he practically jumped to his feet, Walter presumed it was to shake hands, being what most people do when someone enters a room and extends a hand. With the expression of a sphinx and an accusing tone, the young man said, "You are the man I've been waiting to meet. I understand you plan to open a brothel in Pahrump."

By now Walter's patience with the accusation usually said in an insulting tone was worn thin. Besides, this officer of the court was supposed to believe someone was innocent until proven guilty. Angrily he answered, "Well, if I did, it would be legal since you have several others in this county."

Ignoring Walter's response, the young man explained that since it was in such close proximity to Las Vegas, it would cost him "seventy-five thousand dollars up front, and another five percent off the top of the gross, monthly." That pushed Walter right over the edge. He answered, "I never paid a crooked politician a dime in my life, and you ain't never gonna be the first." The young man quickly responded, "Well, you will have the permission of *the people who count* around here, or the only place you'll run a brothel from in this county will be inside my jail." Walter was stunned into silence, not knowing that at that moment, he and the kid who called himself a district attorney reached for their lances, and the joust commenced.

A few days later, Walter saw the woman from the local newspaper again. While discussing equal rights and protection under the law, Walter was dumbfounded when she said, "You don't have equal rights here, Mr. Plankinton, you're a newcomer to Nye County."

He knew at that moment that if this was the local attitude, he was in for political trouble. In the end, it took almost six years to convince him that she did, in fact, represent the mentality of the vast majority of Nye County residents. Walter repeated to anyone who would listen his disgust and dismay over the injustice wielded by an otherwise small-time triarchy who issued their own brand of *law*.

Twice a week, Art and Walter went to a brothel in Lathrop Wells where they met Lisa and Gena (who they later learned were mother and daughter). Art was soon infatuated with Gena. Walter was amused but it seemed harmless enough; there wasn't much for a young man to do in Pahrump. After awhile it became apparent that Gena liked him, too.

September 1976, primary election day finally arrived. Walter ran third out of seven for the Democratic nomination for County Commissioner. Considering that he entered the campaign a total unknown, it wasn't a bad showing. Although he knew from the start he had little chance, he was profoundly disappointed. He considered himself an astute man, smarter than most other men and unquestionably smarter than women. He also believed he had the wisdom of Solomon. A man who thrived on people fawning over him, he vied for compliments, asking questions that would corner people into giving them. In his mind, no one in this desert town could possibly do the job he would, and he was angry with the stupid, blind, brainwashed voters. With all of his face-saving dialogue about there being little chance, he hoped what he viewed as his enormous intellect and charm would win the race for him.

Art and Walter learned the results together. They sat silently as it sunk in. Then Walter spouted facetiously, "Since I didn't get elected, maybe I should open a whorehouse." They laughed but it perked Art up. He thought it was a great idea, particularly if he had a hand in running it. They howled over the outrageous fantasy, but Walter saw that Art really liked the idea. Walter forever claimed that he never had any interest in a brothel except patronizing one, but the more he thought about it, the more interesting the idea became. He said that he felt it would be poetic justice for being accused of planning one. Walter sat down and drew up an agreement that would make Art the manager of the brothel he would establish.

That night in bed, he thought about why he went to brothels: because he could impress a woman, get sexual gratification, and not have to worry about her wanting to pigeonhole him or make any demands on him. He felt that prostitutes not only tried to please him physically, they stood on their heads to build up his ego. They never had headaches, or any interest in using sex to punish him. He was the center of their existence, the target of their total sexuality. He would soon learn why so many types of men patronize brothels. But for the moment, his mind drifted through all the business aspects of a brothel, and of course, the personal side benefits. Finally that night, he later claimed, his mind locked in on the idea and he stopped fighting it.

It is likely that no one will ever know if it was that night when Walter Plankinton actually decided to open a brothel. Anyone talking to him for any length of time on the subject would have to come away concluding that his decision was made before that night. Maybe when his son told him about the first *Chicken Ranch* in Texas; or was it a daydream from his teens, when he first started paying prostitutes to flatter him, whose paid lies would always expand his vanity; or it may have been born as he looked down and saw the lush green valley of Pahrump the very first time, recognizing what a short drive it was from Las Vegas and with his ability to see the possibilities, recognized the income potential. It could easily have been conceived on any one of his trips to Las Vegas where finding prostitutes was (and still is) as easy as hailing a taxi. One of the many reasons it seems viable that he planned it well before this momentous night was purchasing two trailers. Two separate and distinct trailers, not uncommon among brothels, which of course he knew since he had frequented them for decades.

What was most likely was that Walter bragged to someone in the town that he dreamed of opening a brothel, thinking that person would either not take him seriously, or keep it quiet. Walter was a grandstander, by nature. He was also incapable of keeping secrets, as the author can personally attest to, especially if he thought something made him look like a big shot. And running a cathouse was every man's ultimate dream; he firmly believed that. To his death, he denied any earlier interest in owning a brothel, but he knew that by his denial he could forever blame others for his foray into the what the world considered immoral and illicit, however legal. One has to remember that the respect and love of his very straight, earthy parents, sister, and three children were important to him. He had to justify his actions. Blaming crooked politicians was an easy path, and he perfected the story with each passing year. The thing is, so much of his story about the political and judicial structure of the county was true, it made the his own denial more credible.

When the question of a name popped into his mind, he remembered the Chicken Ranch in Texas. As he drifted off to sleep, thoughts of a fancy brothel acclaimed around the world filled his dreams. After all, it was his fantasy, so why not the best. He awoke with the same fantasy. The dream quickly evolved into serious planning. He would soon own and operate a brothel.

While he and Art joined the two trailers, Walter stepped up patronizing brothels around the county, letting as many girls as possible know his plan. Since it would be close to Las Vegas, he assured them it would be busier than those they were working in. Brothel owners didn't appreciate his openly discussing it with their girls, but there was little they could do short of barring him from their brothels, something that is rarely done in most brothels.

The sheriff and certain locals became very open in an attempt to discourage his decision. Although he ignored what they said, some of their rhetoric made an impression. One said, "Prostitution is illegal within the Town of Pahrump's boundaries." Walter knew for a fact that Pahrump was not a town. When he first heard it, he ignored what his instinct was trying to tell him. But recognizing he should handle the brothel like any other business, he hired an attorney.

They went to Tonopah to research the situation. There was no such "Town of Pahrump," nor an ordinance prohibiting prostitution in any part of the area in which Pahrump was situated. But to be absolutely certain, Walter hired an engineer who went to Tonopah to analyze land records, since no one in any governmental office could produce anything showing that a town had ever been formed. The engineer really played detective. He searched everything he could think of to determine the possibility of a town, or any kind of incorporated place anywhere in or around Pahrump. He found no such evidence, trace, or even implied designation.

Walter's attorney told him the district attorney was bluffing and the engineer agreed. They advised him to go ahead and open the brothel. There was no town, and no prohibiting ordinance existed.

Walter and Art finished the interior of the combined trailers. It definitely wasn't going to look like the drawing room of a spinster schoolteacher, but he did want it to be attractive. Walter began to sense the "glamour" this brothel would offer him, personally. He also admitted that the sheriff and district attorney saying that he couldn't open a brothel further fueled the flames of his already soaring determination.

One beautiful, sunny day, the sheriff came to the house. Walter asked him to sit down. Since he had no other way to sit on the low seat, he flopped onto the beautiful new couch, and the massive glob sank deep into the soft, luxurious divan. His enormous jelly-like gut spilled between and around his massive legs. His miniature cannon hung, as usual, to the floor. It was a grotesquely hilarious image.

After a long, dramatic silence—obviously meant to intimidate Walter—he said, "Well, Plankinton, you're plannin' to open a whorehouse I see." Walter acknowledged it. He went on, "You can't because the judge don't want you to open no whorehouse down here."

"You've got other whorehouses running legally in this county. If your judge doesn't think it's legal, close them down," Walter responded.

In a controlled-parrot fashion, the lawman repeated, "Well, the judge don't want you openin' no whorehouse down here." Walter never had any real conversations with this sheriff. It was like talking to a man reciting memorized lines. Walter always believed that when he realized that neither his attempt at a sinister look nor the preplanned monologue were intimidating him, the caricature sheriff knew he had to go back to his programmer for a better script.

NINE

Walter asked around the brothels about hiring a prostitute. One girl referred him to her pimp and told him where to find him in Las Vegas. Walter soon arranged a meeting on the street outside a restaurant. Art went with him, jumping at the prospect of meeting a pimp. When they arrived at the appointed place, the man had a girl with him.

The two bumpkins from Pahrump tried to be cool, to act experienced. They said as little as possible. Walter, being a quick study listened carefully to the pimp's speech and tried to copy the jargon coming out of this slick, fast-talking, flashy-dressed man and his seemingly tough sexpot. If Cathy had had any idea how naive and nervous the two men were, she would either have turned and run or, and more likely, laughed herself into convulsions. They made every attempt to stand in that unmistakable pimp-cool slouch. Although he had never been a shrinking violet, Walter found it difficult to mimic the hard, cold look on both faces. This was one of the few admissions by Walter that a prostitute looked hard.

The idea of such negotiations may seem peculiar to those unfamiliar with the prostitute business. Women don't really need pimps, particularly those working in brothels, but pimps convince them that they do. It's a matter of salesmanship, more often than not coupled with abuse, therefore, fear. Most brothels don't care whether a prostitute uses a pimp; some prefer it because of the added control they may then exert over the girl. A prostitute with a pimp or in a brothel is a commodity, a product to be sold; nothing more, nothing less. With a pimp, however, she usually ends up with little or none of the proceeds from her work.

Walter went to the meeting knowing absolutely nothing about the financial arrangements, but used his business experience to at least put up a pretense of negotiating. He didn't argue since he didn't want the initial contact with these representatives of an industry he wished to enter to go sour. The negotiations were serious, but their speech and body language, and Walter and Art's frenetic efforts to copy, remained in his memory as one of the funniest situations he'd ever been party to.

Cathy was young, but had a birth certificate showing eighteen (which was later revealed as a fake). Walter took her to a hospital in Las Vegas for her health certifications. They then went into Tonopah for her to be checked, her age verified by the county, and to have her registered as a legal prostitute. She was fingerprinted, and her credentials were accepted and approved. Walter saw the sheriff in the hallway. He said, "Plankinton, you still plannin' to open that whorehouse over there, even though I told you not to?" Walter told him yes, the next afternoon. He was tempted to say *at high noon, Sheriff,* but thought better of it. In a particularly menacing snarl, the man said, "Well, Plankinton, I'll be down to getcha, and when I do, don't you resist me." For the first time, he slapped that oversized gun as he spoke. Chills ran down Walter's spine. He asked himself how a man so dull-witted, so threatening, so obese, could be a sheriff.

To relieve his sudden sense of danger, he conjured up images of his trying to chase some criminal down a street. The idea was absurd since it took great effort for him to get in and out of his own office chair. Walter smiled and answered, "That's just fine, Sheriff, I've got the girl all registered and ready, and that must be legal since we did it all here in this legal office. We'll be open tomorrow afternoon."

Gena and Lisa arrived at the brothel to have lunch with Art, Cathy, and Walter. Afterward, they all sat around talking about the plans to expand the Chicken Ranch as soon as it really got going. Gena and Lisa told Walter they wanted to work for him as soon as possible because they realized being closer to Vegas guaranteed more johns. They finally told Walter that Gena was Lisa's daughter. Lisa was a petite Mexican still under thirty-five with a husband and several children back home in Mexico. Both mother and daughter sent every penny home for the husband/father to save for a business. They eventually returned to Mexico to a normal life and successful business. It's difficult to believe that so many women think nothing of living this life to improve their status, but even harder to think of husbands who approve not only of a wife, but a daughter selling her body to any man who came along. This is not only reality, but commonplace in the world of prostitution.

Shortly after four, a car drove up. Walter went to the door and let a man in. They all recognized him as a deputy sheriff from the other end of the county. He was gussied up in his best Sunday-go-to-meetin' clothes. His first words were, "You got any girls?" Walter said, "Sure, we've got Cathy here." It took everything all of them had to keep from laughing since he was obviously trying to play undercover cop. They went along with his charade. Cathy led him into her room, and they went through their financial negotiations. They were in her room for just a short time when there came a thunderous pounding at the door, as if the intruder planned to break it down. The small group hadn't heard another car drive up so they were a bit startled.

When Walter again opened the door, in came the sheriff and a deputy, guns drawn as if there was to be a *Shootout in the OK Corral*.

At almost the same instant, *Agent 007* came out of the bedroom with Cathy in tow. He recited the deal she made with him for her sexual services for thirty dollars. He told the sheriff she was a prostitute and that this place was an illegal brothel. The sheriff recited, in his *Marshall Wyatt Earp* manner, that they were "all under arrest for operatin' an illegal brothel in the Town of Pahrump."

Walter pointed out two important factors: (1) the two girls sitting in the living room were lunch guests and had nothing to do with the brothel; and (2) that there was no Town of Pahrump. Of course, nothing he said made the slightest dent in the mind of this poor, blustering, childlike pawn of the political machine.

They were all herded into the police cars and driven into the sheriff's Pahrump office, which was also the justice of the peace office. After going through their dog and pony show, they came up with a bail package of twenty-five hundred dollars, the maximum fine. Walter was charged with "Maintaining a premises for the purpose of prostitution in violation of Ordinance #2." (Subsequently, none of the professionals Walter hired ever found any such Ordinance #2.) They went on and on about the Town of Pahrump outlawing prostitution, which carried a sixty-day jail term and a five-hundred-dollar fine.

After tiring of their hypocritical proselytizing, Walter demanded his legal right to a phone call. He called Art's father who came with cash and the title to his mobile home. When Walter later tried to exchange the title to the house for cash for the entire bail, the political machine made it as difficult as possible. That day, they used every means to harass all of them. Cathy returned to Las Vegas with her pimp, but Gena and Lisa stayed a week while Walter tried to remove the new obstacle. He made no attempt to open the brothel during this period.

The county commissioners, district attorney, sheriff, and their boss, the judge, had together concocted a mythical town without benefit of law. It encompassed three hundred thirty square miles, becoming the third largest city in the United States. After determining the borders of the town, they wrote an ordinance making prostitution illegal within the enormous city—their justification for arresting Walter. It was pure fairy tale. But these men had the power to make, and obviously break, any law they wished, whether it was to line their pockets, serve their egos, or inflate their power bases.

The final disposition of the case was in the hands of *The Judge*, since they had "sort of treated Tonopah as a town all those years." The judge declared the ordinance valid, although there was no law anywhere stating that prostitution was, in fact, illegal.

Walter went to Colorado for Thanksgiving for a few days hoping to recover some of the money he had given his former partner to set up his wood business. He was running low on cash and extra money would help his situation in Nevada. That year, fall in Colorado was more like spring; he couldn't get a dime, and his income from shrimping stopped—the boat had been stolen. Walter was down to his last ten thousand dollars in cash, and his set income flow during that period was not too great. For the first time in many years, his financial situation looked bleak. He returned to Pahrump.

Walter tried to press his case up to Christmas. It became apparent that his attorney was useless. All he did was to increase his own income. Walter knew he had to change lawyers.

On January 2, 1977, Walter felt discouraged, helpless, and alone. As he sat reading the newspaper, he heard someone drive up. He went to the window and looked out. To his great surprise, it was his son Doug driving his old pickup loaded down with lumber. Walter almost burst with joy. He crashed through the door to greet him. He explained that he had brought wood from the lumberyard investment for a fence to enclose the brothel (Walter had mentioned it to him on his last trip there). It was hard to believe that his son had collected and hauled it all the way from Colorado. The joy was sweet in the knowledge that he cared that much.

Walter filled Doug in on what had happened since he saw him at Thanksgiving. They agreed there had to be some way around the crazy, inequitable situation. They went to Tonopah and began plowing through records to try to find any privately owned land outside of the newly designated, illegally established, so-called town limits of Pahrump.

One day as they drove along the south end of Homestead Road, they noticed a *For Sale* sign on a piece of land outside the alleged town borders. They had to move fast and realized that if he tried to buy it under his own name, instant obstacles (legal or illegal) would appear to prevent the sale. Since Doug's mother had long ago chosen to have him use her second husband's name, they had the solution. Walter paid sixteen thousand dollars.

It was critical to take possession as soon as possible, before *the machine* found out he was involved with the property. Doug rented a tractor and dug the hole for the septic tank. They had legal possession. Two days before escrow was completed, someone discovered that Doug was Walter's son. That started some wheels turning.

The only local person involved with the property was a family member who *liked the grape*. Walter knew he would be easily manipulated by the machine so he did some quick sidestepping. Fortunately, the estate's administrator was an attorney in Fresno. Walter told him that he was aware that the local district attorney was trying to stop the deal. As cool and businesslike as possible Walter told him that if he went along with them to stop the sale, he could count on being sued. The attorney/administrator knew he could and Walter convinced him he would. The man was so removed from the town that the threat loomed greater than anything the machine could do to intimidate him. The deal went through. By then, the entire town knew, so Walter's name was put on the deed. Art left the scene to live in Las Vegas.

Doug, Pete, and Walter finished the septic tank, then split the two trailers, hooked them onto a truck, and hauled them to the new property. They rejoined them and prepared for electricity. Walter applied for it. They were in the middle of nowhere. Poles, trenches, wiring, all had to be done before electricity could even approach the house. Temporarily, they strung wire from the next residence, about a half mile away, making Walter a member of the power company co-op. Soon, men came to dig holes for the poles. They brought the poles onto the land and set them beside each hole. Then it stopped. No men, no digging, no equipment, no wiring, nothing. It just stopped.

Walter made inquiries as to when they would finish the job. No work was scheduled then, nor in the future. He was told the power company was instructed to stop all work on the land, and not to install any power on the property, ever. It took little research to discover that the man Walter had earlier reported stealing gravel from the county and the director of the co-op were one in the same. Walter rented a diesel generator, but only until he could legally force the power company to give him electricity. They had power, although limited. It was late January 1977. Walter went back to the co-op again and again, and got as many different excuses about why they couldn't get electricity. It was cold since the rented generator could pump just so much juice. They had no water.

In early March, the generator broke down. Now there was no power, no water, no telephone. Pete came up with a solution. He had an old cement mixer and an old tanker, which he carefully cleaned out. Twice a week, they hauled a mixer full of water to the house and put it into the old tanker. Pete also had an old five horsepower generator. They had electricity. Limited maybe, but it was electricity.

Walter hounded the power company. Since he intelligently challenged all of their pointless answers, it became more difficult for them to hide the fact that their director told them he should not get power under any circumstance. It is difficult for public employees to break laws without squirming, and Walter made everyone depriving him of his legal rights wiggle real good.

Horoscopes were probably about as interesting to Walter as to the average person. He never took much stock in them but occasionally read them, sometimes paying more attention than other times. In early March he read his horoscope. It said the best time to open a new business was on the eighteenth. The date stuck in his mind.

Walter heard rumors that the county was planning an "emergency ordinance" requiring licenses to operate any new brothels, and that they would allow only three brothels in the county. Only if one closed down could another be opened. There were already three in the county. They were moving fast, but now had to follow some pretense of law because they knew Walter would fight it. Fortunately, they had no idea how little money he had. He moved fast.

All along, he had patronized all the brothels in the area—as much to keep informed as for pleasure. More! One of the maids (women who act somewhat as secondary madams are called maids), Mignon, kept nagging him about working as his madam. Walter didn't like her. She was huge and obviously mean. But he knew nothing about the business, and she did. She would teach him, and could probably bring girls with her. They struck a deal.

Walter was almost ready to open. He had to start before the county found a way to get their ordinance legalized. If he opened before the ordinance, he automatically fell under a grandfather clause, and they'd be forced to give him a license. Mignon told him she didn't want to come until she had some girls ready. Walter explained the entire legal situation and told her he wanted to open on March 18. He explained how primitively they had to live.

Mignon said she would send the perfect girl to open. She was reliable, and although young and only in the business about six months, she was doing well. And she was legally licensed in the county. She would send her over to work on Friday and Saturday, then the next Friday for good.

Walter made certain everyone in Pahrump knew he would open on Friday, and there was absolutely nothing the machine could do about it since it was outside their fictitious town boundary line. He knew if they tried to incorporate him into their bogus township, they would have to legally obtain signatures of fifty percent of the registered voters in the area. Unfortunately for them, the only registered voter in the decisive area was Walter. They finally reached a dead end. Or so he believed.

TEN

On March 18, 1977, Walter answered a knock on the door. There stood a tall, striking redhead. Mignon had made the perfect choice.

There were lights but no heat, and it was a cold, cold March. With only cold water, they used a camper stove to keep teakettles going. Sheri would at least have hot water to wash her customers and herself properly. The only way to stay warm was together on the couch, wrapped in a blanket. They sat waiting, half freezing to death. Doug was set to come in and pay Sheri and lay her so that he could get up in court and honestly testify that he bought sex from her. They could swear they had a paying customer. The rest of the night the trio just sat and talked, laughed, and froze.

The next day, Walter heard that the machine planned to hold an emergency meeting to push through the ordinance to stop him from entering the brothel business. It was too late. They had covered their tracks and made sure the judge, district attorney and sheriff knew it. Walter never revealed to anyone where he kept getting the inside information that the political machine worked so hard to keep secret. It was most likely a woman since he was an expert at charming women, at least those who were not particularly bright.

On Saturday night, one of Walter's neighbors was in a local saloon with a second man, the bar owner's boyfriend. They sat drinking and just carrying on. One said, "Hell, we're going up to the new whorehouse and get laid." They bragged about themselves as great studs and their plans in the whorehouse. The owner/girlfriend finally got so tired of their crowing, she reached into her cash register, pulled out two twenty dollar bills and said, "Here's twenty dollars a piece for you two sons of bitches. I'm gonna lend you the money just to shut you up." They went right down the road, partied with Sheri, and cemented for Walter the fact that the Chicken Ranch was, indeed, a legal brothel.

On Sunday Walter took Sheri into town and put her on a bus back to the brothel where she was still formally employed. During that week, Doug and Walter worked hard to make things a little better. Walter rented another big generator. At least they'd have heat. The next Friday, Sheri came back to stay, and would remain at the Chicken Ranch as long as Walter did.

Word spread fast. The do-gooders were the *Chicken Ranch*'s greatest asset. Walter was on the front page of the local newspaper again and again. While they thought they were damaging the brothel, the opposite was true. Business grew much faster than it would have had they not kicked up such a ballyhoo. Sheri was very soon overworked. It was time for another girl. Walter called Mignon.

Sadie was eighteen (she said) likely going on twenty-eight, but maybe even thirty-eight. While some might have considered her a little heavy, Walter saw her as Rubenesque. She had only one purpose, fast money. She and her brother were ranching in California. They raised prize horses. She wanted to build the ranch with more and better animals. Her goal was to work a few years, then go back and run the business with her brother. She had to make lots of money, meaning lots of tricks.

As green as Walter was in the business, he sensed a winning team. He fantasized about making five hundred dollars a week to pay the bills. The overhead was just about that, particularly renting a large generator.

He hired a local man to drill a well. Soon came word that it would not be considered a "domestic well." One of the *Good Old Boys*, who just happened to be in the well-digging business, told them it was illegal. The official told the well digger that if he didn't stop, he would revoke his license. Walter asked what kind of permit was needed and was told commercial. Walter contracted a commercial well-digging/engineering company. After two months of waiting, the Water Board finally notified him that since there would eventually be more than three trailers on the property, Walter needed a "municipal well," like a city would have. The engineering firm filed new applications. Someone in Carson City was either asleep or was not notified to block the permit. After a month, they had it. In one day, that company had a one hundred forty-six-foot well dug. The *Chicken Ranch* had water. Now anyone who wanted a well within a two-mile radius couldn't dig without Walter's permission. He had a municipal well. He could turn a two-mile radius into a desert and, if he chose, keep it that way; and he could set the rates.

Walter hauled tons of gravel and had his road graded. Subsequently, the county claimed it as theirs even though Walter paid for it.

Frustration without electricity was reaching its limit. There had to be a way. He went to work. At the office of the power co-op, Walter told the clerk he wanted to see the books. She said it was impossible. Very patiently, he explained that since he was a member, he had the legal right to examine the books at will. She refused. Walter went out to a public phone and called the federal attorney general's office and explained the situation. When he returned to the office, no one said a word; the clerk simply presented the books to him.

No one had any way of knowing his expertise in such matters. Having studied highly complicated trucking tariffs and the rules governing them, Walter easily translated the complex, if crude, method of record keeping. It took little reading to determine why the gravel thief devoted so much of his time acting as head of the local power co-op. As a farmer, he used extensive power to pump irrigation water to his crops. As part of the co-op, he controlled the rating structure—to his own benefit, of course. The man pumped water into one thousand acres of cotton at less cost than a family near the brothel with five kids used to cook one hamburger for supper. It was there in black and white. There were about eleven hundred members in the co-op, each with one vote. Yet, only twelve members benefitted from the rate differential. Those few already enjoyed, or were on their way to, huge wealth made on subsidies of the other eleven hundred members whose rates were exorbitant.

Walter was suddenly privy to the secrets in many closets. This clique dominated the entire valley like lords, but he now possessed information that could shake their imperialistic dominance. Equal footing suddenly looked possible. The temptation to throw open this Pandora's box was overwhelming. Walter knew that eleven hundred people were being cheated, but he worried about self-preservation solely, which very clearly revealed his own hypocrisy. He went straight to the director of the local power co-op, wasting no time, nor sympathy, watching his face go from a condescending arrogant sneer to horrified panic. He turned so white Walter thought he might go into cardiac arrest. More amusing and satisfying was his shock when he finally recognized that this trucker from Colorado was no dolt.

Walter had always been fascinated by politicians who take for granted that most people are not bright enough to recognize what is forced on them, and he would add that the blood-suckers draw their conclusions with at least some validity. The citizens of Tonopah were sheep, easily herded by three self-serving men. Although Walter always publicly claimed that he never believed people to be stupid, he conceded that the majority are docile and complacent. In private, he would sneer thinking they are generally stupid, as well, carefully stressing always, that present company was excepted.

He believed that the machine was learning that he was none of the above. He explained to the gravel thief that he had no desire to expose him for the fraud he was. He just wanted electricity. Walter explained in the simplest, clearest language he could find that power was to be hooked up and running at the *Chicken Ranch* by three o'clock the following afternoon. If it wasn't, the head of the co-op could be certain that each member of that co-op would clearly understand exactly what the twelve snakes had been taking right out of their pockets for a long, long time. Walter promised the trembling man that he would dedicate himself to seeing him thrown off the power board, and would call a membership meeting, guaranteeing that the outcome would be a whole new board. Walter also assured him that he would show the entire membership just how the rating should be done. Then he would sit back and watch his cotton fields turn back into desert. Before he left Walter said, "Do we understand each other?" The man replied, "Mr. Plankinton, we understand each other very clearly."

Walter walked out of that office certain that this man recognized that he would go for the jugular. Someone within the Tonopah royal circle finally accepted that he was more to reckon with than most newcomers they whipped into submission. Some years later, the rating was finally changed, however, all of these facts were exposed to the residents of Pahrump by others. Walter never told anyone until after that exposure, and two small books were published about the corruption in the county.

At seven the next morning, Walter heard a noise outside and went to the door. Dust clouds for miles rose five thousand feet into the sky. Over the hill came a long stretch of vehicles; even power trucks from two hundred miles north. Walter would say, "It was like watching the *Seabees* setting up an emergency airfield during World War II." At three-thirty that afternoon, the man threw a switch and the *Chicken Ranch* had electricity.

The generator went back and the power bill dropped from almost two thousand dollars a month to three hundred. He was finally in business and nothing more could possibly go wrong. He had Sheri and he had Sadie. They celebrated.

When Walter initially furnished the girls' rooms, he bought three-quarter beds and other incidental furniture from a second-hand store. As money started rolling in, he started redecorating each bedroom, one at a time, with beautiful furnishings, spreads, chairs. Even the smaller rooms were done beautifully. The larger rooms were given to girls by seniority, so naturally, Sheri had the largest and the best. The larger bedrooms usually had private bathrooms, as well. Eventually, he put sinks into the smaller rooms to make it easier for the girls to deal with peter pans without leaving their rooms.

Right from the start, Sheri was a *cash cow*, but had little purpose and spent her money frivolously. Little by little Walter taught her how to invest. Eventually, she became a rather wealthy woman.

Sadie had one only purpose for being there: to expand her already successful ranch. She made so much money it was almost funny. Men who availed themselves of her company often stopped on their way out, looking foolish and sheepish. They would say, "Could you spare a couple of bucks so I can be sure I have enough gas to get back home?" or, "Could I borrow enough for my cab fare back to Vegas?" or, "Would you cash a check or traveler's check for me? Sadie took my last quarter and I have to pay the cab driver waiting outside for me." The first time it happened Walter struggled to keep from laughing in the man's face, but it eventually became commonplace. Sadie had a way of getting that last dime.

The initial clientele was primarily local. But soon, men came from the Nevada Test Site, not far away; and miners started coming, too. Before long, there were regulars. The calendar could be set by some. They could look down the road on a certain day each month, knowing that an old man who lived a short distance from the Ranch would appear because his pension check had arrived. Then there was a building project to support a mine being opened by a national firm. First land developers and real estate men flooded the area, then construction workers. Some made big money, others less, but almost all wanted to party. Both Sheri and Sadie were happy to be busy. The money poured in and they took on all tricks.

Walter finally learned the origin of calling men tricks. A prostitute does little in the way of originality. Her aim is to convince a man she has the best to offer, then extract as much cash from him as possible. Although an established price is on most brothel menus, when a girl starts negotiating, she'll say anything to entice him to want all the other acts she offers, at higher and higher prices. Maybe she only got fifty dollars from the last customer. If she thinks this man has five hundred dollars in his pocket, she'll talk, and sell, until she gets it all for doing exactly what she did for the man with fifty dollars, or even twenty dollars. Years back, the story goes, some prostitutes sat around chatting about how they "tricked" every dime possible out of their johns. The term spread, but along the way was reduced to "trick." Walter knew there was a lot more to learn, and he looked forward with great enthusiasm to every single lesson.

Walter quickly saw the simple answer to how men are so fooled by these thinly veiled fables. Prostitutes are extraordinary saleswomen. They know they are dealing with men's egos. When men are sexually aroused, or even want to be, they can be told almost anything to create fantasies. And fantasy is what prostitutes sell. Their bodies are little more than the tools to achieve an economic end.

At the beginning Walter cooked; Sheri, Sadie, and Walter shared cleaning. Doug was not living at the brothel. The girls were busy at night, but few customers came in the daytime, giving the trio idle time to fill. They sat around and talked and laughed and planned. One afternoon, *"The Chicken Ranch, we raise the best cocks in the world,"* came up, which was used as long as Walter owned the Ranch.

During a regular visit to the doctor, Walter asked him whether he felt jogging, the newest craze, would be good exercise for his heart. The doctor said no, instead telling him to run as hard as he could for about a block, then sit down and rest—to increase the size of his capillaries, valuable in his case. Not being fond of running, Walter asked for an alternative. The doctor said, "Get all the sex possible, it has about the same effect." Walter knew at that moment he had made the right choice.

Lynn, the third girl hired, was a friend of both Sheri and Sadie. Lynn was married, with a little boy. She always went home to L.A. (girls worked three straight weeks, then left the Ranch for one week). They were trying to buy a new house, so while working at the Ranch, her husband cared for the child. Soon she, too, took home two thousand dollars a week.

After a month, Mignon arrived. Walter had been the *Madam* the first month, and it was fun. He saw that he would be as adept running a whorehouse as he had been operating a trucking company. Mignon knew her business and taught Walter everything she knew, both intentionally and accidentally.

Being a man, he had little trouble comprehending the psychology behind prostitution. Although his own ego would never allow him to stop falling for the con, Walter fully recognized and always admitted that men like to think girls they consider pretty see them as studs. Having spent time in bordellos throughout his adult life, he also knew what was wrong with them. Girls at the *Chicken Ranch* were squeaky clean, with feminine hygiene their number one priority. He knew that most men want to perform cunnilingus, but not on a smelly woman.

A whorehouse is a place to fulfill fantasies. Men who will tell a prostitute precisely what they want wouldn't think of asking wives for the same things. Some think that means that men only want kinky acts. Walter discovered that while some things men want are silly, most are far from kinky. At times it seemed impossible that as little as thirty-some years ago, a woman could get a divorce on the basis of a husband demanding cunnilingus. And if he even requested fellatio—much less demanded it—she had a cut and dry case. Today, a woman would be laughed out of the courtroom. But many men still won't consider approaching wives about oral sex, nor other acts once considered perverted, no matter how simple or harmless.

There remains a battle between many religious denominations. Some highly respected denominations view marital sex as being not only sacred, but a totally intimate thing between spouses, holding to the philosophy that anything between them is normal and acceptable as long as neither harm nor pain are inflicted, and both persons consent. The kicker is the last part. If a wife (it's usually the wife, but not exclusively) has been convinced by someone or something that the only acceptable sexual act is what is commonly referred to as the "missionary position," anything else may seem repugnant. As it is, even in our enlightened, independent world, too many women find even the most basic sex with a husband tolerable rather than pleasurable.

One would assume that at least the young people of our time are not prejudiced and Victorian. But that is not the case. Some who patronized the Ranch were young married men who asked for the same things as older customers, telling the girls much the same stories of provincial wives who were shocked by their desires or sexual actions. No doubt there were, and are, some reversed cases where the man is the inexperienced prude, and the woman endures incomplete, or just plain lousy, boring sex all her life.

One thing is certain: as long as people are narrow-minded about sexuality, there will be prostitutes and brothels. As long as there's a lack of communication between couples, men will patronize prostitutes, in or out of brothels. Prostitution has prevailed throughout the centuries, some male, mostly female. If there were no customers, the profession could not exist. But female prostitutes are treated as if they service themselves. Their customers are ignored by the law, religious groups, and society at large. The customer has always been protected as if the prostitute went looking for the *trick*. Yet, even the least informed among us must know that the johns go into the brothels, and johns go to the corners where streetwalkers are known to be. The propaganda that the prostitute is the perpetrator—as if she walks into homes and physically lures husbands out to this strange territory where she practices her trade—is fascinating.

Walter thought that maybe if men went home and said to their wives, "Honey, get your clothes off, wash your pussy and get on your back because I want to eat you," some of these women would say, "I've dreamed you would for twenty years."

As Walter learned more about running a brothel from Mignon, he began to add his own ideas. He determined that a rigid dress code was a must. His girls had to look like *his version* of ladies. When a "gentleman" was present—and to Walter any man using his brothel was a gentleman—the ladies kept their feet together on the floor. No beaver shots (letting a man get a peek of their genitals) were ever permitted. The girls were not allowed to expose their nipples in the parlor where they met the guests. Neither sex nor money were discussed in the parlor. Profanity was forbidden. Policies established at the *Chicken Ranch* during the first few months were followed as long as Walter ran it.

When a customer entered the *Chicken Ranch*, he was greeted by a maid who escorted him into the living room. She asked him to take a seat on one of the several plush couches. The maid rang a bell which apprised the girls that a customer was in the parlor. The girls, always dressed for customers after one o'clock in the afternoon, entered the room and lined up whether there were two, five, or ten available. As they entered the parlor, the maid *always said*, "Ladies, we have company."

In that parlor, Walter expected them to be what he perceived as "perfect ladies." He repeated to every new girl, "Any man can get a whore off the street for twenty dollars. The *Chicken Ranch* houses no street whores, just attractive, classy ladies who charge a lot more for their time—and their asses."

Each girl in the lineup, at her turn, stepped forward and announced her assumed prostitute name only. She retained a placid look. She could not wink or flash sexy looks, although she was expected to smile. She then turned around so that he could get a posterior view, then faced the front again. Throughout this brief exhibition, she was not permitted to expose any part of her body which might be considered an enticement—at the risk of being fined. And they quickly learned that Walter always meant what he said.

After all the girls introduced themselves to the gentleman, the maid asked if he had made his decision. When he acknowledged, that girl stepped from the lineup, took his hand, and led him from the parlor into her room without letting go of his hand. If she let go of his hand, the girl was fined. Walter knew from his own countless brothel experiences the psychological difference when the girl held on to his hand. He knew that following behind a prostitute can make a man feel foolish. He was determined that each of his customers would feel only delight and exhilaration from the moment he stepped into the *Chicken Ranch*.

Once a customer was in her bedroom, the girl became the whore she was being paid to be. It was each girl's job to get the best price she could. This was done by promising the man anything he wanted, or suggesting things he would never have thought of on his own. She had to be an extraordinary salesperson to get big bucks from each and every john. If she really knew how to sell herself, she could be the worst lay in the universe and he'd never even notice, or much care.

When the price was settled, up front of course, each girl carefully checked for venereal disease. Walter learned from a doctor, himself, then taught the girls how to recognize every disease. If he was free from disease (*clean*), she thoroughly washed the man's genitals. If she saw the slightest sign of any venereal disease, her orders were to hand back the money, and as gently as possible tell him, "You don't need a lay, Honey, you go visit a doctor. After he gets you healthy again, you come back here and see me. I'll be right here waiting for you." During his time at the *Chicken Ranch*, Walter's girls became so skilled at spotting VD, that the potential for their catching anything was one-tenth of one percent of the average high school student's chance.

The girls saw a doctor once a week. He would not allow a *sick* girl, meaning with VD, at the *Chicken Ranch*. And he never relaxed his position regarding cleanliness. He told them, "If you plan to put something in your mouth or any anatomical cavity of your own body, you should want to know that it's immaculately clean." That meant carefully washing each and every customer.

Most prostitutes use vinegar for regular douches since it eliminates odor. But brothels have *peter pans*, which the girls use between each job. When the man enters the girl's room, both strip. After negotiations are completed and she has carefully examined him for lice or VD, she fills the *peter pan*. The john stands and holds the *peter pan* while the girl dunks his penis into the warm, soapy water. She washes it just as lustfully as she knows how because, if he ejaculates, and some men do, her stint with him is done. A prostitute's obligation is to cause ejaculation, nothing more. If he does not ejaculate, she wipes him dry. She then balances the *peter pan* between her own legs while the man watches her finger-douche herself.

Following their *party*, she gets a fresh pan of soapy water and washes him again, although not thoroughly or sexily since he will not enter her again. She then again bathes and douches herself in front of him, usually while he dresses, to remove any semen left inside of her. Most prostitutes keep their middle fingernail shorter than the rest, since it is this finger she uses to douche, again and again.

Walter found it difficult to believe how some customers came into the brothel. Many had what they called *head cheese* around the heads of their cocks that must have been there for a week or more. The girls said the smell alone would gag them, even the admittedly least sensitive among them. At first Walter, being a fastidious man, himself, naively believed that a man would be embarrassed to expose that kind of filth to anyone, or expect women to want them inserted into their bodily cavities—much less mouths. He learned that men are not the least bit self-conscious about it.

One man came in with crab lice so serious, they were in his eyebrows and armpits, which Walter had never heard of, and certainly had never seen before. Although they could see him vigorously scratching his eyebrows, he denied having them.

The girls could offer to de-lice them, which took a very short time, after which the man would go into the shower and the lice would be washed away. It cost about two dollars for the chemical, and they charged fifty dollars for the treatment, then the john could still go into the chosen girl's room and get laid.

One of the girls told of an incident when she washed an uncircumcised man five times with a liquid medicated green soap before the odor was finally gone, and she could be certain the head cheese was gone.

Often, when men were repulsively dirty, the girls would take even more effort to wash them sexily to get them to ejaculate. If they did, she didn't have to lay him. Because most men paid only for the types of lays, and actually for the ejaculation rather than actual time, the girls could get away with it. One of the factors that made the odors so intolerable was the closeness of the rooms. The smallest bedrooms were no larger than nine by twelve feet. In contrast, some men were so clean that they were afraid of catching something from the girls, even though they saw how carefully things were done at the *Chicken Ranch*.

ELEVEN

Those first weeks and months in business were filled with rumored threats about what the district attorney planned for Walter for opening a brothel without his payoffs. They were legal now so Walter was complacent. If he tried, he would have had to close every brothel in the county. He would never forfeit his own free ride. Nor would the judge allow it.   Nonetheless, they wanted Walter out at any cost. He was rocking their money boat. If they allowed him to continue, the *Good Old Boys* might lose control over county residents, nurtured for decades. Walter heard from several sources that he was "a marked man," that he wouldn't "last until summer," and so forth.

After one year in Nye County he began to feel like what Walter called "a country dog: If I stood still, I was screwed; if I turned around and ran, I got bit in the ass. I had only one choice, stand and fight." And fight he did.

At least he finally knew his enemies. There was the godfather: a stately, well-educated, distinguished-looking man of Slavic blood; without doubt, the most intelligent man in Nye County. For twenty-two years, a double-dipper in the most bizarre manner possible. Earlier, while district attorney, he maintained a private practice in the same office. He used county-paid staff, stationery, and facilities. When he represented a client as a private attorney, he also acted as prosecutor, representing the county against the same client he was defending. A genuine *kangaroo court*.

The District Attorney had also been raised in Nye County. His family had come to Nevada to run a gambling hall. After law school he returned to practice, only the second lawyer to remain in the county. He became law partner to the D.A./soon-to-be-judge, and was assigned as assistant district attorney. All court facilities and staff *given* to the D.A. were now also handed to his new assistant/law partner. Pretty good deal for a boy out of law school; an instant, *legal* double-dipper with a guaranteed county salary. In addition to a law practice free of expense, cases were thrown at his feet since it was more expensive to bring an attorney in from Las Vegas or Reno. As soon as the D.A. moved up to the post of judge, miraculously, the county no longer needed an assistant D.A. The new, still young assistant (not considered too bright by any county resident Walter ever spoke with) was elevated to D.A.

An odd couple, indeed. It was obvious that the young D.A. hoped to follow in the footsteps of the judge, but Walter believed he wouldn't make a decent pimple on the judge's ass. So now, they were law partners in private practice, plus jointly prosecutor/defending attorneys/judge. Autocracy? No judge, however brilliant, can remain objective under these circumstances. No man, however well intentioned, can listen to cases where the defendants have, in some way caused him to dislike or just be annoyed by them, and remain unbiased. Some in Nye County believed there were convicts in Carson City, incarcerated by the Nye County Court/Judge/D.A., who wouldn't have been there had they done some serious bootlicking.

Worse, this practice was not only condoned by the county commission, but encouraged. Even more shocking were the people. Walter realized that many people are naive, and like being that way. They have no interest in what goes on beyond their own fenced yard, or square block, or their side of the hill in front of them. And they work hard to raise their children to be as closed off from the world as they are. This would have seemed impossible in the 1970s. The U.S. had already gone from using leeches to nuclear medicine; from six-shooters to rocket fire; from town criers to instant worldwide, satellite visual/audio communication. Walter admitted that some Pahrump citizens were just too intimidated to cry foul. But practically the total population?

Anyone who won't admit that power is not based on some form of intimidation is a fool. But in most places Walter had been, subjugation was unenforceable without full cooperation of the people. And long-term autocracy—such as in Nye County—almost impossible.

The young D.A. seemed even younger than his years. More than once, Walter watched him throw tantrums in the courtroom if a judge berated him for childish behavior. His own law partner/judge never did, however, at least not in the courtroom.

Everywhere else, in the 1970s, people challenged corrupt politicians. Not in Nye County. Walter supposed the geographical vastness created a sort of vacuum. And the judge took full advantage of it. He dispensed favors, justice, and personal retaliations, often capriciously, within his kingdom. Yet, he saw himself as a law-abiding, righteous man, almost saintly. And many others did, too, particularly legal and political cronies who lived in other counties. It's harder to show a man where he can be unjust or wrong when he will not accept even the possibility that he has feet of clay. After a man has been in a position of control of others' lives for decades, it's easy to see how he can forget that it is he who is the servant of the people.

Over the years favors piled up. People around the state either worshipped the judge or feared both men to an irrational level, particularly the judge. No judicial servant, he believed that the simple people of Nye County were not smart enough to handle their own destinies; that he was the one who knew best for these children-people. It is difficult to know whether he was right, or if they were slowly and methodically led to that point by a process of intimidation.

One of the two books mentioned earlier was a very crude publication exposing the judge and Nye County politics, the second was more technical, a documentary-type publication done later as a thesis. They each give more of the abuse of civil rights and unequal treatment of residents of the county during the years dominated by this machine. If the person was loyal, (s)he received favorable treatment before the bench; an adversary or even a nonsupporter was usually found guilty. This kept the public in line, and their constitutional rights be damned.

Finally, to round out the power triad, there was the sheriff. A tough, coarse man, but a simple one. He was an obedient, seemingly almost retarded child who did precisely what he was told. He seemed to know little, if anything, about law enforcement. His department was a reflection of himself: not too bright, mean as hell, and joyfully prone to sadistic streaks.

These three men were born at the wrong time. They belonged in the Old West, before radio, mechanized transportation, before civilization came west, before civil rights were respected. Because Walter always considered himself a model citizen, with exceptional codes and morals, he classified himself as part of what would have been an innocent group who in the past had been run out pretty quickly. But he determined they were not going to run him out. He felt that the judge had finally met his match.

On May 1, 1977, the court ruled against Walter on the issue of there being no town. The judge who had been brought in to hear the case (an old friend of the Nye County judge; Walter later learned there was no judge in the state that was not either a friend or beholding in some way to this judge or one of his countless cronies) ruled that, even though the county had never formed an unincorporated town as prescribed by law in Nevada, it probably had been operated as one for a period of time, so he allowed that it was to be considered a town, at least in Walter's case. It was left that same way, too, which meant that the machine could deal in any manner that would suit them or their supporters, using Pahrump as a town or not a town, dependent upon the whims of those who "ran things differently in Nye County."

Shortly after the ruling against Walter, the D.A. sent a deputy to the Ranch (which still had no phone) to tell Walter that he wanted to see him that day in his Pahrump office. Without preamble, the D.A. told Walter that since the "town" issue was settled, he would soon be on trial for the ordinance violation. He told Walter that the maximum sentence of a five hundred dollar fine and sixty days in jail was "a certainty." He added that if Walter would "close down the Chicken Ranch and leave Nye County, permanently, the charges will be dropped." Walter stood up and said, "You can go straight to hell," and walked out of the office.

Later, he heard that the justice of the peace, the D.A., and the county administrator were discussing the case in a restaurant. They openly declared that Walter was going to jail for sixty days and the five hundred dollar penalty allowed by the quickly and covertly manufactured ordinance. This was how Nye County tried all of its cases. Townspeople on both sides of the brothel issue were disturbed by the way the case was handled, however.

The case went to trial on June 1, 1977. It took the justice of the peace exactly ninety seconds to try and find Walter guilty, as everyone knew he would. The sixty days and five hundred dollar fine were announced with some bravado, like the parrot he, too, was. He went on to try and find guilty the three girls in absentia, without ever notifying them of the court date. That this could happen in the U.S. was inconceivable to Walter and his attorney.

When the trial ended, Walter asked his attorney why he hadn't objected to the procedure, and he said "It's automatically appealable to the District Court, so let them enjoy their fun here." The attorney immediately asked the D.A. how he wished to handle the docket schedule for the appeal. The D.A. told him he would put it on the court docket, then send Walter a notice of the court date on the "regular" calendar.

Before the attorney left to return to Las Vegas, Walter repeated as clearly as he could state it without sounding paranoid, not to trust this D.A., nor anyone affiliated with the district. He warned him to remember that their word meant absolutely nothing, and they believed they were above other men's laws, ruling the county by their own dictates.

Despite the legal chaos the brothel grew every day, and Walter kept learning about his new business; working hard at it, enjoying every minute. He discovered that while all the girls he hired were already experienced fornicators, many were amateurs in everything else. He had to teach them how to examine a man, and some how to lay a man with skill. And he certainly enjoyed honing their overall abilities.

Most applicants were prostitutes, but some were just wannabes. Those girls were promiscuous, but not for money. They wanted to learn to be professionals. A few didn't even know anything about oral sex, usually called "giving head"—a term reserved for woman sucking on and licking a man's penis and balls exclusively for the man's pleasure.

Since Walter was the only man living at the *Ranch*, he had to teach them everything. Not only quality control director and sales trainer, he became sexual guinea pig, as well. Some of the girls had laid every boy in school, but because it was more often than not in the back seat of a car, most had never seen a male anatomy in daylight. They had to carefully examine every body part to become skilled. Walter said over and over, "I'm certain every man understands when I say, it's tough being at the top."

Walter taught them to look at and feel all parts of the genitals for bumps and lesions, crabs and lice. He demonstrated how to feel for little bumps indicating syphilis. Open sore diseases are easy to spot—unless the john is not circumcised. It takes skill to detect problems then. Walter learned that those not circumcised were often dirty. No john slept with any *Chicken Ranch* prostitute without a preliminary exam. During training period, a second girl went into the room just to check the johns with the trainee.

Since each room was wired, the girls were totally aware that Walter spot-checked their preliminaries and financial negotiations to ensure they followed his rules. Pimps teach prostitutes to steal, but they wouldn't steal from Walter Plankinton. Listening in made him horny, at least sometimes, but money negotiations were even more exciting. Just as he learned the tricks in trucking, he slowly mastered brothel trade secrets. Often listening in gave him new ideas about marketing.

He analyzed and categorized his brothel competitors as healthy or dirty foes. Not the type to allow anyone to damage his business, when one of his competitors, Joe Conforte—who later became somewhat (in)famous, appearing on TV talk shows with "his girls"—used some unfair advertising against him, Walter took the first possible opportunity to retaliate.

A new girl came in with the clap, so she couldn't work until she was clean. The *Chicken Ranch* had a young regular who was capable of laying one girl after another —and would have if he could afford it. Walter made a deal with him. He laid the contagious Yvonne free. Then Walter gave him enough cash to lay every girl in the competitor's brothel. Within days, all the girls had the clap, as did most of their regular customers—who, after ridding themselves of the disease, drifted over to the *Ranch*. And once the *Chicken Ranch* got a customer, Walter knew how—and taught his girls—to keep him.

There was no shortage of wannabes at the *Chicken Ranch* right from the start. One day, a woman in her thirties showed up and told Walter she had heard that girls at the *Ranch* were doing pretty well, and asked him to hire her. She had no experience, her husband was long gone, and she had some kids to raise back home. Not one to mince words, Walter told her to look around at all the young, beautiful girls she would have to compete with. No matter how hard looking, misshaped, low-class any prostitute was, Walter always believed she was gorgeous and swore to anyone who would bother to listen that she was virginal looking. He described this "older" woman as very beautiful, and she may have been, but he sincerely believed it was much too late for her to start a career as a prostitute. He also didn't happen to have an opening when Bobbi walked in.

Her eyes filled with tears and she said, "I want to tell you something, Mr. Plankinton. I spent the last dollar I had on the cab getting here. I don't have any money to go anywhere. Please put me to work." Walter hired her. He took her in to be registered and get her health slip. He always kept what he considered appropriately sexy clothes in storage, so they got her clothed. The other girls jumped in and fixed her hair and her nails. They also gave her a carrot to practice giving a blow job. Soon, she was ready. Walter admitted that he could have easily fallen for Bobbi because she was so beautiful.

In her very first lineup, a kid no more than twenty or twenty-one picked her, a trend that never changed. She was pretty and showed class. No one would ever had suspected her to be a prostitute if they saw her on the street. She never took time off, and worked very hard. She proved to be an extraordinary saleswoman, and never made under $2,000 a week once she got going. Her purpose was simple. She had been in business, but because of some minor health problems, she ended up broke. Because she had to support herself and her kids, she couldn't get enough money together to start again. Prostitution became her only answer. She made it. She subsequently went back into business, and last heard of was highly successful.

Tobi was another one in her thirties who seemed to attract the young men. Walter considered her old and sloppy. She had enormous boobs, but when she took her bra off, Walter said, "They were huge flabs that hung to her waist." Although Walter auditioned her and found her adequate but nothing special, he never understood why the youngest of his customers came back and without ever wanting to look at a lineup, asked for Tobi, again and again.

Leta loved to sit on the washing machine. He caught her a couple of times which embarrassed her, at least at first. She didn't give him any explanation. He finally told her to stay off the machines. Only then did she tell him that she had little metal balls, available at any exotic store, which she put into her vagina. By sitting on the vibrating washing machine, she would climax. For those who might wonder why she would need any more sex, rarely do prostitutes climax with their johns. And like any man—which is widely accepted—erotic thoughts sometimes stimulate women, too. Men masturbate in a variety of way, and what's good for the goose should certainly be good for the gander. Every girl in the *Chicken Ranch* owned a vibrator.

Right after Terri joined the Ranch, Walter realized that she was taking up to six showers a day. One day after a solid thirty minutes in the shower,

Walter blew his top. Not only was she wasting his water, she was jeopardizing the septic tank system with all the hot water. He walked into the bathroom (no doors in his brothel were allowed to be locked), and there she was lying in the tub with the shower water pounding away at her clit, a big smile on her face. There was no telling how many gallons of hot water it took to bring her to a climax. Walter told her to go out and buy a vibrator, or whatever it took, because she wasn't going to play on his money.

Linda drifted into town from New York. One day, a regular john showed her a bag full of white powder. Thinking it was coke, she reached in and snorted deep and hard. It was PCP, and her john was gone in a flash, never to be seen again at the Ranch. Mignon rushed her to the doctor who said she must keep moving around. Everyone in the *Chicken Ranch* helped take care of her, day and night. She later took up with a "Jesus freak," and went off to some religious camp in Utah. She became a real fanatic. The new religion believed in getting high so they could recognize Jesus. By the time she tried to go back to the Ranch two years later, having taken every drug there was and gaining twenty-five pounds, adding twenty-five years to her face, she was no longer *Chicken Ranch* calibre.

A surprising number of men paid the girls to give them enemas. The prostate gland is somewhere near the rectal area, and the warmth of the water and excretion cause them to have orgasms. One out of ten men who went to the *Ranch* didn't want intercourse. Some would have the girl move around in various positions, dance, strip, play with her own nipples, masturbate herself, while he masturbated himself. Some of the girls concluded that these men did not have women in their younger years, therefore had masturbated so constantly that after many years of using pictures of nudes, they satisfied themselves better by self-masturbation. When he could finally afford to pay for the brothels, the girls would be the moving pictures of his youth. There were also theories that such men might just be afraid of venereal diseases, maybe having had them in their youth. These men paid like any others. The girls always liked such johns because it was easier on their bodies.

One really odd local man, well known in religious circles, was undoubtedly a homosexual who refused to admit it to himself. He paid to be allowed to sit in a room where he could observe a girl going in and out of her room with another man. When the man left her room, instead of cleaning herself up as she was normally required to do she faked it, then waited until this customer went in for oral sex with her, consuming the previous john's semen as best he could. It was obvious that he was a latent homosexual, but prominent, and quite married. Again, it was a simple job for the girl, took about fifteen minutes, for which she earned three hundred dollars. There were many *pillars of society* with needs beyond what wives and lovers could fulfill.

Occasionally, men who considered themselves pretty smart would try to con the girls into believing they had not had a climax, but the girls could certainly tell. They would argue that they should not have to pay because they were such great studs—actually because the girl had so totally convinced the customer this was so by moaning and groaning as if she was climaxing. Once in awhile, a john would get really angry because he felt if he could convince the girl that she hadn't given him his money's worth, he could get laid again. Walter admitted to trying the same ruse more than once when frequenting countless brothels and prostitutes before he opened the *Ranch*. It never worked. "He never received refund or refuck."

Sometimes, the real story was that a man was embarrassed because he ejaculated very quickly, before he could get laid. If he was an aggressive man, he would swear he hadn't, and try to intimidate the girl or her pimp.

Others, out of guilt (at least that's what the girls were certain it was) could not get an erection. Or if he got one, he'd lose it almost instantly. This happened mostly to married men, and some so-called religious men, who simply wished to experience the brothel situation. It wasn't an ongoing thing, but it wasn't completely uncommon. The girls would discuss it whenever it happened, and Walter was surprised at the frequency.

In his years at the *Chicken Ranch*, Walter said no more than ten men ever tried to get money back from him. Only twice did Walter believe their stories, and gave them another girl at the first girl's expense. It happened only when he knew the girl was moody or temperamental, therefore, the customer's story was feasible. Otherwise, he said the rest were just con men, and it wasn't difficult to tell, no matter how clever the men thought they were.

There was another breed who would come to the Ranch, sit through the lineup, ask a few questions, then say none of the girls interested them. They would then go out to their cars and masturbate. One night Walter remembered seeing one of those outside the kitchen window, so he filled a small pan with scalding hot water and threw it right into the man's lap. He let out a yelp. Walter went about his business, laughing out loud when he heard the squealing of the man's tires as he sped away.

TWELVE

As business grew, more maids were hired so that all hours were covered by hostesses. Mignon was eventually demoted to little more than a maid, herself, since Walter understood the business and took over completely. That was his intention from the start, even before he learned—soon after she arrived—that she had physically abused girls in other brothels, which was considered perfectly acceptable by other owners. He forbade it at the *Chicken Ranch*. He never understood why, with all his charm, suave, and salesmanship, he could not deflate her psychological control over his girls. It infuriated him, mostly because he was very jealous.

As he was learning all about being a pimp, which title he loathed and would turn all shades of red when called one, he somehow found a way to blend his sense of ownership of the girls in with business practices. What was bizarre about Walter was that he exercised as much control as any street pimp or brothel owner. What made him different was that he did not beat the girls up or try to turn them into drug addicts. He never even considered that he was *beating them up* emotionally, or psychologically, however. He treated them like brainless children, and that was how he saw them. The term "girls" is used primarily throughout this book, but Walter referred to them as whores more often than he did girls; and when he did say girls, he always prefaced it with "my." In his mind they were his property, commodities, little different than the most abusive, controlling pimp.

Walter never understood why some looked to Mignon as some sort of mother figure, acting like obedient children in her presence. Sheri was the most surprising. She went to Mignon with her problems, and clung to her every word. This was particularly infuriating to Walter because Sheri was his special property. He considered her his "first whore." Although Mignon's authority was seriously diminished by Walter's presence, he neither reduced her salary nor her "display of control." At least to the girls, she was the madam. However, because Walter was their *pimp*, his orders always prevailed.

The maids present the greatest surprise here. They really came from the staid community of Pahrump. They were housewives, mothers, grandmothers;

to a woman, typical small-town and of good character. They were hostesses at the door and in the living room. But they also enforced the rules of the house. Using these straight-laced women created only one problem: because they would not enter the rooms with naked men, much less consider touching them, they could not act as dual VD checkers with new girls, which would have been ideal. However, Walter never considered demanding it, recognizing the greater benefit of employing such upstanding local citizens. It attested to all the world that Walter Plankinton ran a clean, honest house. How these maids, these women acting as if they were typical Pahrump prim and proper residents, rationalized being *assistants to pimps* boggles the imagination.

Typical of straight ladies with maternal instincts, some assumed motherly roles, exactly like most madams over the centuries. They all seemed to understand, accept, even appreciate the necessity of Walter's rules of the house, and enforced them emphatically, providing them, too, with enormous power over the younger women. They never permitted the girls to smoke or drink in the parlor, or use profanity. They were alert to girls trying to entice customers by exposing their breasts or genitals, or even licking their lips provocatively. They watched as girls led the men from the parlor to their rooms to be absolutely certain they held the johns' hands, and made sure that after a girl was finished with her customer, she led him, once again by the hand, into the *Cat Room*. Whenever even the smallest infractions occurred, they made notes so the girls would be fined. They apparently enjoyed this puff of power over other humans.

The *Cat Room* was a separate sitting room where the girls could talk with the customers. In the *Cat Room*, they were permitted to induce the customers back into their rooms for more sex; paid for, of course. This was done in what Walter liked to call "good taste" under the watchful eyes of the maid—although subtle teasing (at least what Walter considered subtle) was acceptable there, unlike in the parlor. But no girl could smoke, drink, or sit with legs apart, referred to as *dirty hustling*. It was a matter of packaging, and Walter was certain he knew how to package even a human product as well as sell it. This was very serious business to him, and he was incapable of being lighthearted about it. He did, however, admit to enjoying the work more than any job in his life.

People don't realize how many lesbians there are among prostitutes. When the first one came to the brothel, she soon had girls taking trips with her on their weeks off. The minute Walter recognized the problem, he created rigid rules: At no time were two girls in a room alone behind a closed door. If they were caught engaging in anything even resembling sexual acts, both were fired instantly, no questions, no discussion, no argument. He didn't give a damn what they did in a threesome with a customer, as long as it was paid for, nor what any of them did away from the brothel. But at the *Chicken Ranch*, they followed his rules. He was not so naive to think no hanky-panky ever happened, but disobedience so angered him, he was certain it was rare. His rationale for strictness was that he would not allow destruction of the "relative tranquility they enjoyed."

It was no easy task keeping that many women in such close quarters on a twenty-four-hour basis at some level of peace and harmony. Allowing homosexuality to run amuck would have invited chaos. His homophobia became apparent after very little questioning. He loudly condemned homosexuality as personally intolerable, even though he knowingly had sex with every single girl who came into the brothel, and certainly not just once, a good percentage of them lesbians. It was his typical level of self-deceit, both for money and for his own overwhelming desire for sex with prostitutes. He allowed lesbians in the brothel, not that he could actually prevent it, because it put money into his pocket, but he had what he called his own personal limitations, which became law in the brothel. It never once occurred to him that the girls' fear of him had more to do with the relative tranquility he always bragged about than his ability to manage.

Just as a prostitute could actually make him believe that she adored him and felt he was the best lay she ever had, knowing full well that she was lying with every word and move, he was self-infatuated enough to convince himself that in his brothel, he created as much joy and contentment and sense of safety as any genuinely happy family's living room. He was an unsmiling, vainglorious man who found humor almost exclusively in smut or the embarrassment or diminishment of others. If a very funny joke was not dirty, he seemed not to understand it, and even if he did, he still "didn't get it."

Some people might be surprised to know that lesbians act just like female prostitutes. Men who frequent prostitutes generally don't much care, even if they bitterly resent homosexual men, or *gays*, or homosexuality in general. Most don't know, either, that it is quite common for both married and unmarried couples go to brothels asking for combinations of heterosexual-homosexual acts. Walter never cared as long as they were willing to pay for the extra services. But, he never accepted female customers who wanted solely lesbian sex. It was not offered at his *Chicken Ranch*, which gave him a strong sense of moralistic superiority among brothel owners.

A new girl arrived at the *Ranch*. Mignon had met her, socially, in Utah a couple of years earlier. She was a "turn-out" (a girl who had never been properly trained). In other words, an amateur playgirl who may or may not have practiced the sale of sex. Julie had never been a professional prostitute before she was hired by Walter.

Julie was a Mormon with the biggest boobs Walter claimed he'd ever seen anywhere in his entire life. She told him that her good Mormon father worked nights in the mines while her mother worked the day shift. In spite of showing himself to the world as a devout, churchgoing Mormon, Julie's father drank. A lot. When Julie was eight years old, she went home from school one day to find her father in his usual condition, drunk. He convinced her to drink with him, then raped her. He warned her never to tell her mother or anyone else because there was nothing wrong with daddy having sex with his little girl, but mommy might get jealous and punish her; then others would take her away from home and put her into a terrible place.

By thirteen, Julie was an alcoholic who had suffered endless physical and sexual abuses at the hands of her loving, religious father. He also took her into an eerie center where she was systematically abused, both physically and sexually, by numerous other men and women. She was a lovely girl: at least five feet eight inches, one hundred thirty-five pounds; the thirty-five pounds obviously in her boobs. Walter admitted, smiling, that he particularly enjoyed his quality control duties with Julie.

The first night she went into the parlor was a Saturday. It was her practice run, her *debut*. Ironically, during the first lineup, a customer picked Julie and Sheri for a two-girl party. It couldn't have been more advantageous since Walter considered Sheri his best girl, ideal to orient Julie. Sheri, with the largest room which, coincidentally, was the only bedroom that opened directly into the main parlor, was the obvious choice for their party. Since Julie was the rookie, Sheri took charge of the price negotiations and physical examination (a particularly helpful demonstration for Julie whose next customer would almost certainly be solo).

The first part the man requested was a simple, straight lay with Sheri, stipulating that Julie watch them. They all shed their clothes as the john closely watched the two women. Sheri lay down on her bed facing up, eyeing the man expertly as he finished undressing himself. Sheri very carefully performed the physical examination so that Julie would be well trained. Seeing the two girls strip apparently prepared the man because he had a full erection, thus, needed no preliminaries. He happily mounted Sheri's beautiful body.

Sheri not only had the largest and most convenient room, it was the best room in the brothel. It was completely mirrored, including the ceiling. As the john ecstatically bounced up and down on Sherry, she glanced up into the overhead mirror and saw Julie watching them intently. To her dismay, a mischievous Julie realized she had caught the other girl's eye. Julie began making silly faces and motions to distract and tease her, and to cause her to laugh at a time when she certainly could not do so.

Experienced trouper that she was, and aware of the all-around view of her room, Sheri knew that if the customer happened to look just in front of himself into the mirror over the head of the bed, he would see Julie. If he did, he would surely get angry for her mocking his sexual performance. Certain that Julie did not understand that potential, Sheri frantically pointed toward the mirror over the headboard, trying desperately to make Julie understand that the customer would see her if he looked up.

When her charade obviously didn't register with Julie, Sheri continued pointing while the customer pumped madly away. After what seemed like forever, a relieved Sheri saw that Julie's eyes followed the line of the extended finger pointing to above the headboard. Nothing being wrong with the young girl's intelligence and reflexes, she instantly interpreted Sheri's meaning. Without hesitation, she picked up the jar of *K-Y Jelly* on Sheri's bed table (always in reach of every girl's bed), took a large glob of it on her finger, turned toward the bed, expertly reviewed the customer's body, then shoved her beautifully manicured middle finger up his ass, deep and hard.

He lunged forward with such force that the same thought flew through both girls' minds: he must have ruptured himself. He almost tore Sheri's pussy open since he lunged forward just as he was shoving his cock into her. His head smashed into the glass headboard with a loud bang, and blood trickled down his face.

Julie started to laugh so hard she was almost hysterical. Yet, however and wherever the man moved she never took her finger from his ass. Finally, he jumped to his feet and grabbed his clothes. Slightly bent and hobbling, blood flowing down his face, he burst into the parlor naked as a jaybird, with the equally nude Julie following close behind him leaning over with her finger up his ass, howling uncontrollably. The parlor was filled with customers.

In contrast to this pornographic *Keystone Cops,* the ever-humorless Mignon quietly, but quickly, moved to the man and placed her arm around his shoulder. In a most dignified, calm voice she said, "Honey, wouldn't you like to go back into the bedroom and put your clothes on?" She then turned her head toward the still shrieking Julie and in a more sinister voice said, simply, "Julie, take your damned finger out of this guy's ass."

It was then in almost a quick ripple that the men sitting in the parlor grasped the situation. They, too, began to scream and howl. When the man came back through the parlor only partially dressed, apparently not wishing to stay in that room any longer than necessary, they were doubled up on sofas and on their feet holding their sides. Julie stood in the middle of the floor waving her finger in the air, trying, however halfheartedly, to contain herself.

Sheri stood motionless, and stark naked, at her bedroom door, wide-eyed, mouth agape.

Mignon reached out her hand in an attempt to stop the man to ask if he needed first aid, seeing the blood still running down his face and now smeared on the still open shirt he so quickly threw on. He obviously didn't even notice her as he crashed through the front door and into the night.

Hearing loud waves of chaos in the parlor from his office, an unusual sound in the brothel at night, Walter had moved quickly to the room about halfway through the episode. He was grateful to Mignon for staying calm because he, too, stood frozen in the doorway, aghast, unable to react. When he could finally move the man was gone. What he saw then was a room full of customers and girls so caught up in the situation, Sheri finally with them, too, they were unable to talk without resuming convulsive laughter. Walter went from shock into absolute rage, certain he'd lose income that night. The look on his face quickly quieted the girls. His immediate concern was for future losses, maybe even a lawsuit from the man. Little did he know the unusual situations he had to look forward to. He was still a total greenhorn in the brothel business long after he considered himself an expert. They never did see that man again. And Walter never saw any humor in the incident. Some might wonder why he didn't fire Julie.

After all of the customers were gone, Mignon sat her down and coldly balled her out, successfully erasing all of the humor the girl saw in her actions. Then Walter ordered her into his office where he screamed at her, threatened to fire her if she ever did anything like that again, and generally terrified her. But, he was certain she would make lots of money for him, and money always won over anything else. Unquestionably, Julie's sense of humor was diminished. Neither Mignon nor Walter had a whiff of lightheartedness, and did everything possible to ensure that no one else at the *Chicken* Ranch did, either, at least where it involved a customer.

Two months after the trial before the justice of the peace, Walter read in a local paper that he was going to jail for sixty days. The article stated that he had missed the appeal date in district court. He jumped into his car and drove to Las Vegas to see his lawyer. He asked how this could have happened since he never received anything. He couldn't believe what the article said. Naively the attorney answered, "You were there, you heard my discussion with the D.A. about putting it on the regular calendar. You heard him say we'd both be notified."

The lawyer called the D.A. and turned on his room speaker. He asked what the item in the newspaper meant. The answer was slow and casual, "Well, that's just the way it is." Unbelieving, the attorney said, "Sir, you told me that you would put this on the calendar, and that my client and I would be notified of the date." The D.A. calmly replied, "I don't remember making any deal with you. And, your client is going to jail, just as I promised he would."

Anyone doubting the story has to be a fool. Walter had the cash to fight the issue to the highest courts by that time since he was making real money in the brothel. His investments also generated income. He would never have sat back to wait for them to cart him off to jail where he knew he would be in mortal danger. Walter and his attorney knew that all the principals in the charade would say that they were either mistaken or lying about any such understanding.

The lawyer was no match for these despots, nor had he listened to Walter's warnings. Ironically, shortly before this incident, Walter met a newly practicing attorney fresh out of the Clark County District Attorney's office. He went straight to his office. He felt that finding this lawyer was the best thing that ever happened to him. Not only did he handle everything with skill and professionalism, they became friends. After looking at Walter's records, which he demanded the former attorney send over, he told Walter there was little he could do to keep him out of jail, but promised to try.

He filed an appeal and got a stay of the jail sentence. In district court in front of the godfather-judge, of course it was denied. The new attorney appealed to the Nevada Supreme Court but was denied a new trial.

Walter never minded the idea of the sixty days. The Ranch was doing well and could run without him. His concern was what the sheriff told him shortly after the original trial, privately of course. He said, "Once I get you into my jail, Plankinton, I'll kick your balls off every day. You'll be lucky to come out alive." Walter knew he had better believe him because not only did this group want him to disappear, neighbors had told him how abusive, even sadistic, this sheriff was to his prisoners. Walter was no coward, but he had no desire to be maimed or to die at the hands of the tax-paid brute.

Walter asked his new attorney to at least keep him out of the Tonopah jail. He told Walter that jail was unquestionably "cruel and unusual punishment considering the insignificant violation of this purported law." And of course, in light of the fact that there was no such law in the first place, the situation was absurd. Tonopah had no hospital or clinic capable of handling Walter's heart condition, and no doctor closer than Bishop, California. The six thousand foot altitude over an extended period could also be a very real life-threatening factor. The new attorney filed an appeal in the U.S. District Court, where he was certain political pressures could not determine the outcome of the case. He got a "stay order" to keep Walter out of jail.

Word that the *Chicken Ranch* needed girls was out among the brothels as well as in Las Vegas. Walter's Las Vegas apartment address was circulated so they could easily find him.

One day, a petite Chinese girl with long black hair and dark eyes appeared at the apartment door. She introduced herself in broken English with dialogue Walter never forgot. She said, "I Suzie Wong, I from Taipei, Taiwan. I have itty bitty pussy, but go snap, snap, snap." Walter laughed until tears rolled down his cheeks. Contrary to the norm for a tiny Chinese girl, she had large, firm boobs, Walter's favorite female attribute.

During her five years at the Ranch, Suzie netted over two hundred fifty thousand dollars. Yet, when she finally quit she was broke. Every free week she headed straight for Las Vegas and played poker every waking moment, then returned to the Ranch without a penny. Suzie was considerably older than most of the girls, Walter thought probably in her late thirties, but looked no older than early twenties. She was one of the few girls who Walter could set a clock by. Whenever a girl left the Ranch for her time off, she took most or all of her belongings, so that not returning to the brothel was her option (or her pimp's, of course), and many made that choice. But Walter always knew Suzie would return.

She developed a huge following who kept track of her schedule. Only occasionally did she appear in the lineup because she made as much or more money than any of the other girls without it. Fortunately for her, she went into the lineup one day when a man chose her, then spent the next solid two days with her. The man, sixty-some years old, lived on the East Coast but was in Las Vegas on business occasionally. Thereafter, he spent more and more time with Suzie. He fell very much in love with her, and finally told her that she need not remain in the brothel. She left shortly after Walter did.

Eventually, the man retired, and he—and his wife—moved to Las Vegas. At first, Suzie and her sixteen-year-old daughter lived with the older couple, with the wife's blessing. She no longer wished to have any sexual relations with her husband, although loving him no less. They had an ideal marriage, and the wife learned to love both Suzie and her daughter. Eventually, Suzie determined that she needed a private residence, and her aging lover rented Walter's condo for her since Walter was rarely there, himself. The extended family attitude with the man's wife never diminished, however. As a gift to Suzie and her daughter, the couple went back to China to visit Suzie's mother, and her older daughter who still lived with the (grand)mother.

Walter, while impressed with the concubine relationship and the apparently happy family structure of these people, was amazed by it, too. He would laugh and say, "I've had my hands full with one wife at a time; juggling two would be more than I'd ever wish to tackle."

As the Ranch progressed, they all worked to enhance its environment. Doug and Walter's stepson Sam—separated from his wife—came and went, helping to improve the property. They planted shade trees and built a facade on the trailer complex to look like an old ranch house. But after almost a year, they still didn't have phone service, making it difficult to promote the brothel.

Nevertheless, Walter felt compensated by the experiences he was privy to in operating a brothel. Since girls arrived and left, and customers came in all shapes and sizes, life was rarely, if ever, dull. Walter thoroughly enjoyed the people he was surrounded by, the girls above all, of course.

Lynnette was five feet three inches, one hundred five pounds, had dishwater-blonde hair, and blue eyes. She "wasn't gorgeous, but she was pretty." She came from one of the brothels nearby where she had been *turned-out*. She worked there for six months so both Sheri and the madam knew her.

Lynnette had been happily married with a new baby. She and her young husband needed a second vehicle. Greg found an old pickup truck and the two of them went to get it. On the way back, Greg drove the truck with Lynnette following in their car. As they entered the freeway, they naturally increased speed. From nowhere and without warning, two eighteen-wheelers crashed in front of them. As they collided, Greg's pickup seemed to be swallowed up into their vastness. The sound was deafening as she tried instinctively to brake, swerving, missing the twisting mass that tried to engulf her. As she swerved, Lynnette's tire drove over Greg's head, separated from his body, which had been flung out of his vehicle, crushing it under the enormous weight of the car.

Lynnette's mind was all but destroyed. Even after two years at the Ranch, asleep and sometimes wide awake she would see Greg's mutilated, detached head and distorted face. It occurred when she least expected it for no logical reason. For a day or two afterward, she just didn't function. All she could do was cry. Fortunately for Lynnette, she had loving, supportive parents who took care of the baby while she struggled with her sanity.

Anytime Walter talked about this girl, he acknowledged that prostitution is unacceptable to some, but in Lynnette's defense, he would plead that she could have as easily become an alcoholic, a drug addict, committed suicide, or spent her life in a rubber room. It is so easy to judge reaction to unimaginable tragedy, as long as it is someone else's.

In her early twenties, when she could finally come back into the world, Lynnette turned from a straight, sweet, happy wife and mother into a special kind of prostitute. She became what is called in the trade a "come freak." She plunged into her work with gusto and apparent pleasure. Lynnette could get so involved in sexual acts with tricks that she'd fall out of bed with a loud thud. Since her room was just off the *Cat Room*, the entire house would break up because they knew Lynnette had found another guy who turned her on. On one trip home to see her child, she met a young architect and fell in love. They are married with a large family and remain deeply in love; one of those rare happy endings.

Keeping an apartment in Las Vegas made things more convenient for business. It also served as a retreat when Walter needed rest. Trouble was, it also became a haven for strays.

Suzie moved into Walter's condo with her daughter for "a month or two" until she found what she wanted (this was awhile before her future lover would assume her care). It turned into six months. Walter finally moved into an apartment and rented his condo to Suzie. Suzie brought another girl into the apartment, and to the Ranch: Tasha, a beautiful black girl.

Being the first and only black girl, Tasha made lots of money. Many white men go to brothels just for black girls. She cornered that market, of course, but stayed only about four months. Since she and Suzie were good friends, Walter learned that she had gotten into drugs. She was later found out on a median near Flagstaff, Arizona, with her brains blown out, apparently in some kind of drug deal gone sour.

Michon showed up for an interview one day. Blonde, about five feet six inches and one hundred thirty pounds, a bit on the heavy side, but well shaped; another Rubens type. At nineteen, she was already a long-term hooker from Las Vegas. One characteristic stood out. She was dumb, very dumb. *Dumb blonde* could have been coined just for her. But, admittedly, Walter didn't hire girls for their IQs. In Michon's first lineup, she was chosen for an *out-date.*

An out-date is when a customer views the lineup and chooses a girl to take back to town for a night out, a weekend, or even a week. An out-date is the goal for many, depending on how much money they want to make, actually, more often depending on their pimps. The *Chicken Ranch's* minimum was three hundred dollars for an eight-hour period. Since the girls worked three straight weeks without a day off, then got only one week off, an out-date always seemed like a vacation (a foreign word to most prostitutes with pimps). She might go to Las Vegas and see some shows, have dinner, dance, have some fun. Some were even given money to gamble by their johns. Walter learned over the years that what is usually assumed is not always the case. Most people think a customer wants to spend all of the paid period in a bed, but that rarely happened. They usually had only short rolls in the hay.

In a girl's room, the minimum charge for one hour was one hundred dollars. Three hundred dollars was the minimum for an eight-hour out-date. If she thought she could get more before or during, of course, she'd try. While most of them wanted these out-dates, the greedy girls, or those with the meanest pimps, did not. Their fifty percent share of an eight-hour date was only one hundred fifty dollars. A girl could easily turn eight tricks in eight hours, guaranteeing an absolute minimum of four hundred dollars, and much more if she was good at her real trade: sales.

At first, when a customer was sold an out-date, he usually arrived in a vehicle and they would drive back to Vegas, or wherever they were going. He was obligated to return the girl to the front door of the brothel within the contracted-for period (travel time was at his cost). To ensure the safety and return of his girls, the john had to provide very clear information, and leave something of value such as a credit card. He was checked out before he left the *Chicken Ranch* with one of Walter's girls. They knew his real name, home address and phone number, which hotel he was checked into, his room number, and so forth. It was the maid's job to obtain and verify such information. Later, men who came to the brothel in the *Chicken Ranch* plane returned them to the pilot, who held whatever valuables sufficient to ensure the girls' return.

The first time out, Michon sold her trick a twenty-four-hour out-date. He paid eight hundred dollars up front. When they returned she had been wined and dined, and was convinced that she could make lots more money on her own in Las Vegas. She asked for her cash; she had already rented her own apartment. Walter paid her off and drove her to Las Vegas since he was planning on going there anyway. After he'd dropped her off he went back to his apartment. An hour later there was a knock on the door. It was Michon, cut up, black and blue, and crying. Her black pimp threw her out of her own apartment because she quit the Ranch. He took all her money and she had nowhere to go. Of course, Walter let her stay until she was healed and feeling better. A week later she was still there, but once more feeling foxy.

One morning Suzie and Walter went to his apartment. Sarcastically Michon snapped, "I went out last night and made a thousand dollars, and I don't have to split it with you or anyone else." Suzie, the skeptic, laughed and said, "If you got a thousand dollars in cash from some john, let me see it." Michon sneered and muttered, "You'll see," as she turned on her heel and went into the bedroom. She came out waving some bills in her hand saying, "See, here it is, one thousand dollars in cash." She held the bills up in front of Suzie's face. Walter could see them, too.

Walter and Suzie laughed so hard they could hardly stand. Michon just stared at them, bewildered and increasingly petulant, making it even funnier. Walter fell onto the couch and Suzie collapsed into a chair. Finally, Suzie was able to compose herself long enough to explain. Walter suddenly realized he was looking at child standing there, fear slowly creeping into her face because she couldn't understand what was happening. Suzie said, "Michon, this isn't one thousand dollars, it's one thousand yen." The audience of two lost it again as the look on Michon's face slowly turned into rage and disgust. Tears running down her cheeks, her words barely coherent mixed with laughter Suzie squealed, "Some con man screwed you all night for three bucks!"

Michon went back to *Chicken Ranch* with Suzie the same day, along with the funny, tragic tale. She stayed at the Ranch about a year, during which time she was always referred to by everyone as "our three-dollar whore."

Despite minimal ability to openly advertise, customers kept finding them. One became a once-a-month regular. He was around seventy, and so was his wife. He was a successful, retired businessman who had been happily married to the same woman for almost fifty years. They had children who were already well into their forties. Once a month, they would drive in from Utah on Friday afternoon. He would stay at the Ranch while his wife went on to Las Vegas for the weekend. She loved playing the slots, and he loved playing the girls.

One Sunday afternoon when she came back to pick him up, he was still busy with one of the girls, so Walter invited her to join him in the private kitchen for a cup of coffee. Walter admitted to her that he had been curious about their arrangement since they were really among the most unusual of his brothel's customers. She explained graciously, but rather nonchalantly, that they had not engaged in sex for over twenty years. Following some surgery, sex simply was no longer appealing to her. Her husband, on the other hand, thoroughly enjoyed it, and she did not want him to be deprived. In addition, she liked to gamble. She added that they had been very successful, and had more money than they really needed. Their life together was full, with a wonderful circle of friends whom they both enjoyed. They were a content and happy couple. She said they both felt safer if he came to the brothel rather than using some street hooker who might not be safe, or taking up with one woman who might break up their peaceful home and life. Walter said that just five minutes in a room with these two people together showed him the genuineness of their loving relationship. They charmed him and the whole brothel, and everyone there looked forward to their regular visits for years.

Another unusual story was of a mother and son. This was not a kinky situation at all. The son was mentally retarded. The mother chose the girl from the lineup, or in some instances, the girl willing to take him as a customer made the choice. Eventually, she, too, was invited into the kitchen for a cup of coffee, either by Walter or one of the maids. She explained that while he was severely retarded, her son was able to function to some degree without supervision. However, his childlike mind and spirit were trapped within the body and urges of a grown man. Every so often, once a month or so, apparently, he would feel sexual urges. Whenever she noticed his actions becoming a bit odd, she took him to the brothel. When they left, he always seemed more relaxed, and obviously relieved. Some might consider this some kind of sin, but hiding these people from the world, away from training, isolated, deprived of real life is considered an even greater sin by others. This was a mother's act of love, nothing more, or less.

One afternoon, a stretch limousine drove up. A chauffeur got out and went around to the trunk, opened it and removed a wheelchair. Walter, who heard most vehicles drive up was quick to peek out the window, went out to see if they needed help. He and the chauffeur brought the man in his wheelchair up the steps and into the brothel, followed by a young woman who turned out to be a nurse. The man was afflicted with some sort of palsy disease. There was little doubt which girl would handle this john.

Mary sort of specialized in men with various problems such as retardation, those who were severely maimed, or with unusual afflictions. After Mary wheeled the chair into her room, the chauffeur went back to the car, and the man's nurse was invited into the kitchen for coffee, of course. She told the story.

This had been a strong, intelligent, and very successful businessman. He was stricken with this incurable disease which gradually cost him the use of his legs, severely impaired speech, and of course, the shaking. With all this, his mind was not touched, nor were his sexual organs and the usual desires. He had already lost a wife to another illness, and he knew he would not live for very long. One day, he read about the Ranch and decided he wanted to see it before he died. He discovered there was no phone line to ask about anything, but he decided it didn't matter. They traveled cross-country in his specially equipped limo, ending up at the *Chicken Ranch*.

The man spent the entire afternoon in Mary's room, leaving happy and very satisfied. Mary was very well paid for her time and efforts, but more, she was pleased that she could bring this man some pleasure and joy. Along with plenty of sex, they talked, and although he had to repeat some things, she understood every word he said. Helping him back into his car, he thanked Walter for creating such a place. He told him that now he would die happy. The man was in his late thirties.

One day, Walter got a call in his apartment from a man in New York. That wasn't too unusual because he had circulated his number as associated with the *Chicken Ranch*, but his request was just a bit different. His son who was only in his early twenties had some sort of degenerative disease, afflicted since he was a boy, therefore, was still a virgin. His father had read about the

Chicken Ranch and shared it with his son, hoping to amuse him a little. The boy told him that he wished he could go there just once. The father, a wealthy man, called almost immediately. When Walter told the father that his girls were great with men with problems, he asked that the boy be picked up at the airport since he wanted to make the trip alone, as a man. He could stay as long as he liked, and was to be given anything he asked. Money was no object.

The young man became the darling of the brothel. Every single girl and all of the maids clucked around him like mother hens. They fed him steak and lobster, talked to him, pampered him like he was a crown prince, teased him, and played sex games with him, endlessly! After several days, he told Walter it was time for him to go home. While this had been the best time of his life, he was very tired, and he knew it was time to rest. He left with what Walter called the most sparkling grin that ever left the *Chicken Ranch*. After a couple of months, the father called Walter to let them all know the boy had died, but his last weeks were filled with countless stories and wonderful private memories. Despite the tears that fell that day, everyone at the Ranch could feel good about their efforts to make the last days of a boy something special.

Walter associated the story of this customer with his experience in WWII. The boy reminded him of those blown apart by guns and bombs; children dressed up in soldier suits, thousands of miles from their homes and the loving arms of their mothers, the protection of their fathers, teachers, priests, ministers, and rabbis; away from the giggles of girls their own ages; a half a world distant from the soda fountains where the strongest drinks the laws of America allowed them were lemon phosphates and cherry cokes. They lay in the fields of those places they couldn't even pronounce, with cloth arms and legs that no longer covered flesh that had been blown away.

A hospital which shelters some of these men from the stares of the world was not too far from the *Chicken Ranch*. They formed groups and started patronizing the Ranch. They had little to do with their money, so for paraplegics, quadriplegics, quadruple amputees, some of whom had been totally abandoned by families, or had none left, the *Chicken Ranch* was money well spent. Some, who had come to these places after several wars boys, were now old men. After choosing a girl from a lineup which consisted of those who could handle this type of john, some had to be carried to the girls' rooms.

Once on the beds they had to be placed on, those girls, those whores, those vendors of sex, made those heroes believe they were just as desirable, just as sexy as any other man who ever entered that room. They wanted to be laid, have oral sex, to believe they drove the girls mad with passion, to have their penises made hard, then soft, then hard again. To a man, they wanted to hear the pleasure of a woman who begged them to stop, then begged for more.

They wanted to feel a woman coming again and again because he was such a macho, incomparable stud, who made climaxing an experience more erotic, more exotic, more explosive, more intoxicating, filled with furor a woman hardly imagined possible. All this those whores accomplished, even without the benefit of hands, arms, legs, power, or even the ability to climb on top of a woman and overwhelm her with passion.

It would be interesting to find out what the do-gooders, all those pious men and women would preach about how these men of many ages—including very, very young ones—should go to church socials to meet young "good" women for the purpose of marriage. It would be interesting to learn how many of those self-righteous fathers and mothers would like to see their own young, pretty, normal daughters marrying these heroes of our country, considering that they cannot function in the real world anymore. When these men and boys who literally tossed their lives away to protect all of us come back, they certainly have a right to some measure of manhood. The question is who but prostitutes are able, or willing in some cases, to give them back that manhood, if only for moments at a time. No man, however sanctimonious and self-righteous, can possibly believe that after losing everything else, manhood does not continue to be important. And whether they wish to admit it or not, sex plays a huge role in making a man feel like a man.

A Franciscan priest related a personal story to the author about a niece who was engaged to her childhood sweetheart, a young man who left for Vietnam whole, but returned to her with only a part of himself left. She still loved him and planned to marry him, but all of her friends and most of her family pleaded with her to reconsider. She went to her uncle for counseling. The dilemma was whether he should speak to this child he had loved from the moment of her birth as her uncle, or as a priest with understanding and compassion for the afflictions of man. While he told her to follow her heart, he discussed reality with her, and what her life would be like for fifty or sixty years. She finally begged him for his simple, honest opinion of yea or nay. With very heavy heart, he said, "Don't marry him." She didn't. The priest spent a great deal of time with the young man, who ended up consoling everyone else because of their feelings of guilt and sadness.

The compassionate, giving priest who was the object of love by everyone he touched was afflicted, very prematurely, by Alzheimer's. He was cared for and surrounded with love by the community he served for a lifetime. He understood repaying our heros in any way available to them, and us. He knew that while perhaps prayer could quell a hard-on for him, that may not always work for a young man trapped in a body that cannot wear itself out with a daily life. That charismatic, outgoing, kind man finally died peacefully.

THIRTEEN

Walter's stepson Sam came for awhile to help promote the Ranch. They contacted travel agents and every source they could find to market the brothel. Much of their competition came from streetwalkers in Las Vegas. Almost all cab drivers, hotel doormen, parking valets, and bellmen around the world, not to mention Las Vegas, are in the prostitution business. For some reason that fact has always been denied by law enforcement. But any man who has ever traveled anywhere knows it's true, and certainly anyone who ever worked in the hotel industry would have to be deaf and blind not to know. Some bell captains make hundreds of thousands of dollars a year. No one who knows how much they make can possibly be naïve enough to think that it all comes from their share of tips. One Walter knew paid one hundred and twenty-five thousand dollars to get his job, and depending on the hotels in Las Vegas, some are known to have paid many times that amount. Their tax-free *hooker incomes* far surpass their legitimate incomes, and everyone in various contingent industries, not to mention police, around the world are aware of it.

When cab drivers took men to the Ranch, they were not only well tipped by the johns, Walter gave them five percent and the girls gave them five percent right off the top. So, if a cab transported four men who each spent five hundred dollars, which was not unusual, the cab driver made an extra two hundred dollars from the Ranch. This went for limo drivers, too. While the drivers waited for their fares to get laid, they were usually invited into the kitchen for coffee, and Walter or one of the maids would talk with them. Most cab and limo drivers didn't hesitate to take fares out to the *Chicken Ranch*, even though it was at least a four-hour session. Between the meter, passenger tips, and ten percent from the *Chicken Ranch*, they made out like bandits.

It was not easy to expand as fast as Walter began to hope he could. Not that business was bad; they were all making a whole lot of money. It just didn't grow as fast as Walter's experience told him it should, nor for his personal greed. As a result, the girls had time to kill, which they did in more ways than anyone might ever guess.

The *Cat Room*, mentioned earlier, was a room where the girls could take their johns after they had completed their services to sit and chat, giving them the opportunity to talk the men right back into the bedroom for more sex and, more to the point, more cash. During daytime hours, it was also a kind of sitting room where the girls did pretty much as they pleased, within the parameters Walter set; at least when there were no customers in the house.

One of Walter's many rules was that every girl had to get out of bed no later than ten-thirty in the morning, seven days a week, and there were no exceptions, even if she worked the entire night. In the mornings, they did the same things all girls do, of course: bleached, dyed, and washed their hair; fixed finger- and toenails, etc. At one o'clock, they had to be dressed and ready for customers, but they could do almost anything they wanted. They knitted and crocheted afghans, embroidered tablecloths, designed, made, and mended clothes; played cards, watched TV soaps and movies, read magazines, and wrote letters. And just like other girls, they argued, accused each other of cheating in games, told jokes, gossiped about and made fun of their tricks. Sometimes they talked about their lives, either bragging or complaining about husbands, boyfriends, and pimps. Those with children had pictures ever-handy to show anyone indicating the least bit of interest.

One thing they could never do was to lie down because they might mess up their clothes. And since they were expected to appear in a lineup as soon as the bell rang, there was no time to redress. On weekdays, the afternoons were relatively light, although Las Vegas being a tourist town which is well known for its absence of clocks, and the libido of a man is unrestricted by usual daily schedules, that was never guaranteed

Most of the time by three o'clock in the morning customers were gone, and the girls had to go into their rooms. A tally was done by the maid to determine who made the most money, second highest, and down the line. The girl who made the very least money and the second to lowest were "on call" for the night. If a customer showed up after three o'clock, those were the two girls the maid would awaken to appear in a lineup. Most men knew a full lineup would not appear in the hours close to dawn. If two men walked in together, the girls making the three lowest incomes were awakened. The lowest income girl did not undo her bed, but would carefully sleep on top of her bedspread.

A bed was never uncovered for *tricks*. A beach towel, called a *trick towel*, was thrown over the bedspread so that when a man first walked into a room, he saw a bed covered with a beautiful spread as if he was the first one there.

During the night, the lowest on-call girl did not get fully dressed. She would come into the lineup in a negligee. Not the type that would reveal nipples or crotches, but one that was alluring, brief, and sexy. While the john waited for the night girls to line up, the maid would offer him a cup of coffee and sit with him for the few minutes it took for the girls to freshen themselves.

At Walter's *Chicken Ranch*, each girl would get close to a full eight hours of sleep almost every single night. No girl was ever forced to take more than three on-call nights in a row. Walter recognized that even though she might want the money, she also needed rest. He also allowed girls to switch nights if one was very tired, or feeling sick. Many girls wanted the night call because it was a profitable shift. It was called *Early Up*. Walter was also somewhat strict about health. If a girl was really ill with a cold, a virus, or a kidney infection, for instance, she was sent straight to the doctor and was not allowed to work until she was well.

Other brothels did not have some of Walter's rules. Most brothels have girls stay dressed in leotards twenty-four hours a day. Many force each and every girl to go into the lineup right around the clock, no matter how tired or ill they are. Many girls who went to Walter for a job were from other area brothels. They would show up exhausted because they had not had a full night's sleep throughout their three weeks of working.

When a girl admitted she was ill, particularly one with a pimp, they knew she was very ill. If her pimp found out that she spent *his* money to go to a doctor, always twenty dollars, he would beat her brains out. First of all, in order to do it she had to make eighty dollars to just break even every day. Walter charged her twenty dollars a day for room and board. That meant she had to make forty dollars because she only got half of what she took in. Then she had to make another forty dollars to come up with the twenty for the doctor. If there was a pimp involved, that twenty was his, and no prostitute with a pimp deprives him of one red cent or he beats her, at least most do. Working girls in the streets and in most brothels work with high fevers, severe kidney infections, overwhelming cramps, colds, virus infections, chest pains, muscle spasms, back problems, and so forth. Working girls don't take time off during their menstrual cycles, even if they double up with cramps. At least not those in most brothels or on the street.

If a man chose one girl and stayed for several days, she did not have to appear in any lineup. That was one of very few exceptions.

Some pretty loyal friendships were formed in the *Cat Room*. Outsiders might have a hard time accepting that, but each person lives within his or her own personal environment. Prostitutes are no different. They are people with a code; maybe unlike what most people consider reasonable, but they live by it. They laugh. They taunt and tease their friends. They have mothers, fathers, siblings, children, husbands, lovers, boyfriends. Like anyone else, they are exhilarated by music, all kinds of music, some by plays, by ballet. Some are happy most of the time, many are funny and very entertaining. A few are melancholic, sullen, filled with despair. Some commit suicide. Like anyone else, they need encouragement from their friends, or comfort, or just to believe that someone, somewhere gives a damn.

Walter seemed to enjoy talking about how they occasionally needed discipline. Not the abuse that pimps practice, he claimed; to the contrary, the kind loving parents give: scoldings, reminders. The tone of his voice and look on his face as he described this using such bland words, trying to depict his meaning in a loving harmless way, was very hard to swallow. Although his voice would be controlled, you could hear the low, deep snarl, and his facial muscles formed a smile while his eyes were clearly menacing. When once in awhile a girl had to be fined, he insisted that it was always to her benefit. He said he only had to fire a few. There were rules. He made the rules. His rules had to be followed. He stated, without apparently hearing the impact his words had to make, "They were rigid and hard for some of the completely undisciplined women to keep. Of course, some were to either enhance or protect my business. But the way I saw it, most of those rules were meant for the girls' own welfare." The reason he never saw anything wrong or ugly in his admissions was because he had fallen into the garbage pit of pimps, and unquestionably held their standard philosophy, that everything they did *to* "their" girls was for their own good, no matter how cruel. Rape to them is a most common practice, and they don't understand what all the hoopla is about. All women want to be raped according to pimps. They love it. Even ten-year-olds, of course. Walter always held himself above being a pimp for that reason. His upbringing would never have sent him into the streets to convert ten and twelve-year-olds to prostitution. He could easily do a one hour speech on how wonderful and pure he was because he wouldn't do that, no matter how controlling or demanding he was of "his" girls.

Another of his favorite subjects was modesty, which does not exist in a brothel. At the start, he couldn't handle it. Having regularly frequented brothels since seventeen years old, plus the many straight willing women he encountered, he had seen more than his share of naked women before, in every shape, color, and size. And he had seen clothed women who made it their business to expose everything they could and still be out in public. In most of the brothels he patronized, *beaver* shots were the rule rather than the exception. Nevertheless, seeing a flock of nudes casually walking around or sitting talking made him crazy and, of course, horny all the time. At the beginning he'd yell at them, not too sweetly, to put some clothes on. They teased and cajoled him, telling him it meant nothing, and that if it didn't bother them, he couldn't let their nakedness bother him. Little by little, he was more comfortable until he was as oblivious to it as they were to each other's nudity.

Gradually, he became privy to their innermost feelings and secrets, and soon realized he should be flattered. And he was. In the *Cat Room*, they bitched about anything they pleased, including him, within reason, since they all knew how black his temper could be. There were times when he walked in and was startled by the realization that this room was probably like many sewing circles in the world, where women gather to gossip and bitch, sometimes even using their combined power to expel one of their own from a church, or club, or community. Probably the only differences were the vulgar language and total honesty of the prostitutes. They never denied they were gossiping. What fascinated Walter was that while the funny, cute, heartrending, vicious, lewd talk went on, some genuinely beautiful handmade crafts were created.

Prostitutes have their own world, which Walter readily conceded. But they exhibited real feelings for one another, and unquestionably for some people outside of their own lives and world. He was exposed to many examples of how they feel and act when they are touched inside, of their sadness when they hear of others' grief.

One bright sunny day, one of the good town citizens appeared at the brothel's front door. The lady would never have considered talking to any of the girls on the streets of downtown Pahrump under the eyes of her neighbors. The maid, also a straight, local resident, while surprised by the visit, asked her in and what she wanted. After the maid heard her story, she took the woman into the *Cat Room*. Since it was late afternoon, all of the girls in the house were sitting there, already dressed, ready for customers.

When the maid and visitor entered the room, the girls were annoyed since this was their sanctuary, not a place a straight woman was permitted. But they respected the maid enough to know there had to be a good reason for the violation of their coveted privacy. They sat quietly, waiting for the explanation. The maid invited the woman to sit down and explain the reason for her visit.

She told them about a poor Pahrump family with several children, among them a seven-year-old girl who had undergone two operations for brain tumors. The child needed another operation, and soon, although there was little hope. Without the surgery, there would be none. She talked about the sweet, undemanding child who was infinitely patient with her illness and relentless pain. She seemed to know her life would end soon. She was normal in every other way.

She dreamed of going to Disneyland, not too many miles down the road, from the day she understood what it was, much like all children her age. It was a luxury they could ill afford, and she would need a nurse in attendance. Someone estimated the cost at about seven hundred dollars. The visitor explained that it might as well be seventy thousand dollars for the parents who had been financially wiped out, and had already borrowed and begged money just to keep her alive.

Someone heard about it and started a collection in Pahrump to make this tiny dream come true for the doomed child. After canvassing all of the town's population, including all of the do-gooders, some quite wealthy, all they raised was a couple hundred dollars. Then someone came up with calling on the girls at the *Chicken Ranch*, thinking that just maybe their cold hearts could be touched to give this baby her wish.

Walter was working in his office when, suddenly, sounds of crying and wailing reached him, sounds he had never heard in the brothel. He rushed into the *Cat Room* and was confronted with eight girls crying, all trying to tell him the story they had just heard. By the time he understood what they were saying, they had gathered up three hundred and fifteen dollars from their own piggy banks. They counted out the money, their intentions quite clear. They all looked up at Walter with those sad, teary eyes. He reached into his pocket and handed the women the balance, but the looks continued, so he threw in a couple hundred extra. He was choked up, too. It wouldn't have mattered what the cost. Kathy would go to Disneyland because of all the residents in the *Chicken Ranch* that day.

What happened next came with a vengeance. Kathy's story hit the media. Headlines in the *Las Vegas Sun* read, "Chickens Chip in for Disneyland Fling." The wire services picked up the story and before it was ended, it ran in one hundred sixty major newspapers throughout the world, not to mention television. It turned into a human interest story. From that moment, the *Chicken Ranch* was known around the globe.

The British Radio Broadcasting System contacted Walter to do a live telephone interview from the Ranch. He happily agreed. Since they still had no phone, however, they arranged to do it from a neighbor's house. Because of this whole bizarre situation, no one could ever convince any of those who were there that day that the old cliché, "what goes around comes around" is not valid. They were genuinely moved by an innocent child's tragedy. They gave simply to put a smile on her face, if only for awhile. They had asked the woman to keep them informed of Kathy's trip, but never dreamed everything, including what they did, would be as publicized as it was.

The little traveler died a few weeks later. It tore up the entire population of the *Chicken Ranch*. Although they were angry because the child's suffering and death were unfair, they knew they had contributed to her possessing a few moments of absolute bliss. The girls could see in their faces and hear in their voices the joy also given her parents, seeing their beloved child so excited and fulfilled with her heart's desire before she was taken from them. The satisfaction of knowing such a tiny gift meant so much to this innocent child was something none at the Ranch that day would trade for anything.

At first Walter assumed the reasons he couldn't get phones only involved the phone company, and that they had him over a barrel. But after a whole year riddled with problems with the political machine, coping with learning a whole new, rather bizarre business, fighting with one company for water, then another for power, he knew it was time for him to start searching for telephone solutions.

An order had been placed with Nevada Bell as soon as he bought the land for the new brothel. Soon after, their technicians went to the Ranch and staked lines for the trenches. Then nothing. They never returned. Walter went back to the local Bell office and the mountain of excuses began. As fast as he unraveled one tall tale, another took its place. "The half-mile right-of-way has not been dedicated"; "it's twenty-six feet further than we have to lay lines"; "we only have to lay lines in populated areas"; "control is out of our hands, under the jurisdiction of our Reno engineering office"; "our digging contractor is too busy to do the job." During all of the nonsense, Walter kept hearing about what "the tariff" allowed, and all they had to do "by tariff restrictions." He knew tariffs. He obtained a copy and began to study.

At one point he considered having a phone installed in town and hiring a girl to operate it, relaying the calls by some sort of short wave system. It was apparent that would be impractical since it would have to be manned on a twenty-four-hour, seven-day-week basis. Back to the books.

During that year he was discouraged but kept studying. As other difficulties of the Ranch disappeared and he became better versed in his new business, he had more and more time to concentrate on the tariff issued by the Public Service Commission (Nevada's utility control board). Then one day, a light went on in his head. He realized he should also analyze the federal regulations which governed the Public Service Commission.

On one of his countless visits to the local telephone office when the current excuse was that the local contractor was too busy to schedule digging the trenches for his lines, a new question occurred to him. He asked the clerk who the contractor was. With her answer came the bells and whistles. The man with the stolen gravel. He was certain he could handle this the same way he had the electrical situation. But he soon discovered that while the contractor played a role, his part in this situation was minimal.

With all the self-confidence and power he could display which, to anyone who saw it knew, was formidable, Walter went straight to the Public Service Commission and explained that he knew he was entitled to a telephone from someone, and that he really didn't care where he had to go to assure his getting one. He told them he was in the United States, and since phone companies were monopolies, he had the legal right to get a phone, and neither they nor anyone else could deprive him of that right. Where he least expected to find it, there was a ray of hope. They broke down and told him several things. The Mormon citizens of the Valley had made it quite clear they did not want phone service given to the *Chicken Ranch*. The county machine reinforced their stand by making it known they also did not want Walter Plankinton—in a brothel from which they derived no profit—to survive. He soon learned that both factions were well represented within the Public Service Commission.

The same person then told him the final, most important factor: under the law, he could dig his own trenches, lay his own cables, buy his own equipment, and form his own "farmer telephone company." If he did that, Nevada Bell could not refuse a private phone company access to their lines; it was mandatory since they were a monopoly. Walter only need pay a set access fee to have a phone service that would reach anywhere, even though every single call was long distance. No one could interfere with his phone system. He could have kissed that clerk. He left the office determined to create his own phone company.

With trenches dug, he tried to purchase telephone wiring. No one could tell him where to find any. Again he was at a standstill. Then something he had done without thinking much about it came back to roost. Months before he sponsored a trip for a young local girl who wanted to enter a beauty contest out of state. Her father was a phone company foreman. Walter called him and explained his dilemma. A few days later, the man called him back and secretly told him where and how to purchase the federally specified wire.

Walter contracted all of the work required, ensuring that even the most insignificant regulation was stringently met. He was determined there would be no more delays. When it was ready, he submitted the request to hook on to the Nevada Bell System. Of course, the delays began again. They had to "carefully check laws, regulations, and tariffs," and so on and on and on. But, it became obvious that they finally recognized Walter Plankinton as a force to be dealt with, not easily patronized or ignored. When they could no longer justify further excuses to wiggle out of connecting two phone lines, they hooked on to the system.

It was February 1978. The *Chicken Ranch* could communicate with the world, and people from the four corners of the world could reach the Ranch. And no one could take that power away from Walter. One more reason to be grateful for his previous experience with tariffs. It precluded paying lawyers perhaps tens of thousands of dollars for research and court time, and who knows how long before implementation. Word got back that the *Good Old Boys* were raging mad when they learned that, once again, Plankinton outfoxed them.

Walter wanted a local Las Vegas number that automatically rang at the brothel. That had to be arranged with Central Telephone Company, the Las Vegas phone company, never a part of the Bell System. In that process, all Walter could ever conclude was that someone at that phone company had a strange sense of humor. When he (Walter later learned it was a man) heard about the local number being assigned to a brothel, he manipulated the *Yellow Pages* ad to show 125 South Las Vegas Boulevard. Actually, that was the address of a telephone company building downtown housing four hundred operators. For six months after the directory hit the street (Las Vegas is the only city with new *Yellow Pages* every six months), taxis pulled up to 125 S. Las Vegas Boulevard with men looking for prostitutes, day and night. The building had to be locked, a security guard assigned to the door, and a sign posted stating it was not the *Chicken Ranch*—hilarious to most people. Needless to say, the company's management never saw the humor, at least not publicly.

The avalanche of international business that little Kathy's story triggered just kept going. A phone added to it. Walter was kicking even more sand in the *Good Old Boys'* faces in spite of their endless efforts to get rid of him.

In November 1977, Walter was served a summons from the sheriff's office to appear at a hearing before the Nye County Commissioners. The charge was stated as the brothel being a *Nuisance, per se*, yet another ruse intended to close the brothel. In a 1947 Nevada Supreme Court Case, "Washoe County v. Cunningham," the court ruled that a brothel was a Nuisance, per se, and that the county commissioners were obligated by law to abate any and all nuisances brought to their attention. Once again, he was being brought to the attention of the County Commissioners of Nye County. Had it not been so exhausting and damaging, the prejudice and inequity would have been seemed like slapstick.

Three other brothels had been operating in Nye County for many years. But as long as they paid dues to the "people who counted," those the D.A. had tried to explain to Walter during that first encounter, the lawmakers "never knew of those other brothels' existence." This newest insult to the judicial system was so preposterous, it was difficult for Walter to explain his own reaction. With all of his exposure to their "gestapo-like tactics masquerading as a county's legal authority," he was astonished by their audacity.

Many thought Walter a grandstander, and a whole lot more, and he was just that. A small part of the reason he was considered a phony was when he would sound off about how he fought in a war to protect everyone's rights, which many generations had fought and died for before him. But his Midwestern sense of patriotism was genuine. He found it impossible to believe, or accept, that this so-called *legal* process (which was actually a mockery of justice) he kept running into could be happening in the U.S., after so many sacrificed their lives to make absolutely sure such things never could.

The real issue was not prostitution. He was dealing with flexible lawmaking here. But not for normal reasons such as public safety or well-being. It was for one reason alone, to preserve a handful of men's lust for money, power, or both. Prostitution was, and still is, legal in almost all Nevada counties. Only while Walter Plankinton owned the *Chicken Ranch*, refusing to pay off the power structure, were any of these challenges resurrected and/or fabricated [until the late 1980s and 1990, when it recurred, and were voted down by residents; and again in 1995 when the State Legislature postponed it until the next session]. While a very few lawmakers keep trying to get rid of brothels in those counties where they are legal, mostly to satisfy some limited religious or do-gooder groups, the people just keep voting to keep prostitution legal in their counties.

When the hearing finally came up in February 1978, Walter and his lawyer appeared before the Nye County Commission and, just as expected, it was cut and dry. The members of the Commission were openly and wantonly disinterested in listening to anything they tried to say. With predictably few words, they found the brothel to be a *Nuisance, per se,* and ordered the sheriff to close the *Chicken Ranch.* Walter's attorney instantly filed court action to stop the closing. They were to appear before the godfather/judge, but the attorney had him disqualified as being prejudicial. A district judge from another county was appointed to replace him and to hear the case. Through him, they sought and were granted a stay order, stopping closure until they could present their case. This gave them a new lease on life knowing they could continue to operate until the trial.

By the time they appeared, Walter's attorney had discovered that since the 1947 Cunningham case stipulating a brothel to be a Nuisance, per se, the Nevada Legislature had passed a new law in 1971. It stated: "Prostitution shall be illegal in those counties in Nevada where the population is in excess of two hundred thousand." Clark County, which encompasses Las Vegas, had that large a population. By the legislature using that specific criterion, the attorney argued that prostitution was then legal in the remainder of the State of Nevada. The judge agreed and ruled in Walter's favor. It later stood the test when the Nevada Supreme Court upheld his ruling.

The case was a testament to the county's so-called legal attitude toward American law versus Nye County law. Either they neglected to bother researching laws put into effect just a few years earlier; or if they were aware of the statutes, and there is little doubt that they were, they ignored them as if they didn't apply to them. Again they showed their flagrant disregard for law, and contemptuous waste of taxpayers' money, as they persisted in dragging this nonsense though the courts on so many levels, not in any way to restrict or stop prostitution in their county, just in the *Chicken Ranch*. Walter and his attorney never stopped being astonished by their arrogance.

Regardless of their antics, the *Chicken Ranch* was definitely legal as defined in the State of Nevada Statutes. It was out of the closet. The group could no longer pick and choose who would or would not open a brothel, even if the owners wouldn't submit to their self-serving dictates. The word was loud and clear. One more chink in their ironclad sovereignty. Walter felt like he won a great war against a dangerous adversary. He was almost euphoric. Little did he suspect that once again he had counted his chickens before they hatched—begging you to pardon the pun.

Las Vegas newspapers ran to Tonopah to interview the D.A., asking him how he would now deal with the *Chicken Ranch* and Walter Plankinton. He told them: "When I run out of courts," as it appeared he had, adding, "there is a condition in Nevada where I can always go down and burn that damned whorehouse down." When Walter read his public statement, he raised all kinds of *public* hell, stating that it was both irresponsible and reprehensible for the chief law enforcement office of a county to make not only inflammatory statements, but to suggest that a crime would be okay with him, virtually giving license to any fanatic with a match to commit arson and murder, as long as he confined his action to the *Chicken Ranch*. With all Walter had already learned about this man, it was impossible for him to believe that someone in his position would so openly take his personal vendetta to such lengths. In time, Walter would know just how naive he really was about this particular officer of the court.

Walter's Trucking Companies,
Denver, 1960s.
Cowboy Van Lines, Inc.
changed name to
Trans World in 1969.

ELECT

WALTER R. PLANKINTON
DEMOCRAT

**COUNTY COMMISSIONER
DISTRICT #3
NYE COUNTY, NEVADA**

Ran for Office as a
Democrat 1976.

United States of America

State of Colorado   County of   ADAMS   ss.

GREETING:

I, WILLIAM SOKOL , County Clerk, within and for said County, do hereby certify that at a County Election held in said County on the 8th day of September, A. D. 19 70 . WALTER R. PLANKINTON received the greatest number of votes cast for the office of Committeeman of the Republican Party in and for Ward , Precinct 3002 . City of , County of ADAMS , Colorado, as appears from the official canvass of the returns of the said Precinct in said Ward on the 18th day of September, A. D. 19 70 , and that said WALTER R. PLANKINTON is duly elected Committeeman of the Republican Party of the aforesaid.

In Witness Whereof, I have hereunto set my hand and official seal this 21st day of SEPTEMBER A. D. 19 70 .

William Sokol
County Clerk.

Elected Committeeman of the
Republican Party in September 1970.

When Walter ran for Governor of Colorado on the
American **Independent** Party. (October 1970)

It appears that Walter's real political party should
have been named "The Expediency Party."

Chicken Ranch 1981. Behind it shows the orchard Walter planted.

Front Entrance of the Chicken Ranch after the fire.

Elbert Easley,
admitted Chicken Ranch arsonist.

"MENU"

The World Famous

CHICKEN RANCH

"We Raise The Best Cocks In The World"

"Where a houseful of Nevada's Most
Beautiful Girls are waiting just for you,
to cater to your every desire."
Las Vegas' Closest and Most Famous Brothel

APPETIZERS
JACUZZI
MOVIES
MASSAGE
BUBBLE BATH
PHOTO SESSION

RANCH SPECIALITES
VIP LOUNGE
JACUZZI PARTY
VIP JACUZZI COMBO
IN DATE
OUT DATE

A LA CARTE
STRAIGHT LAY
COLORED SHOWERS
BONDAGE
DOMINANCE
FULL FRENCH
STRAWBERRY TICKLE

ENTREES
HALF & HALF
REVERSED HALF & HALF
69 PARTY
PASSION CHAIR PARTY
TWO GIRL SHOW
TWO GIRL PARTY
HOT FRENCH OIL MASSAGE
WATER SPORTS
HOT & COLD FRENCH
FANTASY SESSIONS
EDIBLE BRAS & UNDIES
DRAG PARTY

DESSERTS
CREME DE MENTE FRENCH
FRAPPÉ FRENCH
FLAVORED PUSSY PARTY
SHOWER PARTY
BINACA BLAST

Walter in the Living Room of the Chicken Ranch,
where johns chose their playmates.

One of Hundreds of Resumes Walter Received (Edited)

OBJECTIVE: Seeking an entry level position which offers challenge, career development and personal growth.

EDUCATION: Bachelor of Arts in English—May 1978—GPA 3.45/4.0
- Recipient of the ███ Scholarship
- Recipient of the ██████ Foundation Grant
- Recipient ██████ Oratory Prize
- Awarded ██████████████ Prize for Creative Writing

Member, Student Body Executive Board; member, Academic Standing Committee; columnist for college newspaper

Participated in track, crew, ██████ College Singers and Drama productions.

EXPERIENCE: ██████ **Health Spa**—██████, Arizona
Assistant Manager, 1980s
Duties entailed coordinating operation of the health spa, including supervising maintenance, writing reports, promoting sales activity and good public relations with members.
██ **Public Interest Campaign**—██
Political Canvasser, 1980s
Community Outreach, including conscientiousness raising and fundraising for progressive legislative issues.
Promotion to Field Manager
Duties entailed coordinating canvassing crews in the field.
National Corporation
Sales Representative, 1970s
Duties entailed presenting and selling product line to 96 retail stores and 3 wholesalers.

PERSONAL: Born 1956. Have had articles published in ██████ Magazine and the ██████ Enquirer.

AGE—25
HAIR—Auburn
EYES—Hazel
HEIGHT—5'10"
WEIGHT—145 lbs.
BRA SIZE—38B
MEASUREMENTS— 39-26-40
HEALTH—Excellent—Applicant has never contracted a veneral disease. Birth Control—Tubal Ligation
POLICE RECORD—None

ADVERTISING GIMMICKS

Walter with his plane and pilot.

Some readers may be disappointed in the absence of pictures of *Walter's* girls, of which there are hundreds. They are omitted for one reason: in deference to those who went back to straight lives, who are daughters, wives, mothers, and grandmothers. This book is not used to expose them to what may be a part of their past.

FOURTEEN

Although girls came and went, a few became permanent employees of the *Chicken Ranch*. Regardless of tenure, some provide interesting anecdotes.

There was Pat, who stayed only a few months. Pat was a large-boned girl, but well-built. What stood out about her was that she was just plain mean. Nevertheless, she had a pimp. When she returned from one of her weeks off, she was in terrible shape. Her pimp had beaten her to a pulp. Pat had two brothers who were as mean as she was. She called them right after the beating and coolly told them where to find the pimp. And find him they did. They beat him savagely, showing the same mercy he had shown their sister. They went one step further, however. They put his broken body into his car, drove it into the desert, set it on fire, and left. The brothers are doing life in prison, and Pat spent about two years behind bars for conspiracy.

Very few women get into prostitution without a man, usually a pimp. Many were sexually assaulted as children by their fathers, stepfathers, uncles, brothers, neighbors, friends. But many who came from normal homes without ever experiencing this kind of abuse still started with a man. Every pimp goes searching for women, actually dates them, chases them, makes believe they are falling in love with them. Then, after a girl is hooked, the pimp might start bringing his friends or supposed clients for her to lay as a favor to him, or a help to his "business." Pretty soon, she's a full-fledged prostitute, in love with her pimp, eventually not caring if he has several other girls, since she *knows with absolute certainty that she is the only one he really loves.*

These pimps are a strange and diverse breed. Some are cruel beyond description, yet girls cling to them like a drowning person to a raft in the sea. Most take all of their girls' money, or at least everything but a tiny portion, barely enough to live on. The majority sleep with their girls, at least occasionally; others won't touch them. The only thing they appear to have in common is their Svengali-like hold over these women. Girls, who everywhere else appear independent and very tough, are like obedient puppets for their pimps. Psychiatrists might have a clinical explanation for this, but Walter claimed he was at a loss to understand, even after five years of observation. No amount of discussion ever convinced him that he was as manipulative or as mean in psychological ways as any street pimp. Because he "only" took a flat fifty percent of the girls' incomes, he would dismiss the additional twenty dollars a day he took from them for room and board as natural, necessary expenses on their part. The girls made money at the *Chicken Ranch*, but still not nearly as much as some established, independent call girls.

One odd thing seems to be that the pimps rarely elevate themselves; to the contrary, the majority go from pimping to being drug pushers and/or thieves of one type or another. Although like everything else, there are certainly exceptions, few former pimps ever really live in the real world once they have been in the business.

One girl talked about her pimp in the *Cat Room* one day when Walter was sitting with the girls. Her work name was Serena. Her hair was very dark, but she had the white skin of a Swede. Although she seemed hard as nails, behind the scenes she was sweet and quiet. She had a huge black pimp who always picked her up for her week off. But she didn't get much rest at home. Her pimp stayed with her at least part of her week off, slept with her only on occasion, which she usually had to beg for. But he beat her up regularly.

Most nights, and some days, she turned tricks exclusively for black men in the apartment. In addition, she put on sexual shows for them with very large dogs who were trained to use women as if they were just female dogs in heat. Her pimp filmed those vile pornographic scenes and sold them. The rest of the time, she was out on the street. When she came back, she didn't have a mark on her, but when someone touched her she almost jumped out of her skin in pain. Walter couldn't understand how she could take on tricks without showing her pain, but apparently she did because johns liked her.

Once when her pimp picked her up, Walter made it his business to be outside working on landscaping. When she entered the car, she was happy as a lark, but his hand was out waiting for her money. She gave him every penny. When she came a week later, obviously exhausted, with a couple of bruises on her breasts and stomach still dark, and in even more pain, he let her go. Walter never cared if the girls were beaten up, except for visible marks. What this girl might have brought to the brothel, he feared, was some kind of diseases the dogs might give her. That was his issue, not the girl's welfare if she chose to have a pimp.

Cathy, "just a skinny, flat-chested thing with a pretty face," had a pimp. They were both from Kentucky where they had originally met. Cathy really loved her pimp, and went around finding very young girls to bring into his stable so he would have more cash. Cathy found a fifteen-year-old for him. He shot her up with heroin and took the girl and Cathy to Detroit and put them both out on the street. Cathy trained and supervised her until they were certain she was completely hooked and would continue bringing all the money into the pimp. Somehow, the girl got away from Cathy, went to the police and turned state's evidence. The pimp was convicted and sentenced to four years in jail. Cathy came out west, and for three years worked at the *Chicken Ranch*, never netting less than two thousand dollars a week. She spent virtually none of the money, sending every possible dime back to lawyers in Michigan trying to get appeals to get her pimp out of jail. At about the end of the third year, the pimp's father died, and the prison system allowed him to go to the funeral. Somehow, he escaped and got back to Las Vegas. Cathy kept him hidden in an apartment complex until, somehow, the police recognized that he was around. They went to her apartment, missing him by ten minutes. Cathy knew where he had fled to, and found him. They hung around town after that, although she left the Ranch to support him on the street just to be close to him every day. Walter ran into her one night some time later. She told him she was no longer with the pimp, that she had "wised up" after he broke her jaw in two places with his *pimp stick*, hospitalizing her for six weeks. A *pimp stick*, it seems, is a coat hanger rolled up and used as a whip. It leaves welts which take two or three days to disappear.

It may seem strange to reasonably normal people that johns would not notice welts, black eyes, bruises, and/or assorted fresh cuts or scars on hookers. Well, horny men don't much care, even if a girl cries out in pain. They are with them to be told what great studs they are and how much they satisfy the girl, and to get laid. Little else is even noticed.

Walter quickly saw that whenever a girl had a pimp, even though the pimp was not allowed to enter Ranch property, he had to watch for trouble. Too often, it was a form of slavery, for love. Most people outside of this violent world that exists under rocks, yet right in front of all of us, won't hesitate to say that these women are just plain stupid. But, they are hardly different from battered wives who stay with their husbands or single women with their lovers, many of whom also allow their children to be battered. And not all of these people are of lower socioeconomic status, but upstanding, law-abiding, churchgoing, affluent people, who live right out in front of everyone in the community.

Cathy had been a classic example of a prostitute with a pimp she loved. The very first thing pimps teach their girls is to steal from the brothels they work in or any john they service. Walter learned that very quickly, which was why he had the girls' rooms all bugged, with their knowledge, as previously noted. Certain that Cathy stole, Walter carefully listened in on her. As often as he heard the sounds of crackling paper and other brief but odd sounds, he never found anything hidden in her room. He knew that if she was hiding money, she had to retrieve it before she left on her time off. So, patiently waiting until right before she was to leave one week, he walked into her room at just the right moment. With a coat hanger, she was working hard to retrieve some rolled up bills from the hollow curtain rod. The rule was that everything found belonged to him, so he took fifteen hundred dollars extra out of Cathy's ass for those three weeks of work and, of course, fired her on the spot. She called and called but he never relented. He would give in on some things the girls did, but not stealing, at least from him. In other brothels, girls are brutally beaten for such conduct. To Walter Plankinton's questionable credit, he never beat them. He never considered it.

Barbie had a pimp. Pimping was just a sideline for him—let's call him Joe. Joe was an executive with a well-respected international corporation in Las Vegas. He drove a very expensive sports car. As was the rule rather than exception, Barbie had been trained to steal, and there was no doubt that she was doing just that. So, Barbie's room was torn apart, also to check for drugs which every room was subject to, periodically. Walter always feared local law enforcement raiding the brothel for drugs as a means of closing it down. No matter how many times Walter or Doug, both skilled ferrets, went through Barbie's room, they never found a penny. They went through every makeup container, lighted mirrors, carpeting, linens, everything.

One night sitting in his office, Walter heard Barbie talking to Michon, who was her close friend, in one of the bathrooms. Barbie said, "Damn it, I lost the money I had." Michon asked where she had it, to which Barbie replied, "In plastic wrap, stuffed inside me. I forgot it was there and had to go to the bathroom just as the customer bell rang. I got excited and flushed it down because it fell out when I pee'd." Michon asked how much and the girl told her about four hundred dollars.

Walter turned off his tape recorder, rewound it and made sure everything was there. He then went to the bathroom just as the girls were coming out. He told her that he knew how she had been stealing, and that it was clearly admitted on his tape, and that she should clear out. He added that since she signed the standard employment agreement, all of the money she had not yet drawn out for her week off belonged to him. It was close to six thousand dollars.

For days, everyone in the house buzzed about the six thousand dollars Walter confiscated from Barbie, and that it wasn't worth stealing in the *Chicken Ranch* because he'd find out about it and take everything the girl had. It took a couple of years of this kind of practice, but Walter really counteracted much of the pimps' training at the *Chicken Ranch*.

Once, there were three girls at one time with the same pimp, affectionately

119

called the "old man." Each worked like a fool to outdo the other two to be number one woman to him. In retaliation, the other two would slack off a little until he just beat the hell out of them. Walter would ask them why they then slacked off, knowing he would beat them. They would tell him that it was the only way they could be sure he loved them.

Walter discovered that a successful pimp will have three or four women living together, "stable sisters," all vying for his favors, most working like fools in the street. He tells each girl that when she leaves for the night, she had better not come back without at least a couple hundred dollars. He doesn't care what kind of night it is: if the streets are empty and quiet; if the cops are on the prowl for hookers. No matter what it takes, she is expected to bring back the cash.

Just after Connie went to work at the *Chicken Ranch*, she broke down one night and cried. When Walter asked what was wrong, promising that he would help her if he could, she told him her pimp was vicious, that she wanted to get away from him but he had threatened her. She was terrified of him. He had already come to the Ranch trying to see her, but one of the maids recognized him from seeing him drop Connie off, so she wouldn't let him in when he pretended to be a john. He started shouting outside, calling Connie's name, swearing he was going to shoot the place up. Walter went out to confront him, and threatened him, apparently scaring him sufficiently from ever coming back to the Ranch. What he did do was call Connie's mother, telling her that she was a whore working at the *Chicken Ranch*. While it was terrible for her mother, she accepted that her daughter was a prostitute and assured her that she loved her in spite of it.

On one of Connie's trips back home, she met Linda, another prostitute, and fell totally in love with her. She brought her back to the Ranch, turning totally lesbian. Together, they subsequently met Sandy, a hard-core lesbian, and started partying as a sexual trio. Slowly, Linda's affections turned more toward Sandy. Connie quit the Ranch and went home, but Walter later heard she was in another brothel.

In most brothels, the owners pay the pimps. The girls never see their own money or, if they do, hand it over immediately. They are dominated and regulated solely by their pimps who, in turn, give the brothels orders as to what they want the girls to do, at least to some extent. Between most brothel owner/managers and the pimps, total slavery might be better for these girls. In some of the brothels, when girls were leaving their three-week shifts, there was a caravan of big shiny cars in front of the brothels. The pimps would go into the back room. There, they would be given "all" of the money owed the girls. In one of the brothels, if a girl had not made the amount of money the pimp thought she should, or if a brothel owner complained of problems she had given him related to not making more money, the pimp could take the girl into a soundproofed room and beat her all he liked. Then, if she was physically able, she'd be thrown right back into the lineup without any time off, to make up for "his" losses.

Walter refused to pay pimps, threw several out soon after the Ranch opened, finally banning all from his brothel. They could wait for their girls outside the front door, but that was as close as they were permitted. Slowly, the word spread and girls knew they were protected at the *Chicken Ranch*. Walter no longer looked for prostitutes; they practically beat down his door.

Linda and Donni had a pimp, Donni's husband. He stayed home and took care of their son while she and Linda spent their time at the Ranch working. He had his own plane as well as a lot of other expensive toys. The girls worked the same schedule and Jim would pick them up for their joint week off, and fly off into the sunset. It seems that it was too costly and time-consuming to fly up twice. Walter never found out much about their sex life at home because he wasn't interested. However, he wondered who really was pimping whom. He suspected that Donni, who was a bit older than Linda was the real pimp in the trio because Jim pimped for Linda, but gave all of that money to Donni, ultimately making Donni Jim's pimp, as well as his wife.

Jim had been a jockey for over twenty years, and married Donni when she was very young. She went to work in a massage parlor right after they had a baby, where she met Linda, whom she convinced to work for Jim, which is when he became the pimp. They also had a regular babysitter, Shelly, who knew what Donni and Linda did. She was a disturbed young girl, and they were quickly able to convince her to become a prostitute. She had already been molested by her cruel father, who was on trial for just that. Shelly, being the older daughter of the man who had also molested his younger daughter, had to get up in a courtroom and describe all of the obscene and sadistic acts their father had forced on them. She, too, became one of Jim's girls. She also went to the Ranch to work, and took about fifty thousand dollars to him during her first year at the brothel. He convinced her he was investing it in horses for both of them. But no receipts were necessary because he was, of course, madly in love with her. She never saw her money again.

One pimp particularly fascinated Walter. He was exceptionally good looking, charming, raised in the deep south. He told girls that he had at least a dozen bars back home with many go-go girls, and all kinds of interests which brought in enormous income. He would explain that the only reason he was in Las Vegas was to gather investors for a million-dollar movie he was planning to produce, which would make tens of millions in profits. His line was that the money they gave him from their work made them investors in this huge project, and they would end up rich and famous. One girl after another fell for the same corny, shallow line, and ended up working for him, breaking their backs, on their backs, to line his pockets with gold. Each fell madly in love with this Adonis, and each believed she was his own little favored darling. Of course, not one prostitute will ever question her man once she is hooked because if she does, her pimp might reject her. Prostitutes are weak, alone, frightened little creatures with a desperate need to feel loved, to believe they matter to someone. After all, the life they choose is spat upon by society, and more often than not, they are abandoned by their families.

Here and there was a pimp with scruples. Sammy had them. He had only two girls: Joey, nineteen, and JJ, twenty. Both worked at the *Chicken Ranch.* Sammy lived in a beautifully appointed condo and drove a big fancy car. When they went home, they gave him every penny. All of the furniture and car were in his name. But, he bought them gorgeous clothes, furs, and jewelry. They went to shows and fancy restaurants. They traveled. He took care of the house and cooked gourmet meals for them. They probably handed him four thousand dollars a week between them. He likely took half for himself, and the rest was spent on or invested in the girls. They knew they were safe and secure. Eventually Joey fell in love with one of her customers at the Ranch who was a sous chef, and went off with him. Unfortunately, there was a scene and JJ left, too. Walter saw Sammy a couple of years later in another state where he had taken the money he saved from his time as a pimp. He owned a beautiful cocktail lounge, was very successful, and had a beautiful young girl living with him, one that Walter was certain was not a prostitute.

Another short-term girl was Tracy. She was hooking on the streets of San Francisco. When she heard about the *Chicken Ranch,* she applied. She told Walter she was running from a pimp who beat her regularly and made her go on the street even when she was sick (anyone with any form of VD is referred to as sick). He didn't care that she was spreading disease. When Walter sent her to the Ranch's established doctor to be certain she was clean, he found so many venereal warts in her vagina that it was impossible to get anything inside as thin as a pencil. Both the other girls and the doctor told Walter that the pain when this girl allowed any insertion by a man's penis had to be excruciating. The doctor also told him that the warts were highly contagious. There was no way of guessing how many men in San Francisco she had passed her disease on to.

She pleaded with Walter to let her stay at the Ranch until she was clean. She was willing to do anything, even act as a maid. He felt so sorry for her that he said okay. She was an unbelievably hard worker. She didn't hesitate to scrub floors, vacuum, do linens (a never-ending chore in his brothel), and was great as a maid. After she was determined as clean by the doctor, she stayed on as a prostitute for three or four months, then left. She went to an Ely County brothel for a short time, then left there, too. They never heard of her again.

While Walter was aware of his girls' safety, in and out of the Ranch, he could not protect them outside if they didn't choose to be helped. A few did ask, and he went to their pimps and told them to get lost. There is no doubt that he kept putting his life on the line. But Walter didn't exactly look like a weakling. Nor was he stupid, readily admitting to having known great fear at different times in his life. But he was a difficult man to intimidate. At first he admitted to being totally naïve, not recognizing just how much danger he was in by throwing pimps out, or telling them to stay away from a girl at the Ranch because she no longer wanted any part of him. His bravado was more likely for the girls, whose adoration seemed more important than worrying about those illiterate blood-suckers.

Walter never saw himself as a pimp. He thought of himself more as a teacher, a protector, a businessman. He took fifty percent of what the girls made, plus twenty dollars a day for room and board and maid services. He insisted that salesmen usually get no more than five to twenty-five percent of what they sell, and that some have to pay for all of their expenses, including travel, entertainment and the like. He preached that many, if not most, brothels not only took the standard fifty percent, but found ways to take much more than twenty dollars a day, doped the girls up, and allowed their pimps to abuse them. He saw himself, and was to some extent, a genuine protector. But he also considered himself as the girls' benefactor, and was incredulous when anyone saw it otherwise.

Inside the brothel, of course, Walter was in control and could fully protect the girls. He had a panic button installed at each bedside. When pressed, it triggered lights and bells seen and heard throughout the house. It was there for use at the girls' discretion. In the five years he operated the *Chicken Ranch,* it rang only twice. Each time it was nothing more than misunderstandings which frightened the girls. Of course, they wished they had not pressed the buttons by the time he was finished verbally tearing their heads off for disrupting the brothel and risking upsetting customers. He did, however, make certain that there was always one man in the house so the girls had manpower to protect them.

Walter always found it interesting that the mere presence of a man could have such impact. But it did. He reluctantly admitted that he had known women, many of them prostitutes, who could wipe the floor with any three men. His own mother had certainly proven she could. But it seems in a sexual situation, women are vulnerable, and knowing a man is there to protect them makes them feel safer. Occasionally they had to deal with belligerent men, and Walter used muscle to eject them. He also kept a gun. But nothing ever happened within the girls' bedrooms that put any of them in real danger.

A girl named Candy came to the Ranch from Missouri by way of Colorado. She only stayed about four months and did pretty well. What made her stand out was her tattoos. She had tattoos in places it would seem impossible to draw on, much less use a needle. She often had repeats among the locals. She was so strange looking that Walter never understood the attraction. But he would say: "dry rolls to one is cake to another."

Among the different types of men who frequent brothels are a few common denominators. One which stands out is the introvert. It's widely believed that only less intelligent men are shy, which is rubbish. Many brothel patrons are astute, successful business and professional men, young and old alike. However, if they try to meet a girl some get tongue-tied and trip all over themselves. Such embarrassment is devastating to any man. Women generally seem to believe that all men are makeout artists, with emphasis on *artists*, which couldn't be farther from the truth. Few men are really glib and skilled in maneuvering a woman into a bed. More than are imagined aren't even good at knowing how to approach a woman to take to dance, have dinner, go to a movie, or some such innocent activity. Like everything else, the smaller percentage who get all the publicity create the foolish notion that all men are great lovers.

Men need not be psychopaths or even neurotics to have problems with self-esteem. Most people have to deal with self-esteem on an ongoing basis. Successful, handsome men can become impotent as easily as someone without these attributes. Less affluent or physically unattractive men can be extraordinarily smooth, and great lovers. Some men just find it easier to use brothels with no strings attached and no expertise expected, just as Walter discovered when he was very young. They pay the cost and leave with no feeling of further responsibility for their sexual fulfillment.

Many men who frequent brothels are extroverts, capable of propositioning any woman in sight within their own environments, while others are incapable of asking the least attractive woman around for a date. Some traveling salesmen who are real hotshots when it comes to selling their products, who are flirtatious with all of the secretaries and clerks wherever they go, melt into childlike fear when it comes down to real dating. They go back to their hotel or motel rooms and watch TV, certain that no woman in whatever town they're in would consider even having an innocent drink with them. Some married salesmen would feel guilty asking a woman out on the road, but think nothing of going to a brothel.

In a brothel, a man can pick a girl just like he chooses a tie. Even on the first visit, men know from some man somewhere that the girls know what to do so he has absolutely no responsibility to satisfy the *nameless, faceless whores*. Once there, johns discover what no man talks about, that those same whores will make him feel like a big, important stud, and he's hooked.

There's a different relationship between man and secretary, for instance. He can't talk sex to her or seduce her without possible repercussions. In the brothel, he can say absolutely anything he wishes with no thought of reaction. In a brothel, *he's safe*.

Some of the ironworkers who frequented the *Chicken Ranch* in groups were strong, very masculine, even attractive. In the area bars among themselves, they were witty, humorous, blended in just fine. If a woman caused them to pull away from their protective tribe, they became almost mute—often mistaken by women as *strong-silent* characteristics. In the brothel, the girls took care of everything, from the very first moment assuring them that they were big, gorgeous, macho men. Of course they preferred the brothel, especially where it only cost them cash, not commitment.

There were also types who were highly successful, well-respected, and well-versed when talking within their own business or professional environments. Take them out of that milieu, and they were dull and boring. No prostitute is interested in a john's intelligence or depth; only the number of extractable bills in his pocket. For that payment, however, the girl will feed his starving ego, or his loneliness.

Still other men loathe the hassle of dating a girl over a period of time just to get her into bed. Walter was the classic example of this type. Others don't like to compete for a girl's affections. No prostitute demands or expects anything except being paid.

There was a host of regulars at the *Chicken Ranch*. Some asked for seriously, even dangerously sadistic acts which Walter, *at first*, summarily refused. He never understood how a man could want his penis or testicles brutalized to the level of real and prolonged pain. Puncturing, cutting or burning flesh, or beating to the bloody stage with studded whips was definitely sick. Others were not sadistic, although repulsive. Masochists willing to pay money, lots of money, to have pain and humiliation inflicted on them, are everywhere. And a good percentage of them look much like the man living next door who leaves his house every morning for work wearing a suit.

One such man appeared quite regularly. The first few times, he went through the usual lineup and slowly got to know several of the girls pretty well, in the biblical sense, of course. When he knew that everyone in the brothel knew they could trust him, he asked one of the girls for something special. Although a john was not usually considered a finished job until he ejaculated, some never did, but were still quite happy with the girl and her services. It was always the man's choice. This john finally told one of the girls that the only way he could ejaculate was by lying under a glass cocktail table while a woman had a bowel movement on top of the glass. Don't think that didn't cause a weird bit of timing in terms of competition among the girls. He continued to be a regular as long as Walter was there. Walter considered the act repulsive, but not his half of the money.

Another long-term customer kept in close contact with the maids. He had a favorite girl, which many had, and came every month, often three and four days in a row. The odd thing was that he came only while she was having her menstrual period. He knew her monthly schedule and toward the time called the maid daily to work on the countdown. As soon as she told him his girl was bleeding he showed up like clockwork. For him, while he watched, she would remove the cotton balls they stuff inside of themselves to stop the flow while servicing the customers. He was barely interested in intercourse, he went down on her and sucked up all that blood. A vaginal vampire.

Patty took care of many of the masochistic customers. She was obviously highly skilled in the role of torturer. One man who wished to be severely abused paid thirty-five hundred dollars for each eight-hour period of pain. At some point, Patty would leave her room and ask Walter or whomever was in charge to melt some candles, for example, which she poured all over the john's hairy body. When it dried, she "very roughly tore it off his skin," causing excruciating pain. She poked needles into his testicles, even his penis. On one visit, he asked her to find a plastic pan which he broke a hole in, then had her force it over his head and face. He instructed her to pee all over his head and face. She kept drinking water in order to do it repeatedly during the period he had paid for. These things were in addition to the usual whippings. She also sat her bare ass very firmly on his face almost smothering him, which he particularly liked.

One night, Patty walked into the office and told Walter that her customer would pay him five hundred dollars if he would go into her room and pee on his face. Walter told Patty to tell the stupid john that he didn't need five hundred dollars. The man always paid Patty in cash, so he obviously carried *at least* four thousand dollars in his pocket. He drove a very expensive car and was impeccably dressed. He was obviously educated and successful. Nevertheless, whenever he left Walter had to throw out the girl's mattress.

Walter estimated that ten percent of all of the Ranch's customers were

126

masochists. They did not all want the same degree of pain inflicted, of course. Many wished to be tied to the bed and be slapped, whipped and scratched, and abuse inflicted on their penises. Some wanted collars put around their necks and be yanked and jerked around until it caused extreme pain.

Many, many couples went to the *Chicken Ranch*, but Walter was not too happy about such customers because "most caused problems." They usually requested that the girl service them both in various ways, "oral sex, finger-fucking, anal fucking, objects being shoved into both customers' asses and her vagina; one often watching the other two perform." The husband or boyfriend wanting to watch the two women performing oral sex on one another was very common. Too often, however, if the man was too pleased with the whore, the wife or girlfriend would turn on her and try to really hurt her. To protect his girls, Walter's rule was that a maid stand at the door of the girl's room, and if she heard anything that sounded like a cry for help, she would enter the room and stop the activities.

Contrary to many silly people's ideas, prostitutes did not become lesbians simply by performing this type of sex act. It is as much a common job as a secretary typing a letter, or a janitor sweeping a floor. It's a job, and they think nothing of it. They can usually get a lot more money for such activities, and at the *Chicken Ranch*, these acts cost three hundred dollars an hour, the minimum being three hundred dollars. It should be obvious by now that these were not people from the poorer classes. Often people of stature and affluence came for such games, and stayed for two or three hours. Although there was always the risk of problems, the girls wanted such customers since their prices could easily go from hundreds to thousands. A prostitute, if she's really skilled, can command more money per minute than a surgeon, a lawyer, an entertainer, athlete, or corporate executive. Now that sounds just a bit like *poetic justice*.

FIFTEEN

People often asked Walter if operating a brothel was like living in a candy store, wondering if after gorging himself with every size and flavor in the shop, he could become bored. No matter how much a man indulges in sex, he never tires of it, not for a lifetime. There are exceptions, of course, but they are extremely rare. As for the girls, very few of them climax while they work. They are skilled at faking climaxes, but rarely is it real. They save that for their pimps, boyfriends, husbands, lesbian lovers.

There is no emotion attached to a *trick*. Again, there are occasional exceptions, which are noted in this book. To a prostitute, *turning a trick* is about as emotional as washing a pair of dirty socks. Some are smelly and dirty, others are just lightly soiled. All have to be scrubbed clean.

When Walter helped to polish the skills of some of the less experienced girls, he would explain how much extra money a little moaning and groaning could bring them. He would preach that half the fun of going into a brothel for some men was bragging about how many times he got her off before she got him off. All the girl really did was play a part, giving him anything he wanted to feel, see, or hear. It's another reason the title of *tricks* is so appropriate for men who use prostitutes. The girls are *always tricking* them. Walter even admitted that before he owned a brothel, he was fooled. All those years he believed he was doing those cute young things favors by laying them. He finally learned it was all fantasy, but even then he admittedly, repeatedly, fell under the spell of whatever girl he was with. He believed that almost all men really go to the brothels to have their egos inflated, and that fulfilling sexual fantasies may be in second place. He sees this lineup of cute young things rarely over twenty-three years old, and remember some little cheerleader who wouldn't even let him smell where they sat, much less go to bed with him. Maybe one of the girls in the lineup looks a little like her, or has her smile, or her color hair. She will fulfill his dream of that unattainable girl, acting like he's the greatest stud she ever had. By the time that girl leads him by the hand into her room, he's so inflated he'll give her all the money he's got to be sure he's impressing her, too. By the time he leaves her, his ego, blown up out of all proportion, will hold him for a long, long time.

Some men go to brothels because their wives tell them, in one way or another, that they are lousy husbands, terrible lovers, and a raft of other abusive things. People rarely think of men being abused. Psychological abuse comes in various forms, and Walter was one of many men who believed that most women quickly learn that it's the easiest way to crush, thereby control, their mates. Prostitutes build them back up.

There are men who are smart enough to go to brothels just to learn little sexual tricks that a well-experienced whore can teach him. He can then take those little games back to his wife to use for a lifetime of pleasure for both. Many go into brothels in groups, just for fun. Comparing notes on the way back to their hotels only adds to the kick. A bunch of boys playing a game with his peers which offers an innocent challenge: who performed best, the most, the longest, for the lowest price; or in contrast, paid the most.

Walter never permitted two men with one girl, although they asked. "When two men take one girl, they tend to try to show off, more often than not at the expense of the girl, who often ends up getting hurt." Most brothels allow it. There were multiple parties at the Ranch, but only if the numbers of girls matched the numbers of males, so that each girl's ass could be protected by another girl.

Asian men were the girls' favorites because it took little time and virtually no effort to finish them. After the brothel became popular worldwide, men coming in groups, for what are called junkets to Las Vegas, made *Chicken Ranch* arrangements right along with all of their travel plans before they ever left home. For some strange reason that Walter and the girls supposed had something to do with the code of honor that has always been difficult for Caucasians to understand, an Asian man will not lay the same girl his friend just did. As quickly as the girls learned this, they solved the problem. As a girl would finish with one, she would quickly don a different wig, change clothes and lipstick color, and come back out to the parlor as another girl (prostitutes have no trouble changing their appearances, at least sufficiently to fool strangers). They did everything possible to encourage the men's patronage. They liked them because they had small, narrow penises, were never abusive, and ejaculated quickly. It soon became as important to those men to go to the *Chicken Ranch* as to gamble in Las Vegas.

Everyone at the *Chicken Ranch* was making a lot of money on these Asian men, so Walter was thrilled. He constantly encouraged the girls to treat them right so they would tell friends back home about the *Chicken Ranch*. Walter realized that the girls liked them because they were such easy lays, so he was certain they were using their very best public relations with them.

One afternoon, standing just outside the door of the *Cat Room* as he often did to eavesdrop on the girls, Walter heard explosions of laughter and giggling. It was always nice to hear the girls happy. He stayed out of sight smiling, or so he said, straining harder to hear what they were laughing at. At first he didn't believe what he heard. They were talking about their Asian customers. Walter made deals with most of the travel agents involved with these junkets. He charged flat fees for services at the *Chicken Ranch* of seventy-five dollars per lay. It was a logical quantity discount as far as he was concerned. The girls were not permitted to negotiate. They knew exactly how much they would make on each man. They never would have dared to complain about it, although it wouldn't have made any difference. It was the deal Walter made and he never gave the girls options in such matters—just like any other pimp.

At the door, he heard them discussing which girls had won how much on their bets. He didn't have to hear much of their discussion to understand what they had been doing. They were betting with each other about how fast they could finish their Asian customers. From the moment the girl was chosen in the lineup, the clock started ticking. They had to go into their rooms, strip, examine, and wash the man and themselves, get him to ejaculate, wash again, redress, and come back on the line, when the clock would be stopped. They slowly got the time down to seven, then six minutes. They were howling now because they were beginning to count the time in seconds instead of minutes.

There is no doubt that when Walter walked into that *Cat Room*, they all saw the smoke billowing from his ears. He was white hot. Upon questioning, when they meekly told him how many months it had been going on, he was certain the whole structure shook from his rage. When he finally began to calm down, he saw the fear in their eyes. These were mostly abused young girls who expected him to beat them, or at the very least fire them all. He sat down between them, some quietly whimpering. Knowing their levels of intelligence, believing his was so much above theirs, he patiently explained that if the tour people ever found out about this, not to mention the customers, they'd lose them all. The practice ended then and there. Thereafter, each girl was an international diplomat.

Terry was a sad tale, at least to Walter. One of five children, her father was a career soldier. When she was very small, he committed suicide. After her mother remarried, they moved around a lot, finally ending up in Las Vegas. Her mother was into kinky sex. When her daughters were still very little, four or five, she began to bring them into her bed to participate in sexual acts with her and their stepfather. They were continuously used by both parents, vaginally, rectally, and orally, in both directions. Terry was only twenty when she applied to the Ranch, but old in the ways of sex. She was also as blind as a bat without glasses and always stumbling around. Of course, she'd never think of using them in a lineup. Everyone would laugh as they watched her hanging on to her trick's hand, groping her way back to her own room. She was with Walter for four years.

Girls left for many reasons. Any girl who left on her own was always free to return as long as there was an opening. The brothel reached full capacity with twelve girls working at all times. One night, they were so busy that Walter counted forty-five men waiting in the living room while all the girls had customers in their rooms. As a girl finished her trick, she went straight back out to the parlor and simply asked who was next. When they were that busy, there was no way to use a lineup. Handing the men numbers as they entered may have been more appropriate.

They never worried about the men waiting. Most had traveled fifty-five miles to get laid at the *Chicken Ranch*. When the girl came out and asked who was next, she would also ask which men were interested in her, then whichever man was there first would go in first. Some of them would sit for hours waiting for one particular girl they saw and liked. Occasionally, they would pick a second choice if they didn't want to wait any longer.

This size of backup didn't happen too often, but it was not unusual to have a full house with five or six men waiting. Most of the girls sold anywhere from thirty to sixty minutes. A really good trick was two or three hours. Business usually moved right along. Most men's eyes are bigger than their capabilities when they think they can hold off for more than one hour. And once ejaculated, she had fulfilled the services already paid for and was ready for the next trick.

The waiting list to work at the *Chicken Ranch* grew right along with business. Some girls proved to be enormous responsibilities, even trouble. Kiki was tall and well-built with enormous breasts. She was another true dingbat. Although nineteen, she acted more like thirteen. She had been raised in Las Vegas and was very attractive. It was extremely difficult to watch over girls like her because she was careless. She got pregnant with a *trick baby*. Most people never think about the possibility with a prostitute because they assume all hookers have abortions, automatically. Well some do if they are foolish enough to permit the chance of pregnancy in the first place. There were always ways to keep from getting pregnant; prostitution certainly predates *the pill*, by twenty centuries that we are sure of. But some, like Kiki, don't care if they are, and don't even recognize it until the doctor sees it because they are so far along. She had her trick baby and, fortunately, it was adopted by a wealthy family, the adoption arranged by Mignon. It wasn't until later that Walter discovered that the madam made a pile of money on the baby sale. The only saving grace was that the baby would be raised with love and care.

Yvonne was unforgettable. About four feet nine inches tall, she could not have weighed eighty-five pounds. She genuinely believed she was a witch and scared the other girls half to death. She had all the props sold in mystic stores, used herbs, and stuck pins into voodoo dolls. Her stepfather molested her, then got her to accept and continue the molestation by giving her all kinds of presents. He kept bribing her so she wouldn't tell her mother, or anyone else. His plans backfired when she got pregnant. Her mother had to be told. She was only twelve when he robbed her of her childhood. Her mother divorced the man but Yvonne wouldn't leave him. She decided she wanted the baby and to stay with him, and did for awhile. He left eventually and she gave up the child.

Not only was Yvonne a handful to control in terms of frightening the other girls, she was nasty to customers on occasion. Because of this, particularly, Walter was always punishing her. He kept her for a very specific reason. Her specialty. She took on two types of customers: men with exceptionally large penises, and those who wanted to be chained and beaten. No one at the Ranch ever figured out how this tiny little girl could take on those huge studs. It doesn't take a shrink to understand why she enjoyed abusing the men who came only for that purpose. Whatever it was, she produced lots and lots of money. Her customers came back again and again. They also paid much higher prices for their fantasies. Walter's rule was, "We don't beat anyone up for less than two hundred dollars."

Two sisters, Linda and Terry, were born and raised in Las Vegas. Their mother, a casino dealer, was remarried. She and their stepfather repeatedly molested them from toddler stage, using them in unspeakable ways, certainly in oral sex for their stepfather, long before they were even in kindergarten. Fortunately, at least some of this behavior is being exposed in the media, today. Linda and Terry also became prostitutes but are, of course, condemned for it. Most organizations fighting child abuse are not willing to bring these women forward to expose more of the practice of child molestation, even though they would discuss it more freely than *straight women*.

While many prostitutes were molested as children, more were never raped, or abused, who attended good schools, colleges, but could not make a decent living. Or, when they found that respectable businessmen *expected* extra favors if they were allowed to climb the corporate ladder, which really meant they could keep some two-bit, low paying job, which certainly should be called prostitution, although they pay by hard, underpaid labor instead of being paid, they got tired of free sex and found out that the same sex could bring them a good living in a brothel or as a *high-class call girl*.

Walter received *many* actual "resumes" from women with backgrounds that would shock the average person. They were from respectable women, leading productive lives, raising wonderful children, married to men as prominent as they were, who were former prostitutes. He enjoyed expounding on the contrast in many women he had met in the straight world who were prominent, religious, heads of social-type communities who were feared, hated, and tolerated only because of their great wealth, their family names, their threats, who were "not good enough to lick the feet of some of the whores or former whores."

Walter swore he never meant to sanctify prostitution, only to get people to face the truth about it. He knew that an admired, respected next door neighbor could be a prostitute without anyone knowing about it; he knew many such women. And when it came to its legality, he turned missionary, sermonizing about some human rights for the profession, particularly in view of both politicians and citizens who attack it while pocketing the money or services it brings them, personally, within their own towns or districts. He said, "It's the same hypocrisy as if the Governor of Nevada would openly say, 'Oh, I firmly believe that gambling is sinful, despicable, addictive, and should certainly be made illegal, and I loathe it, personally; but let us all remember that it constitutes the majority of income in our state'."

Walter was once misquoted regarding a statement he made about his feeling that it would be fine if his daughter chose to be a prostitute. What he actually said was that if his daughter ever chose to be a prostitute, he would hope she would find a brothel instead of hooking out on the street. When asked point blank if he would want his daughter to be a prostitute, he said, "Of course not," adding that "no more than would the vast majority of women who are prostitutes want their daughters to follow their career choices." Walter said he watched women for five years who did everything possible to protect their children and families from knowing what they did for a living.

Endless *token* prostitutes are picked up on the streets of our country on a regular basis. Prostitution is not exclusively a Nevada profession just because it allows prostitution in most of its counties. On the streets of any big city or small town in the U.S., including Salt Lake City, Kansas City, Boise, Little Rock, Tallahassee, and so forth, prostitutes are readily available through cab drivers, bell hops, bartenders, corporate officers, salesmen, cops, etc. Yet, police departments of those same cities and towns arrest *only* the women; not the pimps, also known as cab drivers, bell hops, bartenders, corporate officers, salesmen, cops; and certainly *never the customers,* those respected businessmen, mechanics, doctors, construction workers, conventioneers, lawyers, salesmen, corporate officers, cops, etc., etc., etc.

And of course, no one pays any attention at all to male prostitutes—also known as gigolos—or to homosexual prostitution. Prostitution is openly practiced in any gay bar throughout the U.S. Men cruise around grabbing men's asses; women do the same. Even if cash is openly exchanged, law enforcement doesn't care. Some politicians decry its existence, damning anyone practicing it to hell—as if they were God, Himself. But no one thinks of enforcing the laws of any of their states to include homosexuals in prostitution round-ups.

And when was the last time anyone heard about a male prostitute being arrested, or even existing? Male prostitution may not be as old as the female version, at least as far as we know, but then men's closets have much stronger doors than women's. Of course, their title is not in any state's statutes, either. They are called gigolos, even though their profession is prostitution. Maybe because of the old adage, *he's feeling his oats*; or even at sixty years old, *boys will be boys*. Those romantic gigolos, darling little boys, play with as many prominent, wealthy, married "men" and women as those called prostitutes, but only the female ones are condemned, prosecuted, jailed, fined. What is amusing is that they are not exclusively the greasy, sexy con men depicted by Rudolph Valentino of silent film fame. Some male prostitutes are well-educated, clean-cut-looking, and gracious. The ranks of the wealthy, married *johns* and *joans* boast politicians, professors, elementary school teachers, doctors, ministers, and so forth. Of course, there are male streetwalkers, too. Ask any cop you know well enough for him or her to trust you.

The State of Nevada has issued a license plate to a man which displays "GIGOLO." There is absolutely no question that the State of Nevada would never consider allowing someone to display PROSTITUTE or WHORE on a license plate; yet, in Las Vegas, which is in Clark County where prostitution is at least illegal on the books if not in practice, they allow a man to display a synonym for prostitute or whore, which apparently he is advertising he is.

As the prostitutes of Northern Nevada appear to be organizing a union, it will be interesting to see how prostitutes across the country rally to that same cry. Prostitutes who steal, kill, set customers up to be ravaged by accomplices, should all be prosecuted and jailed. But the vast majority who offer a simple service to customers who have been paying them for that service since the beginning of time, should be regulated and taxed, like any other industry. When Nevada glamorizes gambling, which empties people's pockets, bank accounts, lives, one of the most addictive sicknesses which threatens to bankrupt the nation if allowed to spread as those in power hope it will; when the same State of Nevada offers telemarketing, an industry which openly and freely robs the elderly, the lonely who are easily manipulated just to hear a friendly voice; a huge question is how can anyone believe that prostitution is not encouraged, or at least given a wink and a nod, by that State's same *honorable* government.

It took awhile to understand some of the psychology behind prostitution, but after a time, Walter recognized it for what it was. "It's no more exciting than washing dirty dishes. It's a matter of the women conditioning their minds to accept it as a job like any other. They are totally fake with customers, but swear they never con their own lovers. They climax only when they choose to." Walter came to believe that at least while they are practicing prostitutes, there must be a certain amount of faking even with the men they love. And once they leave the trade, it must take a long time, if ever, to return to normal sexual feelings, not to mention trust.

While claiming he only became emotionally involved with one girl during his entire brothel life, his own stories do not bear that out. Nevertheless, with the first one, it took awhile for him to accept her being with other men in the brothel, but when she finally convinced him to look at it as she did, it never bothered him again. Yet, he admitted that if he ever heard that she was seeing a man on the outside during her off time, he would have been very angry and jealous. He finally reached the full measure of being a pimp.

In normal life, sex is the climax to romance—at least it's supposed to be. In a brothel, sex is mechanical. Emotions displayed by any prostitute are completely fake. As in anything else in human nature, there are exceptions; but in this case, there are very, very few. Those few are the *come freaks*. But it still has nothing to do with emotions; they are strictly physical releases.

The same holds true for homosexual acts. As noted earlier, there are many lesbians among prostitutes. But homo- and heterosexual prostitutes are equally as casual and unfeeling about being part of a paid-for lesbian sexual activity as they are with a heterosexual activity. Lesbians who romance other women are as emotional, and can be as violently jealous, as any heterosexual. Some believe even more. They can work in brothel bedrooms, side by side, taking on every *trick* that comes down the road and think nothing of it. But outside of the brothel, if one even looks at another lesbian, the lover can become as violent as any partner in a heterosexual coupling.

In defense of these girls called prostitutes, Walter often got on his soapbox to talk about "wives, supposedly fine, upstanding, righteous women, who are as unloving and coldly submissive, and as much pretenders in their beloved husbands' beds as any prostitute. They just aren't skilled in making their husbands enjoy what is done to them or allow anything even slightly unusual in their beds." While Walter was a narrow, self-serving and self-absorbed man, he was not completely stupid. His opinion on this subject is more widespread than some would like to admit.

Prostitution is often called the "oldest profession in the world." It is condemned, joked about, laughed and sneered at. Yet, when a prostitute falls in love, she can make the best possible wife. At least she knows how and usually continues to make her husband believe he is the most exciting, wonderful stud on earth, even if or when she is bored or tired. How many straight wives can boast about even bothering to learn some sexual skills. Not simply faking, which all women do one time or another, but developed skills, painstakingly used so that a man's ego is constantly stroked so that he never feels like a failure as a man, no matter what turn his life takes.

Of course, Walter never considered that a man should even think, much less worry, that he should have to do anything special or extra for a woman's ego or sexual pleasure. He believed that anything he did was so extraordinary, that it was more than enough for any woman, however little that was. He totally believed all of the fairy tales the countless prostitutes in his life told him. In addition to that, he wholeheartedly believed women were inferior and was only annoyed by women who were strong and independent, admitting that he carefully avoided them throughout his lifetime

He became even more biased about prostitutes after knowing so many, as well as the real people behind the trade, than he was before the *Chicken Ranch*. At the same time, he expounded on having a much deeper understanding of women and their plight in a man's world than most people ever know about. He explained that it didn't make him less manly, just more caring and sympathetic. Over and over again, he admitted that he always felt that men were superior to women. Not only physically, but certainly emotionally, morally, and in most cases intellectually. Prostitutes, he said, only proved to him how right he was.

Money was his primary reason for staying in the brothel business, although he never denied enjoying his work. He believed he experienced every man's fantasy to live in a harem. When confronted with an assertion that of about twenty men asked if they would like that kind of fantasy to become reality they all said no, Walter insisted that every one of them was a liar. He was convinced that every man would have traded places with him because he had used prostitutes on a regular basis from the age of seventeen, and now lived in this paradise. Even with this kind of mindset, he never forgot for a moment that it was a business and his livelihood. His income from it unquestionably took precedence over the sexual aspect.

While Walter apparently despised and would criticize pimps at every opportunity, his desire to use and control the whores he adored was transparent. Walter always claimed he didn't know legal and personal things about some of his girls, but the truth was he didn't care. As long as they were able to produce legal sheriff's cards, he would hire anyone he thought could make money for him at the *Chicken Ranch*. It should be made clear that it was not only Walter; this is the rule of brothels. He would also swear again and again that he became personally involved only once while he owned the brothel. He would then talk about all of the different liaisons he had with girls working for him. Whether it was because he forgot he had told the same people so many conflicting stories, or felt they wouldn't remember, or were too stupid to recognize his changes, remains a mystery. When confronted with such questions, he would squirm, then lie some more, then get angry, then contrite, but a real answer was almost impossible to extract.

Because prostitutes age very quickly from their harsh lives, some of the girls who ended up at the Ranch may have looked older than their early teens, but when Walter kept admitting knowing how old they all were—finding out later, of course—it became more and more difficult to believe he didn't know right from the start.

Justin was sixteen. Since she showed him her legal sheriff's card, Walter hired her, although he admitted suspecting her real age, with that telltale sickening smile of a man who relished the idea of laying very young girls. Frank, who had already been her pimp for awhile, was an exceptionally handsome man. While Walter insisted that pimps were not allowed at his brothel, for the first couple of years some were, by his own account. Justin was an impulsive worker. Although none of the girls had to do any kind of housework, Justin would go into the kitchen and cook, or start cleaning the common rooms like a madwoman.

Soon, Frank tried to tell Walter how to handle Justin, and the rest of the Ranch, for that matter. Walter finally told him not to even come to pick her up, that he would arrange for her to be taken to Las Vegas for her off-weeks. Frank was furious. Walter was often her chauffeur since he went to his condo regularly. One of those times, instead of allowing Justin to get into Walter's vehicle to return to the Ranch, Frank grabbed her by the hair and slammed her into the front seat. That was the last time Walter ever saw Frank. Justin and Frank had some kind of falling out, but Justin soon left the *Chicken Ranch*.

When Walter later spent time in Arizona, he heard that Justin was working in a massage parlor, and that Frank was there, too. Walter went there and spent a long time with Justin, but didn't see Frank. He gave her his phone number in Phoenix. She called him a couple of days later and asked him to meet her. She was cut and severely bruised all over her body. She was scared and said she had to leave Phoenix and Frank, once and for all. Walter took her to Mexico, then Colorado, to Kingman, Arizona, and finally back to Las Vegas. She stayed at the condo with him. He talked about what a great housekeeper she was. Then she wanted to redecorate, so Walter let her change everything: furniture, drapes, even the carpeting.

Walter had a 1972 Eldorado that he loved and had restored, which Justin couldn't keep her hands off. One day, she and Walter had what he called a minor spat. When he went home the next day her clothes were gone, and so was the Cadillac. Two weeks later, Walter heard that Justin was back at the massage parlor, and so was his Eldorado. He flew to Phoenix and picked up his car. Three days later, Justin was at the door of the condo, and moved right back in. Two days later she left, again with his car. Walter flew back to Phoenix, but this time he told her not to try to return. By the time he arrived back in Las Vegas, she was in the condo. She had flown back. She wanted to stay but Walter wouldn't let her. She asked for her job back at the Ranch but he refused. After a little crying and begging he broke another of his so-called firm, fast rules. He gave her one of the best rooms, and she worked hard from then on.

One day, a maid smelled pot in Justin's room and told Walter. He walked into her room and smelled it, too. He searched the bathroom, where he found her high and hysterical. He closed the door behind himself. Justin removed her spike heel and started hitting Walter with it. As blood started running from different cuts, he begged her to stop or he would have to defend himself. As he was finally able to get the door half open another maid came in, saw the blood all over him, and assumed he had beaten Justin up instead of the other way around. The maid started screaming at Walter for hitting the girl. When everything finally calmed down, Walter fired both the maid and Justin, and told Justin this had been her last chance and that he would never take her back again. She packed and left the Ranch. The next day when Walter went into his apartment, he discovered that every piece of crystal, every dish, every small piece that had any value that she could fit into Walter's Cadillac, was gone.

About three months later, Justin's aunt called Walter and told him that the girl was working a straight job in San Francisco. He ignored the call. Two months later, the Nevada Highway Patrol called him informing him that his car was in Lake Tahoe, and torn up from an accident. She had been on coke and rolled the car, then went over a forty-foot embankment. Although she was hardly injured, the car was a mess, and forty-feet down. Walter let the towing company keep the car. He was told that Justin was working in a Northern Nevada brothel, knew a distributor, and had gone to buy coke for all the girls in the brothel.

A few months later, Justin went to the *Chicken Ranch* and convinced Walter to take her back, once again. She insisted that she wanted to get out of prostitution, but the only thing she knew was massage parlors. Walter found one for her in Kingman, Arizona, rented it and had it remodeled, then sold it to her for what he had spent, about twelve thousand dollars. She did fine for awhile, but spent more than she took in, so Walter kept giving her more money instead of her paying him for the business. The Arizona Department of Safety began to show up on a regular basis, watching not only her, but questioning Walter. After an argument, Justin left and Walter, Doug, Sam, and a friend of Sam's went up with a truck and stripped everything out of the interior and took it back to the Ranch.

Justin went back to another Northern Nevada brothel, where Walter would meet her occasionally and have dinner with her. She later met a young man in Reno and was married for a short time. Walter claimed he never heard about her again, but for whatever reason he was apparently lying since she showed up in a 1980 FBI investigation interview at Doug's apartment.

Walter never considered his actions anything but normal when it came to Justin, or any other prostitute. He didn't think it was stupid to keep believing their lies, although most of the time he would swear he knew they were lying all the time. He thought of them as virginal whores, a perception that never ended. Even when he knew the prostitute was a child, maybe fifteen or sixteen, she was "fixable" by him and anyone who would pay him for it— "as long as she had a legal sheriff's card." Nothing else mattered to him. No amount of logic could reach him, could touch his conscience. He loudly and vehemently condemned pimps for *turning out* children, even though he never hesitated to hire and exploit those same children; yet, he never saw flaws in himself. They were criminals, child-abusers; he was law-abiding: the flag, mom, and apple pie. He followed the law. "The girl had a Sheriff's Card!"

SIXTEEN

Quite like any business or job, Walter soon experienced the negative aspects attached to running a brothel. Once in awhile, it was boring and tiresome, although admittedly not too often. Walter had the same personnel problems of any company of the brothel calibre. Some turnover was good for the Ranch, although he quickly learned that it was smart to hold on to a few regulars as long as they were good at their jobs, which simply meant consistent moneymakers for him. Walter liked to pretend that he was in total control, but women came and left at will, or by orders of their pimps, and there was nothing he could do about it except try to hire only girls who had no pimps, and even they came and went like a revolving door.

Some of the girls were not the least bit interested in keeping themselves as clean as Walter demanded, something he found personally repulsive and would fire them without hesitation. With such a revolving personnel door, there were also some who did not get along with others, so they would leave; or if he decided they were troublemakers he fired them. The girls definitely had no union, so just as easily as they could leave on their own, Walter was free to fire them. Since there were so many waiting in line to get into the *Chicken Ranch*, it was more an annoyance than a serious problem. He had a core of long-term girls who suited him very well, and who were apparently happy with him.

Walter often went from being amused to annoyance to anger when people talked about all of the brothels being tainted by the mob. He knew some were involved since they were owned by former hoods; but because he was not affiliated with the syndicate, he didn't like being painted with the same brush. Since he occasionally went into the same bars and restaurants where some of the wise guys hung out, he certainly got to know some of them. Like many straight people, hob-nobbing in the underworld was romantic and glamorous to Walter. And owning a brothel, in his own mind, put him rather high up on the status ladder. He admitted that he was approached more than once by known organized crime members who told him they could instantly stop the harassment he was getting from the quasi-hoods in Nye County. He repeatedly refused them because he knew that kind of link-up would be the

140

end of his control of his brothel. Being seen with this element was one thing, accepting their favors was quite another.

There is an irony in the fact that the mob and most organized religions in Nye County have one powerful factor in common: They both want to outlaw brothels. Of course, their motives are miles apart.

The churches actually believe that outlawing prostitution will eliminate it, or at least lower its practice which is, of course, child-level naivete. All it will serve is to put even more hookers—including twelve- and thirteen-year-olds which is the age most pimps recruit—on the street unlicensed; unchecked medically, thus, spreading disease; adding pimps to the streets of smaller towns surrounding popular gaming areas, thus, increasing crime statistics, and so forth.

It seems absurd that people continue to pretend prostitution doesn't exist everywhere in the country. Walter was incredulous after one incident in Las Vegas when the media was feigning shock because fifty prostitutes were arrested. He claimed to have been told by those who would know that Las Vegas supports up to ten thousand full- and part-time prostitutes, and no one will even venture a guess as to how many invade the area when something big is going on in town like a major convention, or a championship boxing match, or a very popular entertainer or group. The police often rely on those prostitutes, even pimps, to help them solve crimes a lot worse than prostitution. The police know most, if not all, by sight, and are on first-name bases with most or all of the local girls and pimps.

In the real world, prostitution is not a small, select business. There are estimates of around one hundred thousand just in the Nevada, Southern California, Northern Arizona, Southern Utah circle. It is believed that there are one to three million working prostitutes in the United States. For anyone to believe that they are totally hidden is a joke. The media know about it, doctors, housewives, steelworkers, military, they all know about it; Catholics, Protestants, Jews, Baptists, Mormons, Moslems, all know about it. Small-town sheriffs will justify if by saying, "Oh, she's no prostitute. I don't allow prostitutes in my town. She only charges ten dollars, that makes her a whore, not a prostitute."

And when the prostitute is arrested to show the good people of the town or city that the law comes down on these whores, they're out in a matter of hours. The token sweeps do little more than make some extra money for the bail bondsmen, lawyers and, in some cases, the police. And sometimes, a few hours in jail cells, playing cards with the police and each other, gives them a bit of rest from their jobs out on the street. And the money it costs doesn't phase most of them, particularly those without pimps who answer to no one but themselves. It's written off as an occasional fee, particularly for those who make six-figure incomes.

Walter talked about one girl who was "turned out" at the *Chicken Ranch* after having given it away through her teens. She studied everything she could about being a prostitute, including the business aspects. After a few months, she took her money and moved to California, rented a gorgeous apartment and started a marketing campaign. She told Walter she dressed only in designer clothes, went into large offices and conned her way into top executives' offices. She offered her services openly both to them and their clientele, quoting her prices like any other business person. She left her phone number and address. She asked for five-hundred dollars for a couple of hours in the afternoon, or occasionally discounted an evening for regular clients. She worked as little or as much as she pleased, and lived better than most of the world's population even dreams about. The number of prospective customers is mind-boggling. The *Internet* is already cleaning up with the sale of prostitution.

Keeping this industry illegal so that more pimps and the syndicate garner the highest profits is stupid. The IRS coffers would welcome the legal taxes paid on the enormous incomes through prostitution. Instead of taking food out of babies' mouths and making certain the next generation is uneducated, not to mention letting people who can't afford to go to the hospitals die—just like third-world countries—maybe this country should think about taxing something that's already prevalent. The rest of the world laughs at our pretense that it doesn't even exist.

Since Walter was always fending off the Nye County political machine, it was necessary to stay on his toes in case of trouble. Keeping the house squeaky clean in every way was an ongoing challenge. This included making sure that the girls didn't fight too much. It also meant staying in control of Mignon since she was a mean, dictatorial bitch. But the girls' fear of her was to his advantage. There were other disadvantages and problems, but Walter considered them all in a day's work.

Over the years, many people asked why he didn't open a *male whorehouse*. There certainly are plenty of male prostitutes to staff male whorehouses, and everyone in the business knows there are more than enough female customers out there. Walter admitted that he did think about it—briefly. But after watching some of the men who patronized brothels, and listening to endless stories from his girls about their *tricks*, he just couldn't raise any enthusiasm.

What he saw every day were men of every description, age, profession. They were tall, short, fat, thin, bald; some had dirt under their fingernails, others carefully manicured. There were those with dirty, straggly hair, and those coifed by professionals. Probably what he recalled most vividly was the contrast between the impeccably dressed, fastidiously clean and the filthy, dirty men who he couldn't believe could come to a brothel as they did. Equally among all of these factors were young, very good looking men, just plain ugly, as well as very, very old ones. Create any description of a man, and he came through the doors of the *Chicken Ranch*.

The stories the girls told him as they sat around the *Cat Room* created mental pictures for Walter. They spoke of men who had not been circumcised with so much built-up *head cheese*, it was revolting. Although the girls washed every man's genitals very carefully, there was no shower in each room, and certainly no time to waste when a girl was trying to make money, so the customers were never completely bathed.

Every single girl had stories about men whose teeth were coated with scum, discolored tongues from chewing tobacco or cigars, or matted filthy beards creating smells around their heads that were almost impossible to bear. Some men had obviously not bathed in days, or the girls swore perhaps weeks, creating body odors which overwhelmed them being in the same room. Some had feet so black they wondered if they had ever touched soap.

Then there were their genitals. Some were so dirty that while the girls examined the men for VD, they also watched for fleas and lice, which they found many of on heads, chests and underarms, as well as genitals. They said there were men so fat they could hardly find their cocks to do anything with. Most men chose oral sex and paid for it so it was expected. It wasn't bad enough that nauseating smells came from armpits, mouths, heads, chests, and feet, the girls had to lick and suck cocks, balls, and assholes which still reeked so badly, it's a wonder they weren't asphyxiated trying to hold their breath.

The first time someone seriously suggested Walter open a male brothel his first thought was, just as he was quality control manager for the girls, he could be the stud for female customers whenever he was in the mood, or, if they happened to be short of men. He fantasized the possibilities.

When he heard the bell ring, he saw himself seated, dressed in gray silk slacks and a muted mauve and gray print silk shirt with a gray ascot at his neck, wearing black snakeskin boots. As he walked from the *Cat Room* to join the lineup with one other stud, he realized while perhaps not the pretty-boy swashbuckler type, he was a nicely built, intelligent-looking, exceptionally handsome figure of a man. He put on his well-known provocative smile as he entered the room. Then he saw her!

Waiting for them was a huge, lard-like sloven with long, stringy hair so dirty, you could see the matting. Her teeth glistened with yellow, pus-like slime, and she brandished half-polished, broken, filthy nails. Her blotchy makeup was heavy and a vile orange color, obviously smeared on days before. She wore a gaudy print dress, wrinkled and dirty. On her legs, loose-fitting from repeated wear, were drooping stockings. Walter could see black globs in the corners of eyes that flashed with lust for his body. She chose him.

He cringed when he had to take the hand he was certain had been everywhere except a sink, smiling sexily while he tried to whisper sweet nothings through her smelly hair into her even dirtier ears, as he led her toward his immaculate, beautifully appointed, Louis XVI-furnished bedroom with every fabric in the room satin or silk.

After very quickly and easily negotiating the price for what she wanted, he watched as the slimy sludge disrobed in front of him, obviously expecting him to flatter her constantly by telling her how gorgeous, appealing, and sexy she was. Before he could undress and gain control of the revulsion he knew was on his face, or put a towel on his bed, she was down on the beautiful satin-covered bed. She spread her legs apart to the best of her ability, rather difficult considering the ham hocks one might laughingly refer to as legs, all the while fluttering her eyelashes as she waited for him to wash her genitalia, almost impossible to find through the mounds of flab. Recalling some of the revolting smells he had known emanating from men just sitting in the living room, imagining that stench magnified took little effort.

Walter clearly saw her aging tonnage sagging like the science fiction globs we have come to know in movies and TV, laying back on that beautiful bedspread, pointing to the rank-smelling vicinity of her bulbous, pimply pussy. She looked up at him dewy-eyed, panting both from her enormous effort in moving around and her apparent lust for him. In a feigned baby voice she thought sexy, Walter heard her mutter, "Eat it, Honey."

Not only did the fantasy convince Walter that he would never be part of a male brothel, it gave him a fresh new look at and even greater respect for his girls. He realized that sometimes, they really earned their money the hard way.

Walter was a typical farm boy with a thousand stories to tell. One he always enjoyed talking about was not long after he opened the *Chicken Ranch*. They had neighbors not far from the new brothel, whose house they had to pass to reach the Ranch. The family was somewhat notorious in the area since one of the sons had shot his father because of some kind of dope deal; and one of the daughters and her husband had been to jail on some kind of drug charges. This was not a typically good class of people as far as Pahrump was concerned.

One day as Walter was driving to the Ranch he saw the woman out in front of her house waving him down. He stopped and very graciously said, "Good morning, Ma'am," she being a bit older than he was. As graciously, she answered, "Good morning, Mr. Plankinton." Walter asked her what he could do for her, and the woman told him that she wished to tell him a few things about how she felt about his brothel. She said, "You know, I don't really mind you and your son driving up and down this road. It's all those unsavory characters I see coming down to that brothel of yours." Walter, smiling, in his sweetest voice, told her: "Well, Ma'am, next time you see those unsavory characters coming down this road, you look closer, because you'll find that most of them are your friends, your relatives, and your neighbors." Without another word, she turned around and walked back into her house. Walter added that he was forever astonished with how easily the men of the Pahrump Valley convinced people, particularly women, that only outsiders ever patronized the brothel.

While Walter loudly proclaimed that all of the criticism and barbs flung at him by politicians, other brothel owners, straight-laced citizens, and many other groups, did not phase him, anyone talking to him any length of time knew he was lying. He once said, "It's hard when you're talking about yourself not to just plain editorialize about your own reactions to what's being done to you. I'm no angel and don't pretend to be one. I've lived a life that would seem fast to some. I've worked hard, lived hard, and played hard. But I never stole anything, I paid taxes, and I lived by the law. I chose a business in my semiretirement that exposed me to things I would never have dreamed of in my wildest fantasies. It showed me how shielded from many sides of life I had been most of my years on this earth. The world of prostitution is not a simple, quiet, Sunday-go-to-meetin' life. It's hard, sometimes cruel, often ugly, and occasionally deadly, not just for the working girls but for everyone involved in the profession.

"What I find difficult to accept, or comprehend, is how these men who are perceived as upstanding citizens got away with making me an open target. I doubt that I will ever understand how a handful of law-wielding people could treat an entire American county like privately owned domain, with laws made up and enforced by a tiny power structure. They treated my business as though it was an illegal and repugnant operation, beneath their contempt, all

145

the while collecting taxes, deriving favors, and openly associating with and condoning precisely the same kind of operation under the ownership of others in the same community, some of whom were proven murderers.

"By now, everyone knows why they targeted me. My endless question is how an entire community could be so totally controlled that they permitted such open hypocrisy. It would have embarrassed and degraded me to stand and watch such despotism being used on anyone. It makes me realize just how fragile democracy really is."

Walter usually spoke like a Kansas farm boy, limited by the vocabulary, phrasing, and nuances of that part of the country. But sometimes, when caught off guard in a moment of reflection, or talking about a subject which touched him, or recalling things about his family or his childhood, he would drift into speaking almost eloquently. And whenever he wrote about something important to him, at least if it could be brief, he adopted a different vocabulary, an expanded one, and wrote impressively. There was a side of Walter Plankinton that revealed that if he had been educated, he might have accomplished more in his life.

Walter was actively advertising the *Chicken Ranch* in a Las Vegas newspaper (legal then). He was also circulating flyers in California. That added to the unsolicited publicity and satisfied-customer, word-of-mouth advertising which already made the Ranch a booming success.

He sat down one day and wrote the story of the original Chicken Ranch legend in Texas, had it printed, and gave away countless copies at the Ranch, along with fliers which he had passed out everywhere he could think of. He felt that the original story brought a touch of respectability, along with panache, to the Ranch. It was based on factual fragments he had learned, but the rest came from his imagination. He jotted it all down in just ten minutes.

The original Chicken Ranch was established about the same time Texas became a state, December 1845. It all started in a trading post on the beautiful Colorado River at LaGrange, Texas. Little did anyone dream it would operate continuously for almost one hundred thirty years. Cash was scarce in the 1840s, so customers used the old reliable barter system. More often than not, the ladies were paid with chickens. It quickly became known as The Chicken Ranch.

First catering to local farmers and ranchers, it never stopped during the Civil War. The girls serviced generals and foot soldiers alike. Then came the great herds with their cattle barons and cowboys. The cool waters and green pastures of the Chicken Ranch were welcome sights both to footsore longhorns and saddle-sore cowboys headed north to the railheads in Kansas.

Later, the oil boom in Central Texas attracted millionaires right alongside roughnecks. The Ranch endured the hardships of Central Texas during the *Great Depression,* and again flourished during *World War II,* patronizing generals and privates from military bases in the area. Its reputation grew internationally as each succeeding proprietor maintained unquestionably high standards. The Chicken Ranch was so prominent in Texas and Southwestern history that President Lyndon B. Johnson paid a highly publicized visit to the Ranch. Then in 1974, a newly elected, and grossly misguided, district attorney closed the Chicken Ranch down. It seems that it had been operating illegally since Texas passed a law against brothels in the 1870s, ignored by every level of authority, including a President of the United States.

And where did the ladies come from? The same places they have always, from everywhere, from the least significant to the most prominent circles. It is rumored—as dignified gentlemen never tell—that one of the ladies of the Chicken Ranch met a young lawyer from a prominent and wealthy family. They fell in love, married, raised a large family and, some twenty-five years later, she became the First Lady of Texas.

In Spring 1978, Walter decided the brothel business in Nevada needed organization, and a spokesman to represent the industry in political matters. By then there were thirty-six brothels in Nevada. Because they serviced hundreds of thousands of residents and tourists yearly, he was certain that collectively they would have enough financial and vote-getting support to stop at least unfair and unrealistic legislative action against them. And an organization such as the one he proposed could easily single out candidates who recognized the advantages in keeping prostitution legal, at least in Nye County, should the Nevada Legislature ever attempt to end legalized prostitution.

He implemented the first stages to form a Nevada Brothel Association. One early result was an invitation to speak at the Las Vegas Breakfast Club at a Las Vegas hotel. Included in the audience were a number of county and state politicians who seriously encouraged him. He began to call on other brothel owners with his idea.

One day in May, Walter and stepson Sam went to Beatty to talk with one of the owners about the association idea. On the way back, they stopped at the Shamrock Brothel in Lathrop Wells to see Bill Martin, its owner. They entered the small bar at the front of the brothel (the *Chicken Ranch* was the only legal brothel that could not get a liquor license, at least not until after Walter was gone). Martin was sitting at the bar, a slightly built man with a sharp face. Walter and Sam sat down a short distance from him and ordered drinks. When they were served, Walter asked the barmaid to ask her boss if he could have a word with him. She went to him and asked. He replied, loud enough so that everyone in the room could hear, that if Walter would leave Nye County, there would be peace again, and that he had nothing to discuss with him. Martin was apparently not a great candidate for the proposed association.

Earlier (March 1978), Walter had opened another brothel in Lincoln County. He named it the Desert Flower. The Mormon leader of the county decided to hold a countywide referendum on prostitution. On May 15, 1978, they closed all Lincoln County brothels—there were only two besides Walter's. The other two owners were convinced the only reason they were closed down was because he opened a brothel there. Two more votes against the association.

When Walter closed the Desert Flower, he moved the two doublewide trailers he purchased for it to the *Chicken Ranch*, knowing full well that Lincoln County's loss would be Nye County's gain. On Memorial Day, 1978, he took in twenty-five thousand dollars. He had finally made *the big time*.

About a week later he went into Las Vegas to work on organizing the "Brothel Association." At ten o'clock one morning he answered a knock at the door. When he opened it a man shoved a gun in his face and told Walter to come with him. Walter recognized only one thing: fear! Guns were foreign to his entire prior civilian lifestyle. The man placed the gun into his pocket but kept it pointed straight at Walter. He had seen this kind of thing in movies with Cagney and Bogie, but this was real, not up on a huge screen in a dark movie theatre. And the person it was pointed at was him.

They started down to the parking lot, which was usually empty midmorning. That day there must have been a dozen people milling around. It didn't take a genius to know this man was not planning to rob him. Walter was *going for a ride*; probably to the desert where the man would shoot, then plant him. Logic borne of terror suddenly hit him. He stopped walking, turned around to face him and said, "If you're going to kill me, you'll have to do it here and now, in front of all of these people, because I'm not taking another step." The man's look told Walter that he was so surprised he wasn't sure what to do. After a few seconds that felt like forever the man slowly took his hand out of his pocket, leaving the gun inside. He turned away from Walter and started to walk out of the complex at such a normal pace that Walter stood there, stunned. The man never said another word.

Walter counted on his not killing him in front of witnesses; he judged well. But he suddenly realized for the first time just how dangerous a business he was in. He made enemies of the Nye County machine, other brothel owners, and wasn't too popular with the pimps around town. To say he had the jitters for the rest of the day is clearly an understatement.

In the evening, he knew he had to try to get back to being normal so, very cautiously, he left the apartment to go to the store for a few things, one being an electric skillet. By the time he returned it was dark. As he entered the apartment he reached for the light switch. Something darted across the floor. His first impulse was that it was a mouse, or perhaps even a rat. But that was not reasonable. Then he knew. They —whoever they were—had found another way to kill him. There was a poisonous snake in his apartment. Slowly, in the still-darkened room, he crept toward the place where he saw it last, removing the skillet from its box as he moved. He knew it was under the couch. Barely breathing he tiptoed closer to it. When he knew he dare not go any closer even though he was wearing boots, he raised the skillet over his head, at the same time shoving the couch with his foot as hard as he could. There it was. He hit it with all of his strength, decapitating it. He was safe. He pushed the couch further, grabbed the two pieces, went out to the balcony and threw them into the bushes below. He was jubilant even as he shook uncontrollably with fear.

He went to the bar and poured himself a drink, something he never did alone. He downed it and poured another. While sipping the second drink, he went over and over in his mind how he would tell Terri about the incident earlier in the day and the snake in the apartment. He knew she'd be terrified. Terri was one of the many strays needing a temporary home who stayed in the apartment over the years. When she came in later that evening, he hesitated to say anything, trying to psyche himself up for the fear he knew she'd feel.

She popped over to him, kissed the top of his head and happily said hello. She started walking round and round the apartment. Walter knew he had to tell and her and asked her to sit down so he could talk to her. She kept moving around the room, then went into the bedroom, and back out again. She was a happy-go-lucky girl, although not the brightest, and was smiling from ear to ear. Walter dreaded seeing that smile turn into panic, but he knew she had to know for her own safety. He asked her again to come over to the couch and sit next to him. Instead, she said, "I can't find him anywhere. Walt, where is he? Walt, have you seen my little baby?" She was standing in front of Walter. His puzzled look prompted an answer without his having to ask the question. "My little snake."

Walter shuddered, then slowly felt the heat of anger creeping over him, starting at the very top of his head. He had not been in the apartment since he gave her the key a couple of weeks earlier. He had no idea a snake was living in his lovely apartment. When he arrived in the morning, it had not shown itself. He only saw it after the ordeal with his would-be assassin. There was no further discussion with the girl. Walter told her in short, decisive language to pack her things and get out of his home. She was gone in twenty minutes.

SEVENTEEN

Walter didn't often stay in his Las Vegas apartment overnight, but after all of the upsetting events of the day he didn't feel too well and knew he should rest, so he stayed in town. At least now he knew someone wanted him dead, real bad. He would not be surprised again. He tossed and turned for awhile before he fell into deep, exhausted sleep.

As if from a distance, a noise burst through his unconsciousness. The second, a shattering sound, seemed familiar. On its third ring, Walter reached for the phone, looking at the clock through half-opened eyes. Five o'clock. He couldn't identify the voice which brought him full awake as he waited to hear some kind of threat.

The garbled voice was shouting. Then Walter recognized "Dad." Surprised that he didn't recognize his own son's voice, he said, "Doug, is that you? Doug?" Walter finally understood what Doug was trying to say. "Dad, the Ranch is gone." Walter said, "What? What do you mean the Ranch is gone? What do you mean gone?" He heard every one of the next few words. "Someone just burned the Ranch to the ground."

Being jolted out of a deep sleep with this news paralyzed him. He could only listen as Doug, trying his best to calm himself down, talked.

"Someone knocked on the brothel door. When the maid answered it, a man knocked her down without saying a word. He walked past her crumpled body into the living room and sprinkled what smelled to her like gasoline all over the furniture and carpeting. As he backed out of the door, he threw a match into the room. She was terrified." Gasping as he spoke, Walter knew it was hard for Doug to go on. He said no one had been killed but there were some injuries. He was at one of the neighbors. Walter told him not to move, to wait there until he called him back.

Walter woke up his lawyer and told him what little he knew. The lawyer agreed to meet him at his office as fast as both of them could get there. Walter needed his help, but even more, his friendship. On the way there, he remembered that it was Sheri's off-week, so he stopped to tell her about the fire. She was horrified.

The lawyer was in his office by the time Walter arrived. He wasted no time. When he called the number Walter gave him he switched on the room speaker so that Walter could hear, too. Doug told them everything he knew and what the girls had told him.

Twelve girls, two maids, and Doug were in the compound. Soon after the last customer left, most of the girls were in bed. The maid on door duty was in the living room, cleaning. When she heard the knock she assumed it was a late customer, which was not unusual.

Suzie was in bed in that quiet place of nirvana close to sleep. A shriek ripped through the stillness of the house and invaded her peaceful state. Recognition of the terrified screams at the word "fire" made her blood run cold. For an instant, it felt as though someone was strangling her, then the choking dropped to her chest. The inertia lifted and she dove at her bedroom door. The doorknob scalded her hand as she forced it open against the power of the inferno outside. All she saw was a fireball she knew wanted to swallow her. She slammed the door, her heart pounding wildly in panic. She looked at the small window high on the wall. She was never able to remember what she used to knock the window out. She climbed up and started through it, head first, either unaware or not caring about the glass fragments on the edges of the pane. Her body was being ripped as she forced it through the window not large enough to accommodate even her tiny frame. The window was about eight feet from the ground, a long way to tumble for a small woman. But without hesitation, she allowed herself to drop to the ground. With an injured hip causing excruciating pain, she got up and limped away from the hellish threat as fast as she could.

Some girls were awake in their rooms. Kiki had just been paid because she was leaving the next morning for her off-week. She sat on her bed playfully counting out nine hundred dollars. When she heard the bloodcurdling scream of fire, she threw all of the suddenly irrelevant pieces of paper into the air and ran out of her room. Candy appeared. Hand-in-hand they went through the nearest outer door. But instead of running away from the raging holocaust, they dove under a burning trailer to hide.

Doug, still dressed, ran from his room between the fiery walls to an outside door. He only saw a few of the girls at first, but in seconds they all came tearing out of the already flame-engulfed trailers. The first ones out, either nude or in flimsy gowns, shuddered from the night cold of the desert. Doug was unconcerned with their comfort. All he could think of was the fuel tanks which would turn the entire area into a crematorium if ignited.

He quickly herded the hysterical girls toward the desert. He yelled at them to keep going, then went back to find the rest. He brought the second group to the first which was huddled around Suzie, who was obviously badly hurt. This time, he thought of counting them. Two were missing: Kiki and Candy.

His heart stopped. He didn't even want to think of the possibilities. The girls were stricken with horror, easily imagining their fate.

Without hesitation, Doug ran back toward the raging furnace, the roar almost deafening. He saw no signs of life, just flames shooting high into the air and toward him like arms wanting to enfold him in their bosoms. As he screamed the girls' names, he couldn't even hear his own voice. He heard only thunderous rolls of the holocaust which would easily defy Hollywood's finest theatrics. He later realized that had his instincts not kept him moving around, awe for the spectacle could have held him still, a certain sacrifice to the hellfire demon. He heard only the roar but never stopped shouting the names. He knew time was running out. Smoke was beginning to seep into his exhausted, pained lungs.

Still he kept screaming, "Kiki, Candy, answer me." He heard something but was certain it was his imagination. The strange sounds continued, and he turned toward where he thought they came. He saw the two girls crawling out from under trailers being consumed by flames. He ran to them, grabbed each one's hand and pulled them with as much brute force as he could draw from himself, almost dragging them as fast as he could run. A few yards away, they heard a ripping explosion. Still racing toward safety, they looked back to see the trailers they had just escaped collapse into a huge fireball.

When he knew they were safe, neither thinking nor caring if they were hurt, he started shouting at them for being so stupid. He grabbed the shivering, hysterical girls' hands again and dragged them toward the others. Reaching them, both girls were babbling incoherently.

They all stood huddled together freezing, crying, and whimpering, watching in disbelief the spectacle in front of them. Everything was gone, trailers, vehicles, everything. In only a few minutes, all fifteen people had survived a funeral pyre. They were alive, none burned badly, and only one with an injury that would heal in time. And by then, they knew that no one was waiting to shoot them.

Doug knew they desperately needed shelter and help. He started them walking, mostly nude and barefoot, over the desert road toward the closest neighbor a half-mile away. It was four in the morning. As they walked slowly and painfully, they felt the fear and horror of what they had just experienced.

Kiki and Candy chattered with cold as they tried to explain why they stayed under the burning trailer. The terrified girls were instantly certain someone had set fire to the Ranch, and that they had to hide because whoever did it was still out there with a shotgun waiting to pick them off as they tried to escape the inferno. Although they began to feel burns from small flames dropping on them, they were frozen with fear. Then they thought they heard their names through the roar. When they finally realized it was Doug, they crawled out.

Still in shock, everyone on that forced march to safety realized the horrifying death they had just escaped. They felt the numbing cold; their feet began to sting from small pebbles and the rough sand; they felt cramps in muscles rarely exercised by these people who normally walked nowhere. They were freezing and Suzie, whom they helped as best they could, was in severe pain. Doug had absolutely nothing to protect them from the frigid temperature. Although it was June 10, 1978, it was cold, as the desert always is at night no matter how hot the day. By the time they reached the house, a few were faint, their nerves and bodies ferociously battered. Some moaned in agony, others openly cried.

Doug pounded on the door. After a few minutes, the door opened and the neighbor stood in the doorway. As he was assessing the sight before him, Doug tried to explain what happened. He told them the girls needed the shelter of his house desperately. He explained that a couple of them were injured, one seriously, and all were freezing and dangerously close to collapse. While the girls, the maids, and Doug all looked pleadingly into the eyes of this good Mormon neighbor, in a voice they later described as icier than the cold they felt in their bodies, he answered. Looking only at Doug, he said, "I ain't helpin' a bunch of whores; get the hell off my property." With that, he slammed the door shut. They were horrified.

They later spoke of hearing of Nazi soldiers who showed more compassion for prisoners than this upstanding, law-abiding, religious man. The details of this incident were no secret in the community. Yet soon after, this same empty shell became a Bishop in the Mormon Church. While never having been a churchgoer, Walter later said he knew that most faiths only preach compassion, stating, "I cannot believe God dictated this kind of treachery, particularly in light of what we know about Mary Magdalene."

Doug had no alternative than to keep his little band of naked, exhausted, barefoot women up on their feet to herd them still another half-mile to the next closest home, the Koteckis'. Theirs would have been his first choice had the situation been less painful for the girls. Jerry Kotecki was a bear of a man with a heart as large as his huge frame. When Doug knocked on his door, it was a different matter. Fran (Jerry's wife, equally kind and generous) and Jerry quickly stuffed as many girls as would fit into their still warm bed. They pulled out everything they could think of to try to warm the girls and Doug, with no thought to the blood or dirt, or damaging blankets, sheets, pillows, clothes, furniture, etc. They just warmed, comforted, and fed them with hot liquids until the girls were relatively calm and beginning to feel safe. As soon as it seemed reasonable, they drove the scratched, burned, and injured girls into Las Vegas to be treated.

About a week later, an article appeared in the local newspaper about the man who turned Doug and the girls away from his door. To add to his brutality, he attacked the Koteckis as being "non-Christian" for allowing a bunch of prostitutes into his home. Walter's disbelief was beyond description. He said that he could only be certain that, "No real Christian will puzzle over which of these were God-loving and which were depraved."

As soon as the Koteckis assumed the care and protection of the girls half mad with fright, Doug finally began to calm down and function reasonably again himself. He phoned the sheriff, then Walter. After about an hour when neither the sheriff nor his deputies appeared, Doug recognized that the law didn't feel a bunch of whores were important enough to bother with, even though they were victims of a heinous crime. Nor was a fire meant to be their crematory important enough to investigate. When the ashes cooled and all involved began to recover from shock, they recognized that the sheriff, his staff, and their upstanding Mormon neighbor were all of the same ilk.

When Walter's lawyer called Doug later to get a progress report, he asked Doug if the sheriff had shown up yet, to which Doug answered no. He then phoned the sheriff himself. After few words, he knew with certainty that the sheriff had no intention of bothering about the fire, nor a bunch of whores. He called several of his own professional acquaintances. Walter, still sitting in his office, watched as the look of disbelief spread across his lawyer's face. He slowly accepted the reality he was being forced to swallow. With each conversation he learned more about the difference between Nye County law, obviously sanctioned by the State of Nevada, and the justice system practiced in the rest of the country. It became obvious help or attention would have to come from outside. He learned that day that even powerful Nevadans would not risk making an enemy of the judge/godfather who dominated his own tiny Kingdom of Nye.

The lawyer relentlessly searched for someone who cared about the attempted murder of fifteen people. No one wanted to go beyond the fact that these were only prostitutes, and they would be sticking their noses into Nye County power. No one seemed to care that the killers were free to strike again wherever and whenever they pleased. Most of those he called referred him back to Nye County law enforcement as if they didn't hear one word he said about Nye County. No amount of explanation overcame their fear of becoming involved. Finally, almost at a loss for who to turn to, he found someone at the FBI office who seemed concerned. That supervisor dispatched two agents to Pahrump, telling them to go quickly but to work cautiously.

Walter called Doug and told him to go back to the Ranch as fast as he could and make absolutely certain no one stole or disturbed any evidence until the two FBI agents arrived. The agents arrived at the scene soon after he did. They roped off the area since spectators were finally gathering. Apparently someone notified the sheriff that the FBI was at the Ranch. It was now about five hours after the fire. Doug later described the sheriff's arrival in detail.

"The sheriff's police car came roaring down the road at least one hundred miles an hour, sirens screaming, lights flashing. He slid into the area creating a huge cloud of dust as his brakes screeched. *Hi-O-Silver, Away!* He jumped out of his car as fast as he was ever capable of jumping, and waddled toward the roped area intending, obviously, to step right over the rope. As he lifted his huge leg, the agent in charge stepped right in front of him and ordered him to stay behind the rope barrier. The sheriff arrogantly informed the agent that this was his county and that he was there to take charge. The agent, in an uncompromising and authoritative voice, enlightened him fully saying, 'This is now the business of the FBI. Please return to your office and remain there until you are summoned because you, too, are under suspicion, Sheriff.' Visibly shaken by what the agent said, the sheriff obeyed. He sheepishly walked away, got into his car and quietly drove off."

When the sheriff was interviewed by the news media about his action—rather lack of action—he answered, "It happened in the middle of the desert. How can anyone expect arrests?" In reply to their questions about injuries as a result of the fire, his answer was almost unbelievable. He said, "There was a couple of dollies who got their asses scratched going out of windows." He said it in a tone that treated the fire as a big joke.

Walter called Doug at the Koteckis' later the day of the fire and asked if he had talked to the girls about what they thought they would do. Doug said he didn't think anyone had yet thought about it. Walter asked to speak to all of the girls. He explained to each girl that it could be dangerous and he would understand if they decided not to return, but that he intended to rebuild the Ranch as quickly as possible and start again. Walter told them all they were welcome. Each girl gave him the same kind of answer, "You rebuild and I'll be there." He also promised each one that he would not rest until those responsible were punished.

People who think that a bunch of prostitutes are no more important than yesterday's trash, including the hypocrite neighbor, the sheriff, and the rest of the Nye County Machine, could not possibly understand how those girls made him feel. Only those who accept that whores are still human beings with as much right to live as anyone could possibly comprehend his reaction to their loyalty. Only those who believe that everyone has personal rights will

156

understand that prostitutes also have the human right to determine their own lifestyles. Only that kind of person will also understand how deeply touched Walter was by all the girls' and maids' determination to spit in the face of danger and the evil creatures who thought nothing of roasting people alive.

When Walter asked Doug about the madam and her husband (who lived in the compound in one of the spare trailers), he said that in all of the confusion he hadn't thought about them. They should have been in the fire, too, but they weren't. He then remembered and related a series of events which suddenly took on new meaning.

About one o'clock that morning the madam received a phone call. When she hung up she told Doug that she and her husband were going into Las Vegas for groceries. Doug thought little of it because Las Vegas grocery stores are open twenty-four hours a day, and people at the Ranch lived primarily by night. They discovered later that shortly before the arsonists arrived, one of the girls saw Mignon and her husband loading their car with her furs and some boxes. The maids then said they saw her go into the office safe and remove some cash. They watched her count out twenty-four one hundred dollar bills. But when she returned cash to Walter, she only gave him five hundred dollars. When they were able to open the safe there was no cash at all. The day before there was fifteen thousand dollars in the safe. Only Mignon could have removed it.

When the shock really started wearing off, Walter and Doug began to realize other factors. They were at war again. It was quite clear that the arsonists expected Walter to be at the Ranch. He usually returned at night, so they planned to get rid of him too, especially when the kidnap attempt didn't work. Although common sense told Walter to give up and run like hell, all he wanted to do was dig in his heels even deeper. Yes, he would build again. He knew then that either he would win, or die!

He wasted no time. He told Doug to rent a bulldozer just as fast as he could and the FBI allowed, and clear away all of the rubble from the fire. He added that Doug should pile it up in one huge mound within sight of where it was burned. Walter did not want it hauled away. By ten o'clock the same morning, he was in a Las Vegas trailer showroom purchasing two new, double-wide trailers. They would be noticed to deliver the moment the FBI turned back control of the site and the charred skeleton was moved.

This was no small feat since by the time he went to that trailer showroom, everyone in Las Vegas knew all about the fire. No bank would touch financing trailers to replace those just torched. And what insurance company would ever give Walter a policy. The owner of the company took a chance and leased the trailers to him, and carried the insurance as leases. He accepted only two thousand dollars in cash as deposits on each trailer. He inflated the overall cost a bit, naturally, and Walter paid one thousand dollars a month on each trailer for the next thirty months. But on the Monday after Walter called for delivery, there they were: two brand new, double-wide trailers being hooked up to the water, septic tank, and electricity. Surprisingly, the power company quickly brought out two new poles and were there soon after they were called to replace the burned wires and hook up the electricity.

Even before the fire, Walter was experiencing more than usual chest pains, always his warning to avoid trouble or exertion. Doug took on all of the work and responsibility for rebuilding the Ranch, with Pete's help, who used every piece of equipment he owned, as well as himself. They all knew that every time Walter looked at the hideously twisted steel trailer frames it would upset him. But Walter also determined that the sight could not be eliminated, at least not for the moment. Not until those responsible paid for their crimes would it be removed. To Walter, it became a testimony to the unabashed tyranny of Nye County politicians and their personal laws.

Walter finally faced the fact that these people were determined to eliminate him—at any cost. He thought about it awhile and came to the conclusion that if he could get into the spotlight, it might give him at least a measure of protection.

The next day headlines across the country read things like "Masked Intruders Burn Chicken Ranch." Las Vegas papers carried editorials on the facts they knew, and that the *Good Old Boys of Nye County* held the scale of justice in one hand and a fire torch in the other. The publisher of one of the papers arranged a news conference for Walter. Although his paper was a relatively small gaming and show trade paper, it was circulated among tourists from around the world. Most radio and TV stations and all of the daily and weekly papers responded to his call. It was during this conference that Walter first used the phrase, "Tonopah Mafia." When the reporters asked the Tonopah D.A. about the title for the group he was obviously part of, his incredible and straight-faced response was, "Hell, I don't know what he's talking about, I'm not even Italian." This was the country bumpkin mentality of the district attorney of the third largest county in the United States.

Just five days after the fire, the *Chicken Ranch* held its "Grand Reopening." Walter was determined to make the most of the overwhelming publicity. They were back in business, and the eyes of the country, and the world, were on them. He hired a Mariachi band and notified the media.

At four o'clock on the afternoon of June 17, 1978, with newspaper cameras flashing and spectators cheering, they began the ceremony. Everyone walked over to the pile of rubble still there from the old Ranch. Walter had the trumpeter play *Taps*. Then together, they walked around to the front porch of the new Ranch to begin the dedication ceremony. Instead of the usual ribbon-cutting, Walter much preferred the prostitute inaugural tradition.

Sheri, being the first girl at the *Chicken Ranch*, was the only choice to carry out the rite. She wore a beautiful dress which flaunted her figure and added highlights to her lovely red hair. As she walked up the few steps to the porch with photographers' bulbs flashing all around her, Walter ceremoniously explained to the crowd who Sheri was. She turned and faced the audience, her devilish eyes dancing as the rest of her face spread into a wide, beautiful smile. Standing perfectly still, she waited until it became very quiet. Slowly and dramatically Sheri lifted her skirt, under which she wore nothing, and solemnly squatted, displaying all with poise and dignity. For several seconds, the only sounds heard were clicks of cameras and hissing of flashbulbs.

Just as the water began its stream from her stunning body, the band struck up, *Tis My Rancho Grande*. The New *Chicken Ranch* was officially open. That evening under desert stars, Walter's guests drank fifty gallons of beer, six gallons of wine, and two gallons of whiskey. And business inside? Never better!

EIGHTEEN

Before the fire there were six doublewide trailers. Now with only two, Walter couldn't possibly house the madam and her husband, who had miraculously reappeared acting distressed at their losses—except, of course, for the furs, jewelry, and other personal possession which they surreptitiously removed just hours before the fire.

Walter rented motel rooms in Pahrump for them. In light of what slowly became apparent, he was just as happy to have her and her drunken, lazy husband off his property. Mignon's husband talked tough, bragging about having once been a cat skinner, but all Walter ever saw him do was drink. Drunk or sober he strutted around like a peacock.

A couple of nights after the grand opening, Walter was in the kitchen of the new trailer. The *cat skinner* casually stumbled into the room, obviously very drunk. He started his typical grandstanding and belligerent gibberish. Walter watched him closely as he went about his business. Finally reaching his limit, Walter made some snide comment. The man took a swing at Walter but missed. As drunk as he was, he was easy to handle. Walter put a few knots on his head before he even knew what hit him. He staggered out of the room in a huff. Walter couldn't help but wonder how this would effect his wife's business relationship since she was still the madam, if only in name.

While Walter did not reduce the amount of pay they first agreed on, he now knew everything she did about brothels, and had already integrated his own business and marketing knowledge and experience. More importantly, he had long since assumed total command of the *Chicken Ranch*. She was no longer anything more than a maid except for her access to the safe. Walter knew she was bitter, but she never displayed her anger. She continued working after the confrontation with her husband without saying a word. But, she never again did any more than the very least she could get away with.

This woman, according to her own story, was the daughter of an extremely wealthy southern gentleman. She claimed she was raised a southern belle and carried the airs of one. She was undoubtedly well educated. In her youth, she chose to leave home to become a high-class call girl. She remained in the profession until she was too old to sell her body. That's when she turned madam. She was unfeeling and hard as nails. Even girls who had never met her before treated her like a surrogate mother, although all were terrified of her.

A couple of weeks after Walter's altercation with Mignon's husband, she walked into the brothel office announcing that she was going to Utah for a month. She didn't ask for the time off, nor did her tone indicate that the matter was open to discussion. She simply stated it as fact. Seizing this opportunity to rid the Ranch of the mean old hag, Walter told her that since they were just getting back to normal after the disaster, and that all the efforts of both of them was important to rebuild, it was not a decision he could accept. He told her that if she could simply walk out now, it would be a permanent vacation. Even as they talked, he began computing the balance of her salary. By the time their discussion was ended, the check was written. He handed it to her. She took it, turned on her heel, and left the room. Walter followed her. She went to her car and drove off the property for the last time. He breathed a deep sigh of relief. He felt they were all in a little less danger with her gone.

In rebuilding the Ranch, Walter took new and different precautions. They erected a chain link fence encircling the structures, with barbed wire at the top. An automatic gate opener within the entranceway restricted anyone they felt might be a threat to the girls, him, or the Ranch. He retrained the maids to be even more alert than their own new sense of caution dictated.

The property within the fence was his legal domain. He brazenly publicized that anyone coming to the *Chicken Ranch* who appeared suspect or threatening could easily get shot, legally. For a short time, he even brought in a pair of mean Dobermans, and hired an armed guard whose instructions were to shoot first and question later if there was the slightest impression that anyone at the Ranch might be in danger. He had tasted Nye County justice; if they wished to play rough or close their eyes to crimes against him or anyone at the Ranch, he would protect them himself. He soon determined the dogs and armed guards were also keeping customers away, so he removed them, adding them on and off at will.

In trucking Walter saw and was part of self-protecting situations that would shock the crustiest seamen. He never dreamed he would have to consider the same kinds of precautions following retirement.

For those snickering, asking what did he expect from a brothel as a career, his answer would have been that prostitution is legal in parts of Nevada, and that *taxes* are collected from the industry—substantial taxes! It is regulated and licensed—exactly like gambling. Prostitution, called the oldest profession in the world, has employed millions for centuries. And Walter asked, "Aren't men who *sell* their business integrity prostitutes?" His tone became deep and cold with rage when he unequivocally stated that "Women who control husbands with sex are all prostitutes, and all wives do it." "And aren't those who patronize bosses, teachers, each other, all engaging in some form of prostitution?"

If prostitution is truly objected to, then the users should be stopped. No prostitute can make a living without money from truck drivers, politicians, farmers, cops, dentists, athletes, janitors, military men; old men, young men, good men, bad men, and as everyone now knows, even some with backward collars. If pushed, everyone says, "I know the men are bad too," then go right back to talking only about the immoral prostitute.

Occasionally a john is arrested with the prostitute. Occasionally his name is publicized. Occasionally, meaning one-hundredth of one percent of the number of working girls who are picked up, thrown in jail and/or fined. Right behind condemnation of those prostitutes (who, in most counties in the State of Nevada—we keep reminding—are legal) come the pimps.

Pimps are the women's managers and promoters. Some are unspeakably cruel, an insult to the human race. But they are in it for the same reasons politicians run for office: money and power. Pimps, however, are not legal anywhere in the U.S. One thing that irritated Walter was that men who market prostitutes are called pimps, a word causing instant contempt, while a madam doing exactly the same thing is the object of romanticism. She's always presumed to be a once high-class call girl, never a street hooker. He considered it a glaring case of discrimination.

One thing that no one with a grain of intelligence can dispute: without customers the profession would have died long ago. Men keep paying so girls keep playing. Walter ran a legal brothel in Nye County; a clean, quiet, very private brothel. He broke no laws, nor did his girls. He competed with other brothels, except that he used smart marketing methods, no different than any other type of business. He advertised anywhere it was legal, exactly like politicians running for office, plumbers, fundraising charities, the gaming industry, boutiques, you get the idea.

Competition seemed to cause danger around the *Chicken Ranch*, however. There he was in a sleepy little western town in the late Twentieth Century, having to watch the hills for marauders. The people in this tiny kingdom of Nye were even more autonomous than others of the Nevada counties, which are already removed from the law of the land. The godfather-judge could bring in most of the county votes for the State's senators, governors, attorneys general, state legislators, and so forth. In turn, he acquired influence and wielded power throughout Nevada.

Walter's impression of Nye County when he arrived was that a good majority of residents had been born and raised there (truer then, less today), and so were ignorant of the controls imposed upon them. They knew nothing of law nor personal rights afforded by the Constitution. They had tunnel-vision such as he had never seen anywhere else.

The machine did not like its tactics questioned, its motives scrutinized. Pahrump's newspaper editor told Walter, "You don't have equal rights with us, we've been here all our lives. You have no rights of any kind." She was quite correct in her statement, at least according to the county power structure. What never stopped amazing Walter was that some of them were intelligent people who had to understand that diminishing the rights of others risked their own. Yet they allowed horrifying games to be played in that little western town. How sad for them all; how tragic for their children.

Agents from the FBI and the U.S. Attorney's office diligently gathered pertinent information on the fire. When it was in a well-ordered package, they presented it to the Federal Grand Jury in Las Vegas. But after a couple of months it just seemed to fade away. And just as Walter predicted, county law enforcement made no attempt to look into any aspect of the disaster. They justified it by stating that the FBI agent shooed their sheriff away when he attempted to do his job. It was repeatedly and in many ways made clear that in Nye County, arson was no criminal act when perpetrated on a cathouse which sheltered a bunch of whores. What seems inconceivable even now is that they didn't feel any need to camouflage their feelings that they didn't care in the least if everyone in that house was burned alive. They were proud of their callous, inhuman feelings, yet saw themselves as pure, law-abiding, God-loving Americans.

When the Grand Jury failed to return indictments, the investigation stopped. Walter hired a private detective, finally admitting it was the only way to get the evidence that might force action—any action—in this case.

Walter's attorney had introduced Gene to him previously when Gene had done some other work for the attorney. From Walter's own positive impression and his attorney's endorsement, he put Gene on the payroll with the utmost confidence. Imposing no deadline, Walter charged him with finding the men who torched the *Chicken Ranch*.

Gene knocked on every logical door in Nevada. But every lead went up a blind alley. Walter offered a twenty-five thousand dollars reward for information leading to the arrest and conviction of the fire bombers. Throughout that summer no one came forward.

During the same period Walter's *stay order* was running out. It looked more and more like he would go to Tonopah to serve his sixty days. The timing was bad. He didn't need more stress. And, he had a nagging concern about keeping everyone on the Ranch safe. It was more apparent than before that if he went to the Tonopah jail, he would leave on an undertaker's gurney.

In the midst of the turmoil, a young girl named Dolly came to work at the Ranch. She was a tall, beautiful blonde, different than the others he had known in this business (the same words Walter used again and again). He felt the chemistry between them from the moment he saw her. Every day, he felt himself falling harder and harder until one day he abandoned his own—on again-off again—policy not to become involved emotionally with employees. She quickly became his friend as well as lover. Little by little he learned more about her.

By fourteen, she was sexually involved with a boyfriend. Right after she turned sixteen, her parents pulled both of the teenagers into a counterfeiting scheme. They were caught and convicted. Dolly served eighteen months in a federal prison and was on parole. (Once again, the joke of the county's thorough checks on prostitutes hired for legal brothels.) Sometime during their relationship, she told Walter that she married the boyfriend when he left prison, but they were divorced. Walter was thrilled that her trust was growing so strong that she was unafraid to tell him the truth.

One day she went to him in tears. She had to go home to San José because her mother died. She had already made several trips back and forth because of her younger sister. She was trying to hold the family together until she could adopt the child herself. Walter did everything he could to help. He gave her time off whenever she asked.

Dolly and a cute little blonde named Sissy were close friends. When they went out, they often took Sissy with them, so Doug went too. They all enjoyed being together. On a skiing trip to Mammoth Lake, California, Doug broke his leg. The girls continued skiing while Walter took his son to a doctor. When they returned to the lodge, they went to the bar for a drink to help deaden his pain. Walter also thought Doug needed his dad's sympathy, so he drank, too. Walter vaguely remembered the three hundred-mile trip home, but clearly recalled the hangover the next morning.

Upon their return, Dolly told Walter she wanted to go back to school, so they discussed her moving into his condo in Las Vegas. They agreed she could not work at the Ranch if she lived with Walter. He made it clear that he would fulfill her every desire.

The following Sunday they all went to Las Vegas because Dolly insisted that they take Doug out for dinner. Walter thought her sweet to include Doug in their lives. She was leaving the next day to go home for a week, during which time Walter would move all of her things from the Ranch to his condo.

Her flight was eight-thirty on Monday morning. As Dolly and Walter were getting into his car to drive to the airport, Doug called to him from the condo with an urgent phone call; it was one of the maids at the Ranch. Walter ran up the stairs leaving Dolly in the car. The Ranch had just been robbed by three armed men. Understandably close to hysteria, she gave him all the details she could recall. One of the men called another "Randy." It hit Walter like a thunderbolt. Dolly's ex-husband's name was Randy. He listened, feeling his heart being battered once more as he never thought it could be by another woman.

They knocked on the door at three o'clock in the morning, when the girls were all in their rooms. As soon as the maid unlocked the door, they shoved it open and a gun was pushed into her face. The gunman told her to lie face down on the floor. She was paralyzed with fear, certain they were going to shoot her. Two of the men brought in cutting torches and a five-gallon can of water to fill the floor safe so they wouldn't ignite the money inside when they burned it open. One worked on the safe as another held the gun on the maid. The third man, Randy, went up the road as lookout. They communicated by walkie-talkies.

Walter had done the payroll on Sunday morning and put the cash into folders in a paper box, then into a locked closet. No one knew except Dolly who was with him at the time. They went straight to the closet, broke the lock, and cleaned out about fifteen thousand dollars in cash. They continued on the safe for over an hour. The one holding the gun on the maid kept telling the others they had been there too long. The man working the safe kept reminding him that there was fifty thousand in the safe. Making no progress, they finally gave up and left. They must have realized that the fifteen thousand was at risk if they stayed long enough to get caught.

Dolly had watched Walter put the fifty thousand dollars in the safe the previous week. What she didn't know was that he had removed it and taken it to the bank. There was only fourteen hundred dollars in the safe, along with some credit cards.

When Walter silently got back into the car, glaring at the girl, Dolly's only comment was, "Did anyone get hurt?" He answered, "Yes, an old fool I know has a broken heart." Those were the last words he said to her. They both knew she set up the armed robbery with her husband. They drove silently to the airport and just as silently she got out of the car.

Everything she told him eventually came out as lies. Her mother was quite alive and she was still married to Randy. Walter claimed that "The most bizarre part of the whole affair is that if she had asked me for the money, I probably would have given it to her. I was hooked." Anyone who knew Walter knew that was total nonsense. Walter would never hand any woman fifty thousand dollars just for asking. He was never that "hooked" in his entire life. He just had a side which loved theatrics.

Walter was in his attorney's office one day soon after when Doug called to tell them that the sheriff sent four deputies to the Ranch to pick Walter up. One of them was at the back entrance armed with a "high-powered rifle"; another stood at the front pointing a riot gun; the other two came to the door and knocked. When the maid opened it, the sergeant asked for Walter. She said he wasn't there. He told her he would search the house. She asked for a search warrant. The man pulled his gun out of its holster, stuck it up to her head, and cocked it. He said, "Bitch, this is my search warrant."

As the two men swept past her, her heart started pounding as she recalled what the maid on duty the night of the fire had described. She was terrified and went limp, certain she would faint. They opened doors without knocking, and started going through every single room, even those where customers were in beds with the girls. Girls started screaming with rage or crying in terror. Some of the angry ones later described the faces of the deputies. They said it was obvious that they were getting their jollies off by this armed invasion of a brothel. After tearing through the house, finally convinced Walter wasn't there, they left. Walter always believed that if he had been there that day, there would have been an accident that left him dead.

In addition to being familiar with the brothel business because of legal controls, many deputies took full advantage of *freebies* and/or liked to just hang around the Nye County cathouses. Consequently, they all knew that the maids were employees from their own town (they went to the same churches and grocery stores, their kids attended the same schools, their husbands hunted with them). Yet, those chosen by the sheriff terrorized those same helpless women without mercy.

Soon after the call from Doug, two FBI agents arrived at Walter's attorney's office and asked to see him. The agents told them they received a reliable tip that Walter was going to be killed, and that it would be smart for him to make himself scarce for awhile. Within two hours, he was in his car on the way to Arizona. On the road he called Doug, who told him not to worry because he would take care of the Ranch. It was a bad time in his life. He kept moving around, on the run, with no way of identifying who was after him. He admittedly developed paranoia.

His attorney told Walter he planned to appeal his sixty-day sentence to the Ninth Circuit Court of Appeals in San Francisco. But since it was an action unfamiliar to him, he felt it necessary to hire an experienced appeals lawyer. He recommended one he knew in California. Within a day, there was a new *stay order* from the federal court, again delaying the sentence pending

Walter's appeal. Once more, the D.A. could not put Walter into his jail. He returned to the Ranch but remained paranoid for a very long time. His gun was never out of reach, even when he was in the shower.

Walter's first meeting with Roger, the California appeals lawyer, made him feel better. Roger was divorced and very horny. He loved being at the Ranch and thoroughly enjoyed the sex. A friendship developed, so on all of Roger's trips to Las Vegas he stayed in the condo, between excursions out to the Ranch to work on the case, that is.

The detective was still looking for new evidence. One day they met at the lawyer's office. Gene was very excited. He had found something that looked like a lead. Two police officers from Modesto, California, were in Las Vegas investigating a murder case. When they finally picked up their suspect, they found evidence that linked him to the brothel fire in Nevada. They mentioned it to the local police who told them to contact Gene. They gave him all the details. They had also notified the Sheriff of Nye County. It surprised them when the sheriff stated it was impossible since they already arrested the man who torched the Ranch, and he had been in jail for six months.

Gene brought a picture of the suspect, Elbert Easley, to their next meeting. When Walter saw the picture, he recognized him as the man who forced him from the apartment at gunpoint just before the fire. Gene said Easley had been picked up in Modesto for stabbing a man and his wife to death with an ice pick. Roger sat silently for a moment then finally said, "You don't mean Elbert Lee Easley?" Gene said yes. Roger said, "Isn't that the damnedest coincidence I ever heard. I represented him in the arraignment of that case, but subsequently withdrew because he couldn't pay my fee. He now has a public defender."

Roger told the others what he knew about the Easley family. A few years earlier, Elbert's sister was convicted of murder and kidnapping in California. She had served three years of a life sentence when Roger appealed the case and got a reversal of the conviction. Ever since that, Roger walked on water in the family's eyes.

Roger got on the phone and called Easley's father and asked to see Elbert. Mr. Easley arranged with the Modesto police for both Roger and Gene to interview Elbert. Although Easley denied involvement in the *Chicken Ranch* fire, and the evidence appeared rather skimpy, they were all convinced he was involved. The police found a telegram from Bill Martin, owner of the Shamrock Brothel, that asked Elbert to come to Nevada to do a job for him.

Martin, a long-term policeman in the Bronx, had been tried for extortion and thrown off the force. He arrived in Las Vegas a short time later and went to work for the former owner of the Shamrock in Lathrop Wells. Six months later the brothel's owner ended up in the hospital beaten half to death with a baseball bat, afraid to even talk about it. When he left the hospital, Bill Martin was announced as half owner of the Shamrock. After six more months, the original owner disappeared. Relatives said he decided to go to Europe to visit family, but when he never returned the entire brothel somehow became Martin's. He also became one of the *Good Old Boys*. From what Walter was told and personal witness to several incidents, it was apparent that when they needed muscle, Martin was a good friend to have.

The Shamrock was close to Mercury, Nevada, one of our country's nuclear test sites. Between construction and test site workers, Martin did a real good business. It was also the closest brothel to Las Vegas. So over twenty years in business he made a lot of money and built a huge political power base.

Then Walter opened the *Chicken Ranch* forty-five miles closer to Las Vegas and its millions of yearly tourists. It quickly drew some of Martin's established, as well as potential, customers away from his brothel. In addition, as Walter implemented more and better marketing ideas to promote business, Martin obviously lost customers—to Walter.

Over the years, Martin and one of the sheriff's deputies became close friends so Martin could always count on backup from law enforcement. There were always rumors about Martin, the Shamrock, and anyone associated with them, from dope to murder. Everyone seemed to know that he supplied his girls with dope, then kept them in debt to him paying for it. The girls became virtual slaves. If they attempted to run away, he just called on the deputy friend to bring them back. One girl was so desperate she stole a car from the brothel and sped away. Within a few miles, someone rammed her car which flipped over several times, killing her.

The highway patrolman who investigated the case said there was not enough conclusive evidence to make an arrest, so he called it an accident. One of Nye County's enforcement officers tried to give the patrolman some money telling him that Martin was surely grateful for the way he handled the case. The officer reported the attempted bribe to his superior. So much pressure was put on him, he resigned from the highway patrol.

Martin was always surrounded by what appeared to be the criminal element. Walter later learned that the night of the fire there were six convicted felons living at the Shamrock. A virtual army of assassins.

NINETEEN

Being an astute businessman, Walter always recognized the advantage of free publicity; almost any kind. And he knew how to milk it. When he was asked to tape an interview with Tom Snyder for the *NBC Today Show*, twenty-three technicians converged on the *Chicken Ranch* to tape the show. It caused total chaos right there in the middle of the Ranch work day, but they sat in the living room while Walter was being interviewed. As customers came to the door, they were cautioned that a camera was taping so that they could decide whether they would risk being seen on national television. Some tripped over cables, but nothing seemed to deter them. The girls formed the lineup like any other day, and johns walked off with them to their rooms. Apparently, little can deter a brothel day. Walter was later told that the ratings were extremely good for the show. He was interviewed for other radio and TV talk shows. One Florida radio show was done by telephone, and he was told that their ratings went up, too.

The *Chicken Ranch*'s fame kept spreading. In the summer of 1978, it was a feature story in *High Society* and *Cheri* magazines. *Hustler* later carried a feature story. All of the free national and international publicity that Walter admitted he could never have afforded served to accelerate his income. Men from Nevada and its surrounding states constituted bread and butter, but the gambling tourists provided the cake and the frosting. There seemed to be no stopping the prosperity of the *Chicken Ranch*.

In the fall of 1978, the county machine wrote still another new ordinance to outlaw prostitution. Walter knew that the D.A. and commissioners were much too involved in the brothel operations to put Martin out of business, which would also cut off their own cash source. And, Walter suspected that if Martin ever believed they were serious, he would have blown the whistle, or worse, and the *Good Old Boys* knew it, too. Each time they wrote such ordinances, they were either voted down or their effective dates were extended some time into the distant future. Still, they grabbed at any straw to get rid of Walter.

This new attempt was to form unincorporated towns all around each of the other brothels, then declare prostitution illegal in the county itself. They must have realized that would have drawn too much outside attention and public officials. And of course, they knew Walter would see to it. They finally abandoned that idea.

Just before Christmas 1978, three new double-wide trailers were moved onto property which belonged to Sheri, just behind the Ranch. From the start, Walter had encouraged Sheri to invest in real estate, which she did (and eventually made lots of money because of it). Mignon leased the land from Sheri shortly after the fire but before she left the Ranch. Mignon would open her own brothel on that property, called The Filly Farm. Walter discovered that the investors were a disbarred attorney, a doctor whose license had been pulled in California, and Mignon. It also become evident that the D.A. and Martin were involved, as well.

The Filly Farm began advertising and constructed a large sign that covered Walter's to divert traffic to their operation. No matter what they did, however, the house was doomed to fail. It lacked the class and atmosphere of the *Chicken Ranch*. In February 1979, Walter and Doug planted an orchard on the twenty acres around the Ranch. They planted three thousand young peach trees.

Walter watched Mignon and the deputies who failed to respond to the fire developing quite a relationship. They were in the brothel all night, practically every night. One day, a young man called Walter saying he had been the handyman and his wife a prostitute for the Filly Farm. They had a falling out with Mignon. He told Walter he had information about something Mignon and the deputies were planning. He and his wife agreed to meet Walter to repeat all of the details before they left to return to Costa Rica. Walter arranged to meet them at a truck stop near Las Vegas. He called the FBI agent and state investigator who worked for the drug enforcement division.

The couple explained that the deputies and Mignon arranged to plant marijuana seeds around the trees in the new orchard, and when they grew enough to be recognizable, Walter would be arrested. The officers took their statements and the three men went back to the Ranch to look for the seeds. Just as described, they were planted around the trees. Since Walter had not yet irrigated the orchard, the seeds had not sprouted. They quickly and easily collected a coffee mug full. The couple also said that should this ploy fail, they planned to plant some form of drugs somewhere in or around the Ranch which, of course, would be found. Walter lived in fear of false arrest because he knew he didn't stand a chance against them. And the moment it happened, Mignon and the deputies would find a way to close down the Ranch.

Walter was certain the road to the Filly Ranch was on his land so he called in a surveyor. He was right. He went to his lawyer. Since Sheri's lessee had only used the land for six months, Walter could close the road and put up a no trespassing sign. As soon as he put the sign up, they tore it down. Walter asked the sheriff to come out to see him. He showed him the survey results and clearly explained that he had every right to close the road to trespassers. He also made sure he understood that his attorney was ready to start proceedings necessary to uphold the law which gave those rights. He went back into town and obviously consulted with the godfather-judge. He came back, but he went straight to the Filly Farm and stayed there for quite some time.

Within two days they were all gone. Only the trailers were left standing. Walter asked Sheri to sell him the land, which she was happy to do. She had been an innocent pawn in this newest ruse. As soon as the sale went through and Walter had it legally registered, he contacted those involved to get their trailers off his land. When he returned to the Ranch, he and Doug walked over there to look around. The trailer doors were wide open so they went inside. They were more than a little surprised to find boxes with cancelled checks and accounting records that belonged to Walter, all supposedly burned in the fire.

Summer of 1979 was election time for the sheriff and district attorney's offices. Walter had made friends with a rancher-miner in Beatty. Jim was in his early fifties, and six feet of wire and steel. He was an old-school westerner who thought if you wronged him and needed killing, he could take care of it. Yet, to his beautiful wife Effie he was one of the most loving, thoughtful husbands Walter ever met. He had a houseful of big capable boys at his ranch, *The Boiling Pot Outfit*, as it was called in Nye County. Jim and Walter felt the same about the county government, and felt that if they could find a decent, capable man to run the office of district attorney, it might just break the powerful machine and get some honesty into the government.

They put out the word in Las Vegas that they were looking for an honest lawyer to run for the office. One day Walter ran into a friend who knew just the man: a young lawyer who had just moved from San Diego but was not yet established. They met Rick, and were convinced he was the right choice. Jim and Walter filled him in on Nye County and told him they would support him all the way, including financially. All they wanted was for him to offer honest government. Rick signed up as a formal candidate and they began a powerful campaign to get him elected.

The office for sheriff was also being contested by a woman named Joni (pronounced Johnny) Wines. She appeared honest and capable, but Walter didn't feel she had a chance against the sheriff. The girls at the Ranch got interested and, since Wines was a woman, contributed about four hundred dollars to her campaign. That gave Wines gas money. She visited every household in Nye County. Later in the campaign, the girls convinced Walter to give her another four hundred dollars.

Meanwhile, Jim had a conversation with the sheriff who, Walter was certain, had a lock on the election. He was looking for contributions. After thinking about it awhile, Walter decided to kick in a couple thousand dollars. The only reason for the decision was that the sheriff told Jim that if Walter gave him that much, he would leave him alone after he was reelected. Walter thought it good business to hedge his bet. Jim liked the sheriff about as much as Walter did, but they both felt there was no choice if they wanted to stay alive and in business.

Much to their surprise, their candidate for district attorney was defeated by a few votes. The idiot with a quivering lip and character was still D.A. What surprised them even more was that Joni Wines was the new sheriff. She beat the old cowboy by a substantial margin. Walter felt that they had a better chance to survive, even though Wines made it clear that she didn't much like prostitution. Walter felt certain she would enforce the law, and the law said they were legal. Wines hired new, young officers who appeared more capable than the previous regime.

From the moment of the election, the rumor mill said that the *Good Old Boys* began their plans to get rid of her. It was not comfortable for them to lose such an enormous power base, and it was obvious long before she was elected that she would not succumb to their dictates. Smear campaigns sprang up everywhere to discredit her with those who had voted her into office. He only met her once and hardly spoke to her, but Walter heard she started firing deputies involved in activities against her policies. One of the smear campaigns said that she was controlled by Walter. That was one of their favorite ways to discredit anyone who didn't toe the line in Nye County.

Not long after Wines took office, Walter learned that she had started looking into the fire, hitting a real sore spot with the *Tonopah Mafia*. She was told not to concern herself with that alleged crime, but ignored their warnings.

TWENTY

By the summer of 1980, Gene, the investigator who worked tirelessly to find evidence, had found little. Then one day Walter received a subpoena to appear in a Salinas courtroom in Monterey County, California, as a witness in Elbert Easley's murder trial. The maid who answered the door and was knocked down the night of the fire was there, also subpoenaed by the prosecution, as well as two Nye County deputies. They swore that Lieutenant Henderson and Bill Martin told them they were going to burn the Ranch down. They ordered the deputies to go to the other side of the valley and not answer any calls regarding the Ranch that fateful night.

The evidence against Elbert and stories told about his exploits by police detectives convinced Walter of how good he was at his trade. He realized he should be extremely grateful for his own life since Elbert rarely screwed up his assignments as a killer. One story was about Elbert's involvement in cockfighting. It seems one of his earlier crimes was about a wager on a cockfight. A man lost one hundred fifty dollars to Elbert and refused to pay. Early one morning Elbert went to the man's house carrying a baseball bat. The man, who lived alone, began to argue with him about the debt. Elbert started hitting his head with the bat, and just continued pounding until he was dead under a kitchen table, where his brains literally fell out on the floor. Elbert then went calmly to the refrigerator and took out some ham and eggs. He prepared breakfast for himself and ate it on the table with the brains beneath it. When he finished eating he washed the dishes and cleaned up the mess. He placed the man's spilled brains into a paper bag, put the body into his car, drove out to the country, and dumped them into an irrigation ditch.

Later, in Bakersfield, California, Elbert married a Eurasian prostitute named Yoko. Yoko also acted as a pimp for several young prostitutes. The girls went into the fields around Delano, California, servicing as many as eight field hands a night at ten dollars each. Two of the girls owed Yoko some money and were not making any attempt to pay her. One day, she took Elbert to help her find the girls to collect her money. They finally located them in a shopping center in Bakersfield. Elbert and Yoko forced them into their car and drove out of town. They didn't have any money with them so Elbert made them get out of the car and get down on all fours walking around and barking like dogs. When he tired of the game, he shot them both in the head and left them laying in the field.

Shortly after the double murder, Yoko had an argument with Elbert. She went straight to the police and told them about the ruthless killings. The police put her into protective custody then sent her into hiding in Seattle. Elbert had done some time in the federal prison in McNeil Island in Washington, and knew a black man who owed him a favor. Somehow, he found out where Yoko was hiding. He hired his friend to kill her, for which the man was subsequently convicted. Elbert was free, however, since the police no longer had a witness to the killing of the two girls, and they had no other evidence pointing to him.

An earlier marriage had produced three children including a girl named Marty, who was in Elbert's custody, which no one could ever understand. He also had an eighteen-year-old girlfriend named Lori. Lori admitted to having another boyfriend, and Elbert was extremely jealous. He knew of a man named Schneider, convicted of a series of sex crimes in California, who was out on bond awaiting sentencing. Elbert called Schneider and asked if he would kill Lori. In payment, he offered him Marty, then only twelve.

A few days after the discussion Schneider showed up at Elbert's apartment. The two men sat down and had a drink, planning the murder and discussing the payment. Elbert told him that being it was his daughter, he should take her first. They agreed. Elbert took his daughter into the bedroom and raped her. When he was finished with her, he turned her over to Schneider who violated the child in every grotesque way imaginable. After an hour or so, Marty was completely hysterical and tried to fight him off. That so infuriated the monster that he grabbed a filled 7-Up bottle and bashed the girl's head in. It took several days for her to finally die. Schneider was convicted. As Walter learned about some of these unbelievable stories, he began to realize how insignificant life was to men like this who commit unspeakable crimes, yet continue to walk the streets among unsuspecting people.

Much earlier (in the spring of 1978), Elbert had gotten a call from Jack Tatum, another old prison buddy on parole from McNeil Island. He told Elbert he was working for Bill Martin at the Shamrock Brothel in Nevada, and that Martin had a job for them. Elbert needed a viable excuse to give to his parole officer so that he could leave California without becoming a fugitive. Martin sent Easley a telegram asking him to come to Nevada where he had a job for him, satisfying the parole officer. He stayed around the Shamrock doing odd jobs, waiting for the right time to murder Walter and burn down his brothel.

A day or two after he went back to California, he showed Lori the cash he made in Nevada. He told her he got it from Bill Martin for burning down a whorehouse called the *Chicken Ranch* in Nevada. Lori later testified to that at his trial.

About six months after the fire, Elbert was in Fresno with his cousins, the Davis Brothers, when his sister's boyfriend, Westmorland, contacted him about a job. They told him a man named Pinka needed his partner in an insulation company killed, and Pinka would pay Elbert four thousand dollars for the job. Pinka had already agreed to pay twelve thousand dollars, but the Davis Brothers and Westmorland were keeping the difference as a broker's fee. Pinka and his partner, a young German engineer named Johann, had a serious dispute. Johann was industrious and Pinka was a playboy. Johann gained the confidence of the other stockholders in the company and was about to have Pinka thrown out of the firm. A man in his early fifties, Pinka saw his world about to crumble. He looked for someone to murder Johann. Elbert accepted. Told that Johann had a young pretty wife, he just arbitrarily decided to kill them both in their home.

Elbert went to hardware store where he bought two rubber balls and an ice pick. He learned in prison that an ice pick leaves very little external blood, instead causing the victim to bleed to death internally. He borrowed a shotgun from his cousin. Later, he picked Lori up and they drove out of town until they came to a cattle feed lot. He got out of the car and walked over to some stacked bales of hay. With a wire cutter, he cut several lengths of wire from the bales. He had all the tools needed.

When they returned, he cased the house situated in the middle of a quiet, tree-lined street. The job would have to be done on the weekend since he was still restricted to a halfway house in Fresno, and could only get away at night with an occasional weekend pass.

It was November 1978. At about seven o'clock, the couple was getting ready to go out for dinner. Elbert knocked on the door. When the young German innocently opened the door, Elbert stuck the shotgun in his face and pushed him back into the house. When his young wife walked into the living room, Elbert shoved her against the wall and told her not to move or he would blast both of them. He tied Johann up with the baling wire then put the small rubber ball into his mouth. He tied the young woman's hands behind her back with the baling wire and put a ball into her mouth. She tried to run to the back door to escape. Elbert caught her in the kitchen where he threw her on the floor, pulled down her pantyhose, and raped her. When he was done with her, he stabbed her fifty-two times with the ice pick.

Elbert knew Johann would have the company payroll at home. He tried to get Johann, who didn't know his wife was already dead, to tell him where he hid the money. He stuck the ice pick through Johann's eyelids, ears, face, and his testicles and penis when he wouldn't tell him where the money was. Elbert then stabbed the man fifty-seven more times. He left the house and drove to a hamburger stand about five minutes away. From there he called his cousins to tell them the job was done and to bring his money. While he waited, he " . . . sat down and enjoyed a hamburger, french fries, and a malt."

At the trial for this gruesome killing the defense, attempting to illustrate what a nice person Elbert was, his defense explained that he took two hundred seventy-five dollars of the four thousand dollars received for killing the young couple and bought a headstone for his raped and tortured daughter's grave .

The jury in Monterey found him guilty of the couple's murders. But under California law, to get a death penalty, the prosecution had to prove that Elbert was involved in other crimes of violence. The prosecutor was sure he could prove Elbert was involved in the *Chicken Ranch* fire during the penalty hearing. He put several investigators on the case. He called Walter to the stand and asked him to explain his problems in Nye County to the jury. It was his first opportunity to tell, under oath, about the D.A.'s attempt to extort money from him to operate a brothel there.

As Walter looked at Elbert while he spoke, he could see this was a man without a soul. He also saw his parents' faces. The family originated from the Cookson Hills of Oklahoma, home to a few other notorious criminals including *Pretty Boy Floyd*.

A gray-haired lady he knew to be the current Sheriff of Nye County was seated in the courtroom as well. She was there with her husband and the two young subpoenaed deputies . Walter could not guess that his testimony would enflame her sense of justice to the point that she would begin an investigation, in earnest, as soon as she returned home. Sheriff Wines was determined to find and bring to justice those responsible for the most heinous crime committed in the county in the past one hundred years.

One of the Nye County deputies was called to the stand. The prosecution asked him about the interrogation methods used in Nye County. He used a story to explain.

He and another deputy suspected a man of selling a controlled substance so they decided to do some undercover work. After setting up a deal with the suspect, they went to a local casino and borrowed five hundred dollars to make the buy. The deal went through as planned, but when they analyzed their purchase, it was aspirin. A couple days later they saw the suspect and picked him up. They took him to the old Johnnie Mine where they threw a lariat to create a pulley on the old head frame over the shaft. They tied it around the man's ankles and hung him upside-down over the six hundred-foot deep shaft. The sergeant tied the rope to a post. As he started to question the suspect, he whittled away at the rope with his knife.

Just then the judge asked, "Deputy, did you read the man his rights?" "Oh yes, Your Honor, we read him his rights just before we told him that the sergeant had to keep whittling on the rope until he told us what we wanted to know." This caused a wave of laughter in the room until the judge hammered his gavel and told the witness to continue his story.

It sounded like a horror story someone made up from the Nineteenth Century American West days. It was also reminiscent of the torture stories perpetrated by the Ku Klux Klan in the old south. But it was neither of these. This was a description of how law enforcement was handled in the late Twentieth Century in a county in the middle of the State of Nevada, U.S.A.

Finally Barbara, the maid on duty the night of the fire, was sworn in. When asked, she related everything she knew about the fire, including seeing Elbert that night at the Ranch with the man who pushed her down to the floor and lit the match.

The jury was out for a very short time before they returned with a death penalty decision for the murders Elbert had so brutally committed. The hearing also clearly proved he was guilty of torching the *Chicken Ranch*.

Walter observed Elbert's mother's face as she walked from the courtroom. She sat down on a bench in the hallway and he quietly sat down beside her. Walter told her that if there was a chance to save Elbert's life, he would need the best appeals lawyer available. He told her that he wanted Elbert to tell the truth about the fire and to tell him who else was involved. He made it clear to her that if Elbert did that, Walter would pay Roger to handle the appeal. He knew, instinctively, before he left the woman that she would deal.

Walter returned to Las Vegas. As he left the plane two Las Vegas police officers were waiting for him. They said that someone was going to try to kill him. The paranoia returned. He didn't sleep even with an officer in his living room sitting on the couch with a shotgun on the cocktail table in front of him. After about ten days, the police withdrew their protection. A few nights later, ten o'clock at night, the security guard in the complex, who had been alerted, came to the apartment door and said he thought someone had been in Walter's car because he saw the dome light on and the passenger door open. Walter told him not to touch anything and called the police. They found a bomb wired to the driver's door powerful enough to level a city block, an exaggeration, perhaps, but the bomb was real. It took them most of the night to disarm it. It was then that Walter began to feel he had an angel on his shoulder. It was not yet his time. Maybe there was something more for him to do.

Early one Saturday morning Roger called. Easley accepted the deal to give information on the fire. They arranged to meet with Easley on the next Saturday, where Gene, the investigator, would also be present. Walter phoned Sheriff Wines, who said she would send two of her trusted deputies to Modesto to attend that meeting.

Walter decided it best not to attend the meeting. The week was long, but the hours during the meeting were agonizing. Walter hardly moved away from the telephone. Finally at about four in the afternoon it rang. Roger was calling from a phone booth just outside the prison.

He said, "We just finished talking with Elbert. He signed an eight-page written confession giving us the names, dates, and all the details he knew surrounding the fire. He's now talking to the deputies on tape. They should have a real story when he finishes." He told Walter that all of the information was great, but now they had to somehow corroborate the story. Once that was done, they would have to find someone to prosecute them since it was unlikely it could ever be done in Nye County. If they allowed it to be done there, they knew there would never be convictions. Roger sent the detective back with a copy of the confession, and said he would meet with them in the Las Vegas attorney's office.

They were all in the office on Monday morning, including Sheriff Wines and her two deputies. It was mutually agreed that the evidence should go to the FBI and the U.S. Attorney's office. An extremely capable Assistant U.S. Attorney was assigned to the case. He worked tirelessly to pull the case together since there seemed very little federal jurisdiction in the matter. He soon recognized, however, that if the federal government did not prosecute, no one ever intended to do anything about it in the county or the state. It was certain that all of those protectors of the people would happily allow the criminals to continue living and working in their county, and go unpunished; anything to rid themselves of a brothel owner who wouldn't share with them.

The FBI set about finding corroboration for Elbert's confession, and subsequently brought him back to Nevada to retrace the steps that he, Jack Tatum, and Kenneth Kolojay (manager of the Shamrock Brothel) had taken the night they burned down the *Chicken Ranch*. Slowly, everything began to fall into place.

With evidence now in hand, Assistant U.S. Attorney Leavitt presented his case to the Grand Jury. Mignon Clayson was brought into the Grand Jury. Walter was later told that a few days after her testimony, the FBI gave her a lie detector test which indicated that she lied about almost everything, including her name. She was never indicted for anything. About six months later, she went to work for the Shamrock as the Madam. She stayed there until her health forced her to retire. Walter never stopped believing that she was directly involved in the fire.

When all of the people and evidence were heard by the Grand Jury, they brought back indictments of perjury, firebombing, and conspiracy against Martin, Kolojay, Tatum, and Sergeant Henderson. The FBI agents went to Nye County and arrested all of them.

When they appeared before Judge Roger Foley, who set bail at forty thousand dollars, Martin very calmly took out a stack of bills from a brown shopping bag which he had carried into the hearing and counted out forty thousand dollars. Kolojay's was set at fifty thousand dollars. Within a few days, his family came in with it. Tatum's bail was also fifty thousand dollars but he had no way of raising it. He threatened to talk so Martin's lawyer, in conjunction with the public defender, got the judge to reduce his bond to thirty thousand dollars, which Martin promptly posted.

Both Nye County and Las Vegas newspapers carried stories on the arrests and indictments. When the newspapers went directly to Judge Beko and asked his opinion, he told them he would never believe that Henderson and Martin were guilty, "even if they were convicted." People openly discussed how irresponsible and reprehensible the Judge's statement was, considering his position as a District Judge. What made it even more absurd was that he was not privy to any of the evidence presented to the Federal Grand Jury which issued the indictments. His well-known form of Nevada justice was his only law, even allowing murderers to go back on the streets to potentially kill again.

This was shortly before Christmas 1979. Knowing there might finally be some justice, Walter threw a big Christmas celebration at the Ranch. They had a huge, festive dinner and exchanged lots of gifts. It was the first real Christmas some of the girls at the Ranch ever experienced.

In January 1980, Walter decided to build an airstrip so customers could be flown in, day or night. Doug handled most of the project because it had been his trade. When it was finished, a twin engine could easily land and taxi almost up to the front door of the brothel. Walter knew it would be good business since it took about an hour by car. Walter started shopping for a plane and finally settled on a new Cessna which carried eight passengers. A man named Billy became his pilot, and eventually a good friend. He was exactly what Walter needed: one-third pilot and two-thirds salesman.

The plane was in service no more than a week when the *Las Vegas Review Journal* did just a small story on it. After all, it was the only flight in

179

the entire world which took passengers directly to the door of a whorehouse. Dame Fortune once again smiled on Walter Plankinton when the wire services picked it up, ending up in eleven hundred newspapers around the world. The publicity turned the aircraft into an instant, smashing success. Billy flew as many as seven trips a night between Las Vegas and the Ranch. While the *Chicken Ranch*'s pilot, he made over four thousand landings and takeoffs on the Ranch strip. It became the most popular aircraft to McCarran Airport personnel. The tower became so familiar with the craft they often saved time and expense by giving Billy the best approaches in and out of the field. The flight took about twelve minutes each way. While generating lots of money, the plane proved to be an expensive toy. But it brought a lot of what Walter perceived as class to the *Chicken Ranch*. The flight was taken by many who would otherwise not have considered a visit to the Ranch because of the time spent driving there and back. It proved to Walter that the biggest difference between men and boys are, indeed, the price of their toys.

Spring 1980 was a very busy time. The *Chicken Ranch* employed up to fifteen girls, available around the clock. Because of great press, it became the most famous whorehouse in the world. It got so easy to get girls for the Ranch, Walter received resumes in the mail from around the U.S. Word was out about how well he treated and paid his girls.

In May, several people in the Pahrump Valley asked Walter to run for County Commission again. After serious thought, he decided to do it, even though he felt a brothel owner had little chance of winning. He put a lot of effort into the campaign. When the primary was held, he came in second in the county as well as in the Pahrump Valley. That was a big, big surprise.

When the stage production of *The Best Little Whorehouse in Texas* appeared in Reno, star of the show June Terry invited Walter to see it. At that performance, he learned that the show was going next to Las Vegas. As soon as the opening performance date was announced for September 1981, Walter called for eighteen reservations for himself and his girls. The hotel was a little skeptical about it, but sold him the tickets. The media was alerted, of course, and Walter had earlier arranged to have four dozen long-stemmed red roses delivered just before the show to June Terry with a note that said, "If you want to see the 'real cast' of the *Chicken Ranch*, during the last show tonight we'll be there."

He had his pilot fly everyone into Las Vegas in shifts, and had limousines ready at the airport. They formed a caravan down the *Strip*. As they left their limos, cameras flashed wildly. The hotel's owner was there with his publicity man shouting, "No pictures, no pictures." Their panic was understandable considering a pimp was appearing with almost twenty known prostitutes in

180

a town that swears they are illegal. Walter assured him there would be no problems since they were there only to see the show. They walked through a human corridor of spectators with security men surrounding the group of women bedecked in furs and jewels, accompanied by their very showy, also diamond-bedecked pimp. As the gaudy group entered, silence fell over the garish showroom—a rather unusual occurrence. Walter always believed it was because he and his girls were such a gorgeous picture; nothing could ever convince him that it was because it looked like a pimp and his whores converging on a showroom. He swore that from all sides he heard *Chicken Ranch* being whispered, but that is highly questionable since Las Vegas hotel showrooms are never exclusively filled with locals, and most tourists would have known little or nothing about them since they don't go to Las Vegas to read their newspapers or watch television.

As the lights dimmed, June Terry came out on stage and announced that Walt and the girls from the current *Chicken Ranch* in Pahrump were in the audience, and because of it the cast was going to give its best performance. The house lights went back up and they were given a round of applause. At the end of the show, the maitre'd went to Walter and asked him to stay until after the audience was gone. They were surprised when the doors of the showroom were locked, and servers came out with champagne, followed by the show's entire cast and crew, which joined them for a private party. Walter, of course, insisted that his girls were perfectly gracious ladies, and that the cast's actresses seemed like the real whores. It's doubtful that anyone at that party other than Walter and his girls would agree with his characterization. The party lasted until dawn, when limos returned them to the airport for their short flight back to Pahrump. If anyone might question Walter's willingness to forfeit all of the money lost during that evening, don't be confused. Since twelve prostitutes were always in residence, that meant there were more employed so as to cover the off-weeks. Consequently, the Ranch was not closed down that night. However skeleton, there was a crew at the *Chicken Ranch* that night.

In the general election that November, legal prostitution was again on the ballot. Walter knew there was at least a chance that the citizens of Nye County would vote to close down the brothels, but was again surprised by the outcome. Seven out of ten voters chose to continue the legal houses of prostitution.

All during this period of politicians decrying prostitution, Walter went over some of the hypocrisy which men live by. In the State of Nevada, County of Nye specifically, an eighteen-year-old cannot legally drink or gamble, or serve liquor in a bar, or work in any place around gaming. But, an eighteen-

181

year-old girl can be legally licensed as a prostitute. Any man who wishes to go to a brothel can enter the room of any eighteen-year-old prostitute, remove his clothing, watch her remove hers, and do just about anything he wishes to do on or with her or his body. He may put his penis into her mouth, her vagina, her anus. He may simply tell her to use her tongue to suck, lick, or enter his mouth, penis, or anus, all within the law. But if he buys her a drink in the same county, he can be arrested. Those men who do this each and every day are not all the dregs of society because those men cannot usually afford a brothel. The dregs use streetwalkers who are unlicensed, may be as young as twelve, are controlled, directly or indirectly by organized crime, and well known by the police. Men of at least some means use brothels.

Walter frequented every other brothel in Nye County, as well as all of those in the adjoining counties, extensively, before he opened his own. As he learned more about the politics of the county and recognized the faces of its residents, he was astonished by how many of the men he had personally seen in brothels, and knew about through others, were the same men who cried out against prostitution, alcohol, drugs, gambling. Some were lawmakers, elders of churches, pious, righteous husbands who demanded—and got—strict obedience and *respect* from their wives, children, neighbors, employees, and co-workers. He wondered how those men were able to look into the eyes of their children, their mothers, their spouses, or mirrors, and justify their hypocrisy. They were out whoring in the night, but when the sun came up they were loving fathers, sons, leaders, honored men. Walter firmly believed that he never pretended to be something he was not. His family and friends always knew exactly who he was and what he was doing.

TWENTY-ONE

When asked about being involved with any of his girls, Walter almost consistently said no, or only once. Yet, he told story after story about different girls he had "lived with at the apartment." After awhile, one recognized that Walter's truth didn't always match all of the facts. If something was provable, you could be fairly certain of his honesty; but if it was hard or impossible to prove, he cared little for what the truth meant. Of course, his form of honesty is well understood in political and business arenas around the world: call it "selective truth."

In the summer of 1980, Walter started living with a little blonde named Lauri. He described her as a bubbly, highly intelligent girl who helped him with publicity. Any time Walter was smitten with a girl, which was often, she suddenly acquired about a thirty point increase in IQ. To her credit, Lauri did get an article written about the *Chicken Ranch* in *Cosmopolitan Magazine*, which meant national publicity. She worked hard at her full-time job as a prostitute at the Ranch, and saved her money. Once again, Walter was involved with one of his girls while she continued working at the Ranch. Lauri was from the East Coast, and had been a successful prostitute there. Shortly after she arrived in Las Vegas, she met a young man who claimed to be the nephew of a noted syndicate boss, although everyone who met him doubted it. He played the role of a tough little *wise guy* and was a genuine low-life.

When she married him, she was in a reasonably good financial state, driving a paid-for *Lincoln Continental*. Just one week after they married, the imitation *wise guy* insisted they needed more money and put her into the *Chicken Ranch* to work. After her first three weeks, she had a hatfull of money and went happily home to her waiting new husband. What she found was that he had sold her car and all of her furniture, which he had gambled all away. He beat her up, took the money she had just earned, and went right back to a casino to gamble it away.

Lauri went back to the Ranch so bruised and beaten that she couldn't work for awhile. Walter convinced her she didn't need an ex-con, gambler husband who had illusions of being a big-time mobster when he was nothing more than a lazy pimp. Walter took Lauri to his lawyer who got her a quick divorce. The ex-husband kept calling her but she finally convinced him he wasn't going to get any more of her money.

Lauri never wanted to be a prostitute. She always wanted a bar because she felt she would do well in business. She asked Walter to be her partner. They found a neighborhood bar in Las Vegas and decided to buy it. They submitted an application to Clark County for a business license. However, a problem was growing. Lauri was jealous of every minute Walter was not in her sight. She assumed he kept sleeping with all the girls, and it soon became tiresome to Walter.

After about two months of applications, discussions, and waiting, Walter hauled a truckload of records into the sheriff's office for them to investigate his background. Soon thereafter, he received a summons to appear in court. He was being charged with a State of Nevada law prohibiting a brothel from advertising in Clark County, since prostitution was supposedly illegal there. It didn't take long to find out what happened.

Previously, Walter hired a distributing company to send brothel brochures to California, Oregon, and Utah. In billing him, they inadvertently added Nevada. He could only conclude that the typist assumed it was also for Nevada since the invoice was being mailed there. Walter was arrested. He eventually believed that the investigator assigned to his license application was a friend of the Nye County D.A. After all, the population of the entire State of Nevada was just over eight hundred thousand at the time, and county authorities were small and knew each other. They knew if Walter was convicted of the charge, he would be in violation of his brothel license in Nye County, making it simple to get the brothel license revoked. The distributor was intimidated by county officials and signed a statement that Walter paid him to advertise in Clark County. It wasn't too difficult since he, too, had a license he wished to protect in Clark County. Walter was sure they had finally found the crack to pour him through.

His lawyer dove into the case. It smacked of collusion and he went to meet the president of the distributing company. After much discussion, he finally convinced the man that since he had done nothing wrong, his license could not possibly be revoked. He made him realize that it would be best if he told the entire truth about the case. There can be little doubt that the attorney scared him even more than the county representatives. The man went back into court and told the truth. As a result, nothing ever came of their bogus case. But it did serve to cause Walter to finally face some hard, cold facts. The Nye County machine would never give up on him, and that their arms reached well into Clark County, and all of Nevada.

Shortly after the court incident was resolved, the owner of the bar Walter and Lauri were to rent refused to give them a lease. He told Walter, "You've had one business burned down, a whorehouse. I don't want my property burned." Lauri and Walter gave up on it and finally went their separate ways. Walter later hired Lauri to run a bar he bought in Arizona, giving her a salary plus a bonus percentage of the business. He also bought a house to stay in whenever he was in Arizona. He did not know that Lauri had started up with her ex-husband again, and became pregnant. The ex decided to move to Arizona. At that point, Walter told her he wasn't going to be involved in their problem again, and sold the business and the house. Walter tried to relate this story rather glibly, but with some questioning, it became very obvious that he was serious about Lauri and twice thought he would end up married to her, or at least living with her long-term. His disappointment was again profound.

Throughout 1980, several articles were written about the "Nye County Brothel War." Walter was constantly in the limelight, which he thoroughly enjoyed. The *Good Old Boys* were not given good press, however, and were not too happy about it. Normally, if a skeleton happened to pop out of one of their closets, they just swept it away. This new publicity changed that. Walter stood in their way and it became a collective obsession to get rid of him.

Finally in November, Bill Martin, Kenneth Kolojay, and James Luther Tatum went to trial in the U.S. District Court in Las Vegas for firebombing as well as perjury. The Assistant U.S. District Attorney explained that they might lack jurisdiction in federal court, but assured Walter that he would not give up until a decision was made. He was a meticulous prosecutor. Quiet in demeanor and sure of his facts, he began weaving a web of truths around the defendants. He showed the jury that they were quite guilty.

Bill Martin sat in the courtroom for seven weeks sneering at the jury as he sucked on one Lifesaver after another. His face showed the contempt he held for everyone there. He had amassed a great deal of power in Nevada and acted as if he was disgusted with those who dared challenge him. Agent Bailey of the FBI assisted Leavitt and was obviously good at his job. He helped present facts the FBI had put together. Walter was the first witness called to the stand.

As he walked up, he felt a rush of pleasure knowing he would finally be able to tell his story to the right people in the right place. Walter explained about going to Nye County and being asked for seventy thousand dollars to be permitted to open a brothel and five percent off the top monthly. He talked about the D.A., the sheriff, and the county government, and explained their indifference after the fire. He related how it became necessary to appeal to federal authorities when he discovered that no one in the State of Nevada would even listen, and the apathy he met on all governmental levels. He even included his offer to Easley's mother regarding paying for Elbert's admission of the fire.

When Walter finished his testimony for the prosecution, he was excused from the courtroom since he could also conceivably be called by the defense.

Elbert Easley followed Walter. He explained every detail of the plans and implementation of the brothel fire, and the various failed attempts on Walter's life. He described how Tatum called him to go to work for Martin in Lathrop Wells and about the telegram Martin sent so that he could leave the jurisdiction of his parole.

Elbert never destroyed the telegram because it was his excuse for leaving Fresno. It was what led the Modesto police to expose his other crimes of violence which, in turn, would help them to get the death penalty for his crimes in California. Together they planned the fire and were sure Walter Plankinton would die in it. They decided that Easley, Tatum, and Kolojay would handle the arson together.

Kolojay borrowed a Chrysler from a friend in Las Vegas to make the one hundred-mile round trip between the Shamrock and the Chicken Ranch. Tatum and Kolojay found a couple cans of gasoline and kerosene-based liquid dish soap to devise an explosive fluid to guarantee a massive fire. Elbert and Tatum drove to the Ranch a couple of days before to case it and discussed several different methods they might use to burn it down.

They thought about going into the Ranch as customers with douche bags filled with gasoline under their coats, then taking them into the bathrooms to set the fires. Had they used that method, customers might have perished. In the end, they decided all three men would enter the Ranch early in the morning when fewer customers were likely to be there. Kolojay and Tatum knew the layout well so they decided Easley should drive the car and they would do the job. Kolojay would carry a rifle. Alibis were already established at the Shamrock. They were fixing a broken water pipe at two-thirty on the morning of June 10, 1978.

They stopped at Martin's house to tell him they were on their way to burn down the Ranch. Martin, jumping up and down with delight, shouted, "Burn the son of a bitch down to the ground with Plankinton in it." Easley went on:

We left the Shamrock Brothel. About two miles from the Ranch, we stopped to mix the gas, coal oil, and dish soap until it was the right consistency. Kolojay poured some on the gravel road and lit it to see how it burned. When we were satisfied with the mix, we got back into the car and went on to the Ranch. We arrived in the front yard a few minutes after four o'clock.

The maids just changed shifts and most of the girls were in bed. The maid on duty had worked on the Ranch only about one week. She was in her early sixties, a petite, grandmotherly type. The early-up girl was Maria, a tall, dark-haired girl.

Easley said they pulled the car up within a few feet of the porch. Kolojay carried the rifle in one hand and a large can of the explosive mixture in the other. He stood to the side of the porch out of sight of the front door. Tatum placed another can of the mixture on the floor to the left of the front door so it would be out of sight as the door opened. When everything was in place Tatum rang the doorbell.

As the maid was sliding the door open, Tatum burst through the small opening and hit the maid square in the face knocking her to the floor. Tatum and Kolojay had black tape over the lower part of their faces and wore old hats pulled down over their foreheads. The maid screamed as she lay on the floor watching them spread the mix around the living room. They soaked the couches and the rug. When they finished, they backed out of the front door as the maid jumped to her feet and ran screaming into the other trailer. Tatum lit a book of matches and threw it onto the floor through the open door. It exploded into an instant inferno.

Elbert told the jury of the fear they all suddenly felt so close to such an explosive fire. As Kolojay jumped into the car, he inadvertently stuck the rifle into the steering wheel, jamming it. It was impossible to move the steering wheel as he tried to turn around to get back to the road. When they finally were able to release the rifle, they sped away.

As we approached Pahrump, we decided not to return the same way we came. Instead, we took Hwy 52 to Shoshone, California, then north through Death Valley and on to the Shamrock. A few miles north of Death Valley, the water hose broke. It was about seven in the morning. The car started heating up so we coasted into the yard of a trailer house. The old couple who lived there helped us tape up the old hose and cool off the radiator so we could fill it up with water again.

The couple later took the stand to identify the three men in the car that morning, collaborating their part of Easley's story.

The three men drove back to the Shamrock and told Martin the job was done. Martin had agreed to pay fifteen thousand dollars to burn the brothel to the ground. After he was assured it was done, he handed Tatum an envelope with ten thousand dollars and told them he would give them the balance later. Tatum handed Elbert one thousand and kept the rest to split with Kolojay.

Easley went back to California a few days later.

The prosecutor asked Easley if he was ever concerned about being caught if he went to Pahrump and burned the Ranch. He answered that they were assured by the sheriff that if they burned it, he wouldn't investigate much, and the D.A. would never prosecute them. It was evident that he was absolutely right since no attempt to investigate or prosecute was ever made.

The defense attorney challenged the federal court's jurisdiction since both arson and attempted murder came under control of the State of Nevada. An expert brought in from D.C. showed the judge and jury that under the right conditions, gasoline became a potent explosive, and that such explosives came directly under federal law. The judge listened to both sides and concluded that the federal court had no jurisdiction in the firebombing. He dismissed both the firebombing and conspiracy charges, but let the charge of perjury stand against all three defendants. The trial continued and the prosecutor proved that they had, in fact, lied to the Federal Grand Jury when they denied, under oath, that they had anything to do with torching the Ranch.

The prosecutor then called Vickie McKool to the stand. She was a "cute twenty-two-year-old blonde with a nice figure and a chipped front tooth." She had called Walter at the Ranch to ask for a job. When he met her, he was sure she'd fit right in, but gave her the name of Summer. She worked about six weeks but left suddenly in April 1978. He never heard from her again until the summer of 1980, when she called him and asked if he could meet her in a cocktail lounge in Las Vegas. She sounded frightened. She told Walter she was married to Kolojay and they had a son two years old. Walter agreed to meet her but was afraid that Kolojay might also be there waiting to blow his head off.

Walter called the FBI to tell them about the plan. When he arrived two agents were already there. He went to the end of the bar and sat down. About five minutes later, Summer came in, sat down beside him and ordered a drink. She told him she was afraid for herself and her son. Kolojay threatened to kill her because she knew about the fire. She needed money to leave town. She told Walter that her husband made her go to work at the Ranch to kill Walter. Kolojay gave her a bottle of digitalis, a heart medication lethal in the right dosage. She was to put it into Walter's coffee or something he would be sure to drink. Knowing his heart problems, they were certain an autopsy would make it appear natural. Fortunately for him, she was not a murderer and couldn't go through with it.

She repeated that she desperately needed help. Walter told her there were a couple of men sitting in the booth he was certain would help her. He went to the two agents and briefly repeated to them what she told him. He walked back to the bar and lead her back to the two men in the booth. They asked her to sit down. They told Walter they had questions to ask her but that he should not be present. He sat at the bar while they talked with her. When they finished, she asked him if he would drop her off at *the Strip*. He did, and never saw or heard of her again until that day in the hall outside the courtroom.

She told the court about her relationship with Kolojay and Martin, and her time as a prostitute at the Shamrock, before and after the period spent at the *Chicken Ranch*. She also spoke of Beverly Burton, her husband's girlfriend. Summer was originally prepared to give Kolojay an alibi, but later realized he might kill her anyway simply because she knew too much.

Beverly Burton was then called to the witness stand. She admitted that she was Kolojay's girlfriend, and told about the drugs he forced on her and abuses she suffered at his hands. After Summer left the *Chicken Ranch*, Beverly was ordered to replace her in order to poison him. Walter recalled hiring her, but she didn't last long. She was very dirty, personally, and would not bring her standards up to the cleanliness of the house, so a maid fired her after only three nights. Walter became agitated when he heard about her testimony because he was certain Beverly was capable of murder, and he realized he had survived still another close call.

After the maid discharged her, Beverly returned to the Shamrock and was there the night of the fire. She was to give Kolojay his alibi, swearing he was with her all that night. Shortly after the fire, however, she and Kolojay had a fight. One day, she showed up at the Nye County Sheriff's office. By then, Joni Wines was the sheriff and she interviewed Beverly. She told the sheriff how afraid she was of Kolojay and Martin and how, with the help of drugs, she had been kept in virtual slavery. She said Martin ruled the lives of many of his prostitutes using drugs. She explained the planned alibi for the night of the fire. She corroborated Easley's story about Martin jumping up and down yelling at Tatum, Kolojay, and Easley to "burn the son of a bitch to the ground with Plankinton in it."

Sheriff Wines took Beverly to the FBI in Vegas. They sent her to her home state until the trial, when she was sent for as a witness for the prosecution. Beverly, like Easley, lacked credibility. Still, the defense could not dispute the facts being submitted by other witnesses the government found.

Although she was not called to testify, Walter was able to obtain a copy of the FBI's interview transcript of Justin, directed by Assistant U.S. Attorney Leavitt. Justin (Walter's former employee-girlfriend) explained to Leavitt and FBI agents how she met Walter, then in February 1980, two months before this interview, with Kenneth Kolojay. She told Leavitt and the agents that she was afraid to testify because Kolojay would kill her if she did. She explained that she was told that Kolojay wanted to talk with her, and she was given his phone number, which turned out to be the Shamrock brothel. She said that Mignon Clayson gave her Kolojay's home phone number. He told her he wanted to meet with her. Note that Justin's real name is not being used as it appears in the transcript.

[Justin] contacted a friend of hers, Thomas H. Jones, who was also acquainted with Kolojay, in an effort to learn something about Kolojay and inquire as to what he wanted. Jones set up a meeting with Kolojay at the Plush Horse Bar [in Las Vegas]. From talking with Jones, she learned that Jones had recently been arrested and had a trial date set in April on a rape charge in Las Vegas. Kolojay was attempting to help Jones by contacting someone who knew the judge or had some influence over the pending charges on Jones.

[Justin] met Kolojay at the Plush Horse Bar; however, they talked very little. From what she could determine Kolojay wanted to talk about Walter Plankinton and her relationship with him. She next met Kolojay at Billy Jo's on Industrial Road [in Las Vegas]. She stated she was drunk at the time and really did not converse that much with Kolojay. . . .

A fourth meeting was set up at Billy Jo's. Kolojay told her that she could trust him and that he wanted her to testify about Walter Plankinton's character. Kolojay said that Walter Plankinton was a Federal Agent and since she lived with him for a period of time she could testify about that. He wanted her to testify to certain things that would degrade Plankinton and make him out to be a bad witness. Sometime during or just after this meeting, Tom Jones told her that Special Agent P. [another agent] and Kolojay had recently met at Billy Jo's Lounge and discussed Walter Plankinton. Jones told her that Special Agent P. was on Kolojay's side and they wanted [Justin] to be on their side. . . .

At a subsequent meeting, Justin added that Kolojay wanted her to . . . testify that sometime after the fire Plankinton made the statement in his sleep, 'I should never have burned that place.' Kolojay offered her a new custom Seville Cadillac and offered to fix up her car which had broken down in San Francisco. . . .

She went on to tell them that Kolojay had papers for her to sign but she refused. Kolojay offered her lots of money but she still refused. The transcript continues:

Kolojay indicated that Bill Martin was in all probability going to be convicted for the arson of the Chicken Ranch. The plan was that Kolojay was going to use Justin and others to beat the rap; therefore, allowing him to continue running the Shamrock brothel. Kolojay stated that the reason that Plankinton was burned out was because he would not play the game with [District Court Judge] Bill Beko and [District Attorney] Peter Knight. He related that Plankinton did not give any money to Peter Knight who had requested it for allowing Plankinton to open up his brothel. Knight then called upon Martin to burn Plankinton out. Kolojay stated that Martin owed a favor to Knight and he agreed to burn down the Chicken Ranch. Kolojay also indicated that he was going to plant a girl into the Chicken Ranch to learn what was going on to further discredit Plankinton.

The defense called Nye County District Attorney Peter Knight to the stand. Upon cross-examination, the prosecution asked him about other brothels in Nye County. He was asked if he lived directly across the street [in Tonopah] from Bobby's Buckeye Bar for eight years, and Knight said he did. The prosecutor added that he assumed the D.A. was aware that it was a brothel. Under oath, he denied ever knowing it was a brothel. The prosecution stated that he discovered that Knight had grown up in Beatty until he left for college, which Peter Knight acknowledged. The next question asked was if he knew that Fran's Star Ranch, a known brothel, had been operating during this period. Knight stated that he never knew it was a brothel, even though it was right upstairs from the casino which his parents operated.

The prosecutor asked if normal duties took the D.A. to Pahrump on a weekly basis, which was also affirmed as being reasonably correct. He asked if this did not necessitate driving past the Shamrock Brothel in Lathrop Wells where there was a sign four feet high and forty feet long clearly stating that it was a brothel. Once more, the D.A. said he really didn't know that it was a whorehouse. When asked how he knew the *Chicken Ranch* was a brothel, his response was "I just knew, that's all."

The prosecutor asked about Walter's previous testimony stating that the D.A. tried to extort money from him which, of course, Knight denied. When asked if he would submit to a lie detector test by the FBI, he agreed. The local newspaper, very much controlled by the Nye County machine, prominently printed his willingness to take the test. But somehow, the results were never published, or even mentioned again, anywhere.

The trial dragged on for seven weeks. Finally both the prosecution and defense gave their closing arguments. The jury quickly returned with verdicts of guilty on all counts for all three defendants. It was December 31, 1980, and Walter couldn't think of a better way to start a new year.

The *Las Vegas Mirror* made certain the outcome was well covered. They made Walter feel great when they wrote, "Jack Tell, a respected reporter for the *Israelite Newspaper* once stated that 'One man and the truth constitute a majority,' but it took Walt Plankinton to prove the statement true."

TWENTY-TWO

It was only a matter of days before Walter was served with a summons to appear before "The Brothel Board" to show cause why his license should not be cancelled. Their review determined that he had advertised "illegally" because he appeared on the local *Dick Maurice Show* (a Las Vegas TV celebrity talk show), and permitted an interview by *Cosmopolitan Magazine*. Their charges included that he was written up in several other magazines, and that the Vegas World Casino was running a production called *The Chicken Ranch Follies* in their showroom, and was advertised on their marquis. Both Walter and his lawyer were astonished by the preposterous lengths to which these politicians would go to put him out of business. The taxpayers already indicated they did not intend to allow the state laws governing brothels to be changed. But they wouldn't stop trying to prove that laws could be twisted and molded in the Kingdom of Nye County to suit their own personal desires.

Walter's attorney could find no basis for the charges and no law that would permit such a travesty. They appeared before the Board as instructed. When they walked into the room, both Martin and Kolojay (who, just days before, were proven to have caused the arson at the Ranch) were sitting at the table. They were out on bond awaiting sentencing.

The entire meeting had been carefully orchestrated by the D.A. Although he had no evidence of any wrongdoing, he told them that it was the policy of the Board that anyone holding a brothel license must keep his head down and his mouth shut. He admitted that this policy had never been written in their bylaws, but it was "just understood." He continued on with his complaint stating that the *Las Vegas Mirror* printed numerous editorials about the *Chicken Ranch*. Walter's attorney showed that he had no control of the editorial policies of any newspaper. But the D.A. went droning on. Finally, Walter jumped up in front of the D.A and said, "Maybe you can stop the newspaper from editorializing. You can get 'Billy the Torch' Martin and Kenny 'Gas Can' Kolojay to go down to Las Vegas and burn that damned newspaper down."

The outburst finally shut the D.A.'s mouth and the meeting was ended without a determination of what should be considered advertising. Just a few days later, Walter received another summons to show cause why his license should not be revoked on exactly the same charges as the last hearing, word-for-word. Waiting for that meeting date, members of the Board made it publicly known that regardless of the evidence, they would revoke his license, and if he ever could get it back, it would be only through a lengthy and costly court battle. In the meantime, the Ranch would be closed which, of course, would put him out of business. No matter what the final outcome in court, they were certain all of his cash would be swallowed up, with no way to replenish it.

On April 4, 1981, a second hearing before the so-called Brothel Board of Tonopah was held and, of course, the results were already publicized before they entered the room. No evidence was presented to show Walter violated any Nye County Ordinance. He was not asked any questions nor allowed any comments before the vote was called. They unanimously revoked his license, effective April 7, 1981.

Walter's attorney filed an action in the federal court in Las Vegas, immediately, contending that his civil rights were violated and that he was denied due process of law. He requested a stay so that he could continue to operate until the federal court date. It was denied, so Walter was forced to remain closed until the court date before Judge Harry Claiborne of the Eighth Judicial Court.

There was no way to know how long the Ranch would be closed, although Walter expected no more than a few weeks. While waiting for the court decision, which Walter knew would be in his favor, he decided to keep his girls entertained and together so that when the Ranch reopened, he'd have the same crew.

He recalled the other fantasy of most truck drivers when they retire: if they couldn't own a whorehouse, they would settle for sailing the seven seas in a yacht with a harem.

He rented a houseboat which accommodated fifteen people, and filled it with his girls. They cruised Lake Mojave on the Colorado River. He was the rare truck driver who fulfilled both fantasies. Maybe it wasn't a yacht or the seven seas, but knowing this was a lifelong dream, the girls worked overtime to make the cruise everything a man could ever imagine. Walter was waited on hand and foot, and anything he wanted was his.

He was surrounded by young, shapely women who enjoy walking around naked. Because he was used to their nakedness, they worked to tease him day and night. Multiple sex was the rule rather than exception. They performed for him with each other while several nibbled or sucked all parts of his body, simultaneously, making his cock hard again and again. The girls made up contests trying to determine which kinky acts made him harder or gave him the most pleasure. It was sexual fantasy night and day. "Between bouts of playing with every inch of my body, outside and inside every cavity with their tongues, hands, feet, nipples, or my touching, sucking, or fucking one after the other, we waterskied, fished, ate steaks, drank the best wine, and listened to beautiful music." If ever a man felt like an indulged mythological god, it was Walter Plankinton.

But no dream lasts forever. They were closed six weeks when Judge Claiborne sent down his decision. He determined that the Board violated Walter's legal rights, specifically, and showed "the most blatant disregard for due process of law" he had "ever seen in the manner they used to revoke his license." The date of his decision was May 19, 1981, the same day the *Chicken Ranch* reopened. [Claiborne was subsequently convicted of various paper crimes and removed from the U.S. Bench. Nevertheless, he was, *and remains to this day*, a highly esteemed member of the Nevada *Good Old Boys*, thus, eloquently vindicating Walter for his years of accusations and criticism of the closed Nye County Mafia. If one from their own ranks saw irresponsible behavior and stated it so critically, how can anyone else ever again pretend it didn't exist.]

Certain he would have to start over again to build the business, only three girls were put on duty the first day, with the others on call [no pun intended—well maybe just a little one]. The news media were again kind to them. In Las Vegas, their reopening made the front pages. In less than a week, twelve girls were back on full-time, and business was better than ever.

Within another few days, Walter was notified the Ninth Circuit Court of Appeals in San Francisco had made a decision on his appeal. They instructed the Eighth Federal Court in Las Vegas that the facilities of Nye County, where he was to be held for sixty days, were not qualified to handle a person with his medical history. They ordered the County to find a more suitable place for him, ensuring his physical well-being.

The D.A's office immediately inquired as to facilities available in Clark County (the Las Vegas area). They asked about city and county jails, and their willingness to incarcerate Walter for sixty days. Although the godfather had good friends among the Las Vegas *Good Old Boys*, none of the agencies were too anxious to get involved in this Nye County brothel mess. The D.A. turned to state prison officials in Carson City to have Walter placed in the State Penitentiary. The moment they became aware of this turn of events, his attorney appeared before U.S. Federal Judge Foley who informed the D.A. he could not go there. Prolonged confinement in the higher elevation of Carson City was a definite threat to his health. In addition, his conviction was for a misdemeanor, and imprisonment in a state prison would be cruel and unusual punishment.

Walter knew all along he would eventually have to serve those sixty days somewhere. Finally, the judge suggested a federal half-way house in North Las Vegas. Walter was delighted. The judge ruled that from seven in the morning to six in the evening, he was free to go anywhere he wished to continue running his business. There were no guards. Confinement was based on his word that he would be there by six each evening. He would have a two-bedroom apartment with his own TV, telephone, kitchen, and all the comforts of home. Walter and his attorney were ordered to appear before Judge Foley on June 1, 1981, to stipulate acceptance of the facility. The D.A. knew it was the best he would ever do, although it was a hollow victory considering the facility. He agreed since he was given no other choice. The space would not be available until October 6, when Walter would begin to serve his sixty days.

It seemed like poetic justice that on the very same day (June 1, 1981) when Walter appeared before Judge Foley, exactly one hour later Bill Martin, Kenneth Kolojay, and James Tatum stood in front of him to be sentenced for their perjury convictions. Aware of the scheduling, of course, Walter remained in the courtroom to witness that sentencing. He sat in the front row. He wanted to hear every word.

Only Martin and Kolojay appeared. Tatum had another eight-year sentence hanging over him before he could even start this one. But he had jumped bail and was a fugitive, appearing on all national *Wanted* lists.

Martin was called to the bench first, where all of the usual arguments were made by his lawyers about possible probation, and so forth. It was obvious by Martin's more haughty than usual stance, that he had been assured he would get nothing more than probation. His attorney was the then Nevada Democratic Chairman Charles Waterman [also one of the *Good Old Boys*, although not a too highly respected one], so it was a shoe-in. At the end of the arguments, there were a few moments of silence. The judge then pronounced his sentence. "Five years in the federal penitentiary and a ten thousand dollar fine."

Martin stood absolutely silent, the look on his face certain the judge had not been referring to him at all. He then went white as a sheet and his shoulders visibly drooped. His attorney had to assist him back to his seat. Walter could see his hands were shaking. It was the maximum allowed. Walter knew the judge was aware of the other charges which Martin had beaten, and this was the very best he could do to serve justice. For the first time since Walter met him, Martin's arrogance was gone, vanished. He almost felt sorry for the man. Walter later decided that maybe it was his manhood he pitied. He had watched this bully strut around at the peak of his power. Here, now, he was just another convict. And ironically, little to show for his unrelenting, vicious struggle to what he considered the top.

Next was Kenny *Gas Can* Kolojay's turn. Kenny always seemed like a dumb farm kid who watched too many episodes of *The Untouchables* on TV, and thought he was Al Capone—or at least one of his privileged henchmen. Kenny was visibly shaken by Martin's sentence. As he stood before the judge, his head was bowed and his hands shook. Probation arguments were once again submitted which included the fact that he had a three-year-old son to raise, and had never been convicted of any crime before. Apparently the judge bought their story. He sentenced Kenny to only three years, but the same ten thousand dollar fine. The court permitted both men to remain out on four hundred thousand dollars in bonds while they appealed their convictions to the Ninth Circuit Court of Appeals in San Francisco.

How ironic it was that although the *written* Brothel Ordinance of Nye County specifically forbade anyone convicted of a felony to work in, manage, or own a licensed brothel, the Shamrock's license was never challenged, much less revoked, at least during the appeal period. Walter also found it interesting that the Nevada State Gaming Control Board, with the same basic rules, never moved in any manner to revoke, nor even question Martin's license to run the gaming operation he owned. Maybe Martin's grandiose crowing that if he went to jail he would take many Nevada politicians with him had something to do with it.

Within a few months, Tatum was picked up in California and returned to Las Vegas for sentencing. The judge gave him the maximum sentence of five years in the federal penitentiary and a ten thousand dollar fine. He then sent him before the federal grand jury which indicted him for jumping bail. He was convicted of that charge for which the judge added another five years. The combined sentences meant that it would be fourteen years before he could ever be eligible for parole. Tatum was in his late fifties and also had a serious heart condition. The sentence probably meant dying in prison.

Walter and many other people living in the area were convinced that the Nye County Machine was involved in the *Chicken Ranch* fire, and it's likely that no one could ever convince any of them otherwise. It was also suggested that there were many dope deals and countless other illegal activities in which they and Martin were partners; or at the very least that they knowingly ignored Martin's criminal activities.

Shortly after the sentencing, Walter learned that Martin began making arrangements to be gone for a few years in the event his appeal failed. He leased the Coachman's Bar and Service Station in Lathrop Wells near the

Shamrock to two young Pahrump men. They immediately began remodeling and expanding the facility. For some reason Walter never discovered, the lease arrangements went sour. Martin tried his best to cancel the lease, which included a purchase option. Hard feelings quickly developed since the two men had used up all of their savings in the deal. And now Martin, whose power was well known in the community, was apparently trying to screw them over. The two men had legitimate reasons to be outraged and distraught.

One of them, Gerald Aesop, showed up at Martin's house behind the Shamrock one night. The two men got into a shouting match. Gerald pulled out a gun and shot Martin three times in the head. Then trying to recover his losses, Gerald got into Martin's safe and took eighteen thousand dollars from it. He grabbed Martin's current girlfriend as a hostage before driving away. A *Flight for Life Helicopter* was sent in an attempt to save him, but Martin was DOA at the Las Vegas hospital.

Gerald drove south on U.S. Hwy 95 toward Las Vegas with Nye County deputies in hot pursuit. He headed toward California. By then, California deputies and highway patrols joined the chase. They finally cornered Gerald in a field a couple of miles south of Shoshone. For the rest of the night he held them at bay with threats to kill the girl.

Someone found Kolojay and brought him to the scene. He finally convinced Gerald, with whom he had become very friendly, to surrender to the California officers. He was taken to the County Seat at Independence where he was charged with kidnapping, armed assault of police officers, and several other charges. Nye County, of course, desperately wanted him returned to their jurisdiction so they could prosecute him for Martin's murder. They finally extradited him to Tonopah and he was arraigned in Beatty. His bail was set at one million dollars.

One fact always seemed suspicious. Martin's girlfriend said that throughout the period she was his hostage, Gerald never threw anything away. Yet Kolojay swore he must have taken the money as well as all of Martin's alleged secret papers from the safe before he left the Shamrock. Walter wondered what Gerald said about the cash and papers. Somehow he doubted the man ever saw them since nothing was ever said publicly again. Nor has anything ever been mentioned about exactly what Kolojay meant by "secret" papers.

Just twenty-four hours before Martin was killed, he had been notified that his appeal was denied and he was going to prison. Kolojay was definitely on his way to prison, too. Walter was vengeful. He sent Kolojay a jar of Vaseline to take to prison with him. Walter knew that like everyone else, Kolojay must be aware of the gruesome situations which pretty boys like him faced inside at the hands of powerful, lustful men, not to mention strong homosexuals. Walter always felt cheated regarding Martin. He was lucky. He would never face prison knowing how inmates treated cops, even ex-cops.

The fifteen people who were in the Ranch the night of the fire filed suits against Martin, Kolojay, and Tatum, as well as Nye County and several of its officials. Walter joined them in the suit asking for twenty-one million dollars in damages. They felt that the evidence presented at the trials offered them a basis for a suit that would be hard to beat. The suit infuriated the County machine, so once again, they turned their attention back to finding any infraction which might serve to revoke the *Chicken Ranch* license.

TWENTY-THREE

Soon after Martin's murder, District Attorney Peter Knight announced that he would not run for reelection in the upcoming election, and that he had purchased a home some two hundred miles away. Then word got out that the godfather was going after a seat on the Nevada Supreme Court, and was calling in his countless political markers collected over many decades. There was endless buzzing about his having the inside track for the seat, and that all that was left was the formality. He would certainly be moving up to Carson City very soon.

Over the years of strife with the *Chicken Ranch*, Walter got to know several of the state's newspaper publishers and editors. What most of them told him privately was that they were appalled that such a man could be placed into a position to make rulings which would affect people throughout the state. They were determined to prevent his election. Several editorials were written. The Governor and Judicial Committee, all of whom already knew Judge Beko very well since most were either *Good Old Boys* themselves or umbrella'd by them, were made very aware of what the press, and citizens of Nye County, thought of his potential appointment.

Not only was he not on the list of candidates, he was not even mentioned as ever being considered. All of the favors owed him, used up to get this prestigious appointment, were apparently valueless. Now he was just another loser. He was no longer feared to quite the degree he had been, and the respect he once commanded diminished enormously, except for the inner circle of *the Good Old Boys*.

The only state magazine wrote an article about Walter with the caption, "Rooster of the Chicken Ranch," causing a great deal of controversy. The Nye County Brothel Board issued still another summons for Walter to appear before them to show cause why his license should not be revoked again for advertising the *Chicken Ranch*. They went so far as to repeat the same stupid game they played in the previous spring. By now, not only were Walter and his attorney beginning to question the intellectual ability of this Board, but the mental competency of its members. The hearing was set for September 8, 1981, but his attorney succeeded in having it postponed.

Just about the time Walter was certain he had seen every kind and shape of girl making her living as a prostitute, up popped something new. Most people want to believe that *all* prostitutes are raped, abused, poor, underachievers. On the contrary, many are college students or graduates, from upper-middle class or affluent families, who have never been abused in any way in their lives.

Walter talked about one college student who worked at the Ranch almost every summer that he owned it. A English History major, she was an extremely serious student. Being a full-time student was made possible only because she was a paid whore. Once she graduated, he never heard from or of her again.

Another college graduate's academic achievements were exceptional. Her father was a prominent banker in their home state, and her home was not only affluent but happy, at least her family believed it was. After finding her way to the *Chicken Ranch*, her father somehow tracked her there. He took her home, but she was back in no time. Walter knew she was a drug addict, but swore she never took anything while at the Ranch.

After some time, her father returned and took her with him, again; but this time, she went straight into a psychiatric hospital. Somehow, she got out of the hospital and back she went to the brothel. Because she was twenty-two, her father had no legal right to control her life. Each time he went after her, he convinced her to go back with him.

The third time he returned to the Ranch, the girl's father was at his wit's end, and he talked with Walter. This time, he left without her. She stayed at the Ranch for awhile, then left. Some time later, Walter heard that she met a Las Vegas casino dealer who started working two jobs to keep up with her drug habit. He finally started pimping for her with some of his high-roller customers, all just to keep up with her addiction.

After a few months, some police detectives from Las Vegas interviewed Walter about her. A young man she was having an affair with embezzled $97,000 in cash from his own father's company. When he got drunk and fell asleep in her room, she grabbed the money and disappeared. They were trying to find both her and the money. Walter never heard any more about her.

Danni was a writer from California. She was at the Ranch only about two months to write a movie script about a prostitute. Walter started getting strange letters saying that another woman was determined to destroy Danni, and that her career was stealing her (the letter-writer's) lovers. One day, a man who Danni lived with came to pick her up. While he waited for her, Walter talked with him. It seemed that Danni had a split personality: the one at the brothel was tough and fearless, and sounded almost like a long-term

201

prostitute; the second character, the professional, was an intelligent, charming, successful writer. They left and she never returned.

Ginger had a sister, Amy, who was mildly retarded. Each sister had a baby—Amy's was illegitimate. Their father was a drunk who hung around them all the time. Walter always suspected he also fathered Amy's child from things Ginger said. Ginger's income totally supported both girls and their two babies. Ginger left the Ranch to return to the Midwest and a straight life. She met and started living with a young man. One day, Ginger's ex-husband appeared at their house shouting that he was going to beat the hell out of both of them. When the ex finally kicked the front door in, the boyfriend pumped eight bullets into him, including one into his head, but the ex didn't die. He ran down the street, with the boyfriend chasing after him, hitting him with two more bullets, one in the back of the head, finally killing him; and thus, forever eliminating the possibility of a case of self-defense. He was, of course, convicted. Ginger returned to the *Chicken Ranch* after it was all over.

Melodie arrived in Las Vegas to live with her sister who was a dancer in one of the big Las Vegas shows. Her sister had a small child, whom both sisters cared for. Although Melodie's sister was not a hooker, it was clear that she probably slept with every casting director (and others who only claimed to be) in Las Vegas, trying to get into a show, even though she was genuinely talented. At least some of the dancers are used to entertain high rollers, and if they refuse, they might not keep those jobs too long. This is a fact always denied in the Las Vegas gambling industry, but one owner was refused a license when Atlantic City opened its doors to gambling because he was considered pandering, or "pimping" for high rollers. Although technically prostitution is illegal in Las Vegas, it is practiced openly and freely among "high rollers," and all of the so-called regulating controls turn away if the man is dropping thousands on the tables. There are many, many gamblers, particularly from the Middle East—although not exclusively—who drop millions in one night.

One day Walter went to his attorney's office to discuss the newest, ridiculous Nye County Mafia charade. As he entered the office, he sensed something serious was happening. His instinctive reaction was concern even though he knew there was little chance that the Board could do anything, at least this time around. They had not changed their dialogue in any way. There were no new or different charges. Nevertheless, Walter felt a shiver rush down his spine. The attorney asked Walter to sit down. Walter sat down across from him, waiting for more bad news. He was unable to read anything in his face.

Quietly, the lawyer said, "Walt, would you consider selling the *Chicken Ranch?*" Walter was very surprised and a small cynical laugh escaped. The attorney went on to explain that another of his clients, a real estate agent, had someone interested in buying a brothel. They asked him to find out what Walter would take for the *Chicken Ranch*. This time Walter laughed out loud and told him he was an old farm boy barterer, and would sell anything if the price was right. Jokingly, Walter said, "One Million Dollars. I'll sell it for one million dollars, but it has to be cold, hard cash."

Walter knew they would laugh in his face when the lawyer delivered the offer, but from lifelong habit, his business mind went into high gear. He figured that after taxes he could invest the balance in municipal bonds and have a good income for life. Walter suddenly thought, sitting in that office, that he was certainly a long way from that little Kansas farm and the poverty he experienced during *The Great Depression*.

He left the office smiling, absolutely certain he would not hear anything more on the subject. But this had opened a bit of a *pandora's box* for him. Driving away, he began to fantasize feeling one million dollars in his hands, and all the things he could go on to do with it. He knew he would never just sit somewhere and collect interest on the money. He would find something bigger and better to do with it.

As he drove back to the condo, he thought about the people in Nye County and saw no end to the battle. He knew that if they threw enough shit against the wall, sooner or later, something was going to stick—especially considering the fact that they were not above manufacturing the shit themselves. The law of averages was in their favor if they continued and Walter, at long last, admitted to himself that they would never give up, even if it meant putting him into a grave. There was little doubt that when it finally happened, he would be out of business with probably little more than press clippings to show for his efforts. He didn't like that prospect.

All through the evening, he thought back over the last few years. He was proud of his accomplishments. He felt that he had elevated his brothel to the same plateau as the bordellos which existed in earlier centuries (and still do) around the world. Whether he accomplished that is in the eye of the beholder. He made some small effort to put a facade around the Ranch so that it looked nicer than just four double-wide trailers [sixty-six hundred square feet]. But, it was just trailers, nothing more [and still is].

After completely gutting one of the units, he rebuilt it into a massive room covered with deep-piled, luxurious, blood-red carpeting, and red, crushed velvet drapery. Crystal chandeliers with light reflecting from prism pendants. Custom-made white, silky couches with gold legs and trim, glass-topped rococo-based cocktail and end tables of clear glass being held by gold, naked bodies were all over the room. Paintings, mostly depicting scenes from bordellos of old, ornately framed in baroque style adorned the walls. Two lamps of bronze naked women with Tiffany shades, bought at auction from the original Texas Chicken Ranch were among Walter's most prized possessions.

The Twentieth Century seemed to fade within the walls of this room that can only be described as garish. Historical references and pictures bear out that this was certainly the decor of early bordellos, admittedly theatrical, creating a setting in which seduction could be played out with an air of flamboyance, titillation, sensuality, yet dignity, in stark contrast to the raw sale of sex by women in the streets of red-light districts flourishing around the world.

There were certainly no dark, dank-smelling rooms in the splendid *houses* easily accessible and patronized by the nobility of France, Italy, Spain, England, and the rest. Some of the *ladies* of bordellos in earlier centuries became the mistresses of great estates through marriage to lords, marquis, and barons. In some cultures in the far east, and even as close as South America, a girl taken from a brothel to become a concubine, or second wife, is respected, as are any children who come from such relationship. In those bordellos, great pains were taken to create the same atmosphere of luxury as the aristocrats had within their own homes. In some places around the world, use of such decor has survived the centuries, but very few brothel owners in the United States bother to use it as an enticement to men to keep returning to the same *house*. Walter seemed to understand this psychological impact, and he went to great pains to accomplish as close an imitation to early bordellos as he could; at least within the budget he was willing to expend.

He was still at the condo when a couple of days later, Walter's lawyer asked him to come into the office to meet with his other client. The broker naturally tried to bring the price down, but Walter told him that the price was not open to debate and that it was one million in cash, or nothing. He told the broker not to bother him again unless the price was accepted. When Walter left the office this time, he headed back to the Ranch. The very next day, his attorney called and told him it was a deal. They would pay Walter one million dollars in cash.

On December 8, 1981, two days after he finished serving his sixty-day sentence in that little apartment prison, he sat in his attorney's office signing the papers which would turn the Ranch over to the buyer. He felt like he was signing away part of his life. They told him it would take sixty days for the transfer to be final.

Walter flew to Kansas to spend an early Christmas with his parents. He then went to Denver to see his daughter and her family. Finally, he returned to the Ranch to spend Christmas Day with his family there, just as they had done from that very first year. But this would be their last together.

Many of the girls, some from sad beginnings, told Walter that the best Christmases they ever had were with their family at the notorious *Chicken Ranch*. During January 1982, they were extremely busy because of all the conventions held each year in Las Vegas. While there were many moments of sadness and melancholy, even regret, Walter knew it was time to find another mountain to climb.

The old sheriff was long gone, District Attorney Peter Knight was leaving, and Judge Beko's balloon was just another tiny pile of rubber—or in this era probably cheap plastic. The story was finished. Maybe Walter could have stood alone at the top, at last. New people were moving into Nye County every day and, maybe someday, the *Good Old Boy* machine would be no more than a bad memory. At least he hoped so. But he knew after many hours and days of soul-searching that it really was time for him to move on.

One beautiful, bright day in February 1982, the nineteenth to be exact, the *Chicken Ranch* was legally turned over to new owners. Walter left his lawyer's office and drove out to the Ranch. When he walked in, he went straight to the safe and put his briefcase into it. Slowly, he collected all of his personal belongings and took them out to his car. When he finished, he removed the briefcase from the safe and went into the parlor to say goodbye to his friends, his surrogate family.

The maids and all the girls were there, even those on their off-weeks. A lot of tears flowed in the parlor that day, Walter's among them. When they finished saying everything any of them could say, he turned to walk out the door with a huge lump in his throat. As he reached the car, he turned around to take one last look at the old girl he had built from his wonderful dreams. He clicked his heels and, in true marine fashion, threw the finest salute he knew how to give.

Walter got into his car and glanced back once more through tears as he drove slowly away. He looked down at the briefcase beside him and patted it, affectionately. He could feel the precious leather which held one million dollars in cash nestled against his thigh. With a big smile breaking through the tears, he turned out of the driveway and headed west into the most beautiful sunset he ever saw.

EPILOGUE

The *Chicken Ranch* was purchased by a small group. One of its owners, a California high school biology teacher, left his academic position to assume Walter's role at the brothel. Soon thereafter—and for the first time since its inception—the *Chicken Ranch*, like all other Nye County brothels, was issued a liquor license.

Walter deposited most of his money in Arizona banks. The State of Arizona soon froze his bank accounts, claiming that since gambling and prostitution were illegal in their state, he was breaking their laws, even though the gambling/brothel ship he arranged to purchase was docked in and would operate in neutral waters. Since Arizona is pretty much landlocked, and there is no known ownership of any bay or ocean by the State of Arizona, he was completely puzzled by their outrageous and flawed pretense. His attorneys were equally mystified.

Whatever others may think of him, it was Walter's nature to stand up for what he believed in. But he was finally becoming convinced, much to his dismay, that laws were passed to conform to whatever politicians in control of various geographical areas decided they should be, to their own advantage and profit. Once again fighting for his Constitutional rights he was, nevertheless, depressed and exhausted.

On August 9, 1984, at his ranch in Santa Rosa, Texas, Walter Plankinton finally lost the long and bravely fought battle with his heart. He was fifty-six years old.

On April 15, 1995, Judge Beko, still on the Bench, also succumbed to a heart attack. Wherever they are, which surely is the same place, maybe they are finally friends, or, maybe not.

THE END